SHL
WITHDRAWN

HONECKER'S CHILDREN

MANCHESTER
1824

Manchester University Press

For Mum and Dad

Honecker's children

Youth and patriotism in East(ern) Germany, 1979–2002

Anna Saunders

MANCHESTER UNIVERSITY PRESS
Manchester and New York
distributed exclusively in the USA by Palgrave

Copyright © Anna Saunders 2007

The right of Anna Saunders to be identified as the author of this work has been asserted by her in accordance with the Copyright, Designs and Patents Act 1988.

Published by Manchester University Press
Oxford Road, Manchester M13 9NR, UK
and Room 400, 175 Fifth Avenue, New York, NY 10010, USA
www.manchesteruniversitypress.co.uk

Distributed exclusively in the USA by
Palgrave, 175 Fifth Avenue, New York,
NY 10010, USA

Distributed exclusively in Canada by
UBC Press, University of British Columbia, 2029 West Mall,
Vancouver, BC, Canada V6T 1Z2

British Library Cataloguing-in-Publication Data
A catalogue record for this book is available from the British Library

Library of Congress Cataloging-in-Publication Data applied for

ISBN 978 0 7190 7411 0 *hardback*

First published 2007

16 15 14 13 12 11 10 09 08 07   10 9 8 7 6 5 4 3 2 1

Typeset in Sabon 10.25/12 pt
by Servis Filmsetting Ltd, Manchester
Printed in Great Britain
by Bell & Bain Ltd, Glasgow

Contents

List of tables and figures

Tables

Figures

Acknowledgements

The research for this book has been inspired by numerous and often lengthy conversations with east German friends who grew up in the GDR, to whom I owe much time, patience and friendship. I would not, however, have embarked on this project without the impetus provided by Mark Allinson, whose enthusiasm for GDR history inspired me as an undergraduate and postgraduate, and whose guidance and support proved to be invaluable during my PhD, out of which this book has grown. I would also like to express my gratitude to all members of staff in the German Department at Bristol University for their help and encouragement throughout my time there, as well as my colleagues at the University of Wales, Bangor for their support and good humour.

This project would not have been possible without the generous financial support of the Arts and Humanities Research Board, which funded my postgraduate research, and enabled extended periods of time in Germany. A number of institutions in Germany have also been invaluable in helping me to track down the necessary documents and resources for my primary research; I am indebted to the staff of all the archives I visited, particularly Frau Dittmer (SAPMO), Frau Dr Basikow (BBF) and Frau Schaarschmidt (BStU) for their patience and advice, and Frau Dr Kornemann-Weber for making her private collection available to me. I have also been greatly aided by numerous youth clubs and organisations in Magdeburg, who helped me not only to find interviewees, but also to gain an insight into east German youth culture.

My primary research in Sachsen-Anhalt would have been impossible without the help of numerous individuals, whose interest and enthusiasm for my project have been central to its development. Above all I would like to thank Kurt and Sabine Onnasch for their tremendous generosity and friendship, and for sharing so many of their experiences in Magdeburg with me. My time there cannot go without a mention of the *Magdeburger Domchor*, many members of which proved essential points of contact, particularly Ulrike Jerratsch, whose help in finding interviewees and resources was invaluable. My thanks also extends to Frau Herbig (*Interessenvereinigung Jugendweihe e.V.*) and Herr Beyerling (*Junge Humanisten*), both of whom allowed me to attend a number of *Jugendweihe/FEIER* ceremonies, and most importantly to my interviewees, who provided me with endless inspiration, and whose time made this book possible.

I am indebted to numerous flatmates throughout the years, who not only put up with the frequent disarray of German Democratic Republic (GDR) literature scattered around the house, but also offered valuable friendship and advice. Special thanks go to Joanne Saynor, Hilary Brown, Hannah Hickman, Lara James and Helena Miguélez-Carballeira for their careful reading of various drafts at different stages of this project, and for their thoughtful comments which have been instrumental in shaping the end product. I am also grateful to my PhD examiners, Mary Fulbrook and Clare Flanagan, for their valuable comments and suggestions on how to take this research further. Needless to say, all imperfections and faults remain my own.

Most importantly, I would like to thank my friends and family for their inspiration, humour, patience and friendship, and above all Mum and Dad for their constant love, support and encouragement.

List of abbreviations and key terms

Abgrenzung	delimitation (GDR policy in response to *Ostpolitik*)
Abitur	A-level equivalent
APuZG	*Aus Politik und Zeitgeschichte*
APW	Academy of Pedagogical Sciences
BArch	Federal Archives
Bausoldat(en)	GDR term for young men completing military service without the use of weapons
BBF	Library for Research of the History of Education
Bezirk(e)	county (counties); GDR administrative region (1952–90)
BStU	Federal Commissioner for the State Security Records
BV	County Administration
CDJ	Christian Democratic Youth
CDU	Christian Democratic Union
CPSU	Communist Party of the Soviet Union
CVJM	Christian Union for Young Men (YMCA)
DA	*Deutschland Archiv*
DDR	see GDR
DJ	*Deutsche Jugend – Zeitschrift für Jugendarbeit*
DJI	German Youth Institute
DLZ	*Deutsche Lehrerzeitung*
DM	Deutschmark
DRK	German Red Cross
DSF	Society for German–Soviet Friendship
DTSB	German Gymnastics and Sports Association

DVU	German People's Union
EOS	*Erweiterte Oberschule* ('extended high school', for *Abitur* students)
EsP	Introduction to Socialist Production (school subject)
e.V.	registered society
FDGB	Free German Trade Union Association
FDJ	Free German Youth
FDP	Free Democratic Party
FR	*Frankfurter Rundschau*
FRG	Federal Republic of Germany (West Germany)
GDR	German Democratic Republic (East Germany)
GEP	*Geschichte-Erziehung-Politik*
GP	*German Politics*
GST	Society for Sport and Technology
Jugendweihe	secular coming of age ceremony for 14 year olds (containing an oath of loyalty to the GDR state prior to 1990)
JuliA	Young Liberal Action
Junge Gemeinde	Protestant youth groups in the GDR
JuSos	Young Social Democrats
JW	*Junge Welt*
Komsomol	'Communist Union of Youth': youth wing of the CPSU
Kreis(e)	district(s)
LA Magd.-LHA-	Central Land Archives (of Sachsen-Anhalt), Magdeburg
Land (Länder)	administrative region(s) (1945–52 and post-1990)
M-D-A	Matthias Domaschk Archives
MfS	Ministry for State Security (Stasi)
MMM	trade fair for young people in the GDR
MV	*Magdeburger Volksstimme*
NATO	North Atlantic Treaty Organisation
ND	*Neues Deutschland*
NVA	National People's Army
Ostpolitik	FRG policies working towards rapprochement with the East

PDS	Party of Democratic Socialism (successor party to SED); from July 2005, *Die Linkspartei*
POS	*Polytechnische Oberschule* ('polytechnic high school', obligatory ten year system)
SAPMO	Archive Foundation of the Parties and Mass Organisations of the GDR
SED	Socialist Unity Party of Germany
SOWI	Social Science Institute of the *Bundeswehr*
Sozialkunde	Social studies/civics (school subject)
SPD	Social Democratic Party of Germany
Staatsbürgerkunde	civics (school subject)
Stasi	see MfS
taz	*die tageszeitung*
UN	United Nations
Urania	society for scientific knowledge
USSR	Union of Soviet Socialist Republics
Wehrdienst	military service
Wehrunterricht	military school classes
Wende	'change' (term used to describe the political changes of autumn 1989)
ZIJ	Central Institute for Youth Research
Zivildienst	civilian alternative to military service
ZK	Central Committee (of the SED)
ZR	Central Council (of the SED)

Introduction: Honecker's Germany – a world of the past?

The GDR lives on . . . (*Good Bye Lenin!*, 2003)

The GDR exhaled its last breath on 3 October 1990, with the uni-fication of the two German states. Its final year was one of intense emotion, turmoil and, ultimately, resignation; the one-time jewel in the Soviet crown disappeared from the map with few apparent mourners, and was expected by many to become little more than a footnote in history. Yet within less than a decade, the GDR had made a come-back, albeit repackaged to meet the consumer demands of *Ostalgie* (a conflation of the German words for 'East' and 'nostalgia'): shops marketed T-shirts, postcards, mugs and numerous other items of memorabilia featuring East German traffic light men (*Ampelmännchen*), the much-loved children's character *das Sandmännchen*, GDR slogans, and even the face of Erich Honecker (affectionately branded as 'Honi'), the leader of the com-munist party between 1971 and 1989. Away from Berlin's tourist trail, many east Germans began seeking out eastern products again, such as *Schlager Süßtafel* (chocolate flavoured bars) and *Rondo* coffee, erstwhile discarded as substandard and inferior to western products. Others restored their old Trabant cars, or Trabis, which had rapidly become a cult symbol of the former socialist state. The release of Wolfgang Becker's hugely popular film *Good Bye Lenin!* in early 2003 further prompted a new wave of *Ostalgie*, and was soon followed by *The GDR Show*, aired on national television, as well as the unveiling of plans for the construction of a 10,000m^2 GDR theme park in the Berlin suburb of Koepenick. In this atmos-phere, publications of nostalgic childhood memories, such as Jana Hensel's *Zonenkinder* and Claudia Rusch's *Meine freie deutsche Jugend* have enjoyed widespread popularity.[1] On the eve of unification, however, few could have suspected the influence that the GDR was to have from beyond the grave.

The legacy left by forty years of German socialism, however, clearly consists of more than *Ostalgie*. Unemployment rates in the east have soared since 1990, reaching over twice those of the west; eastern townscapes are commonly characterised by developments of mass-produced concrete architecture; and the political sphere in eastern regions is distinctive for the relatively strong presence of the Party of Democratic Socialism (PDS; renamed *Die Linkspartei* in July 2005), successor to the GDR's Socialist Unity Party (SED). The catalogue of physical and mental differences between east and west is lengthy, and one which is frequently charted as a measurement of difference in the east. Indeed, numerous publications have profited from the polarisation of *Ossis* (easterners) and *Wessis* (westerners), from joke books and tongue-in-cheek guides through to more serious psychological investigations of both populations. The presence of a distinctive eastern identity is, however, often regarded as something which must be overcome in the interests of inner unity, for the 'wall in people's heads' threatens to undermine the recent narrative of 'normality', endorsed by numerous politicians, journalists and intellectuals, who view unified Germany as 'the natural and normal, self-evident area of reference'.[2]

Yet the experiences of the young generation, whose lives have straddled the 1989/90 caesura, appear to be anything but 'normal'. As the second generation born in the GDR, young people in the 1980s knew nothing other than the 'normality' of division. Schooled to show loyalty to the GDR state through a comprehensive programme of patriotic education, few things could have seemed more abnormal to this generation than the fall of the Berlin Wall. From one year to the next, pupils were confronted with textbooks lauding the praises of the West German state which only months before had been portrayed as an imperialist repressor; soldiers were expected to swear an oath of loyalty to their former enemy; and whilst dissenters became heroes, loyalists were denounced as opportunists and informers. For these young people, 'normality' had been turned on its head, and not only had their country of birth disappeared, but their adoptive state was far from familiar, often leaving a sense of insecurity and inner turmoil. Over the following years, spiralling unemployment rates were accompanied by increasing instances of xenophobia and right-wing extremism, growing apathy within the political sphere and feelings of resentment towards western dominance; the new daily normality was, for many, far from desirable.

The influence of Honecker's Germany clearly did not end with the demise of the GDR, yet to what extent has it lived on in the identities of its youngest generation? Where have young people in the wake of the *Wende* (the change brought about by the GDR's demise) turned their loyalties amidst trends such as *Ostalgie*, unemployment and discourses of normality? This book will examine the relationship between young East(ern) Germans and two German states (the GDR and post-unification Germany) during a period of unique change, exploring the extent to which each state has attempted to form a young generation loyal to its image and ideology, and how, in turn, young people have responded.[3] It will ask how far a young generation's loyalties can be regulated from above, through official education and socialisation, and in the face of cultural and historical traditions, material conditions and social circumstances. Specific to the context of East(ern) German identities, it will therefore pose two central questions: firstly, to what extent has GDR socialisation and socialist patriotic education influenced the formation (or rejection) of loyalty to, and identification with, unified Germany? Secondly, how do the young generation's loyalties help explain the (in)stability and the demise of the GDR? This study thus aims to deepen our knowledge of the functioning of the GDR and its longer-term impact, but also to advance our understanding of the ways in which collective loyalties, frequently understood as 'patriotism', are formed in a broader sense.

Eastern identity in the wake of the GDR

Issues of identity inevitably dominated the unification process, and were no more prominent than during the weeks following the fall of the Berlin Wall on 9 November 1989, when euphoric choruses in both East and West were inspired to chant 'We are *one* people' (a permutation of the GDR demonstrators' original slogan 'We are *the* people'). The victory of capitalism over communism was welcomed by the majority of East Germans yet, as this slogan demonstrates, the basis for unification was clearly predicated on ties of ethnicity and kinship. There was, after all, no reason why a reformed GDR could not continue to exist, in the same way that other socialist

countries, such as Poland and Hungary, emerged intact from communist rule. Yet the bonds of a common ethnic identity drew both
halves of Germany together. As a result, some critics, such as Günter
Grass, feared the essentialist basis of a unified Germany, instead
proposing a 'cultural federation';[4] for others, the rapid rise in right-
wing extremism since unification, particularly in eastern Germany,
provoked fears that the new German nation might once again
become too powerful. The initial euphoria of national unity was
above all dampened, however, by consequent identity problems in
the east, and as the dream world of unity became reality, the Berlin
Republic was increasingly marked by continuing division rather
than an overbearing sense of unity. As Heinrich Jaenecke typically
observed in *Stern*: 'Twelve years after the fall of the Wall: the alienation of west Germans and east Germans has not been overcome. It
is growing.'[5]

Alienation between east and west has commonly been attributed
to the growing regional identity of east Germans, frequently
ascribed to GDR socialisation. Matthias Matussek, for example,
claims that east Germans have remained GDR patriots following the
demise of the GDR, stating: 'The fascination for a strong state
remains unbroken, and at the same time many people are still convinced that the SED regime was more human than other dictatorships.'[6] Whilst this opinion suggests that East Germans were strictly
compliant with the party line, others take a more differentiated view
in recognising the influence of the GDR. Marc Alan Howard, for
example, describes east Germans as an 'ethnic' group marked by elements such as common history, collective symbols and myths and
territorial integrity. In contrast to Matussek, Howard regards identity developed in the private, rather than the public sphere of the
GDR to be most significant, claiming that the anti-political niches
which developed in society created a specific 'GDR culture'.[7] In a
similar way, Helmut Meier identifies the conflict between the projected image of the GDR and everyday life there as influential. Like
Matussek, he claims: 'For these citizens, socialism was in no way fin-
ished with at the end of the GDR.'[8] For him, however, the problem
is not over-zealous GDR patriots, but rather the way in which the
reality of socialism, and the memory of it today, compared and compares to the state's official image. Whilst the reality of life under
socialist rule severely undermined official socialist propaganda
during the GDR, the tables have now turned, and instead today's

official image of socialism undermines the reality east Germans remember. As a result, many experience confusion over their identity as former citizens of a socialist state, unable to accept the identity bestowed upon them in a new society. In suggesting that east Germans accurately remember their socialist past, Meier rejects the notion that attachment to the GDR is mere nostalgia, yet *Ostalgie* clearly conveys a longing for the comforts of a fictitious, rosy past, aptly described by Kerstin and Gunnar Decker as 'the ability to lament that things are no longer as they never used to be'.[9] In reality, few people actually want to return to the GDR, and nostalgia for the socialist state is only partial, focusing on certain aspects of the regime, such as childcare provisions, social security, full employment, low prices for basic foodstuffs and rent and a less competitive atmosphere. Whilst the positive memory of such elements may indeed be a result of personal experience, this also depends on the conditions of life in contemporary Germany, for a direct comparison between the past and present systems is inevitable; in areas of high unemployment, nostalgia for the GDR is thus likely to be higher.

Experience of life in unified Germany is perhaps the most important aspect to consider when discussing east–west identities. Lothar Probst, for example, dismisses the idea that the cultivation of an eastern identity is the result of either social heritage or nostalgia for a lost nation, but rather corresponds to the feeling of being misunderstood by western compatriots.[10] Commonly referred to as a 'we-identity' or a 'we-feeling', this has emerged only since confrontation with life in west Germany, and perceptions of western arrogance and political colonisation, as well as the persistence of economic inequalities between east and west, have doubtless contributed to a sense of inferiority amongst easterners, and the feeling that they are 'second-class Germans'. Jens Reich coined the phrase *Trotzidentität* (an identity of defiance) in the early 1990s to describe this phenomenon, for fuelled by their disappointment and resentment, many east Germans have transferred the practised distance that they had maintained from their socialist state onto the new German society.[11]

Similar arguments have been used to explain the rise in right-wing extremism in the east since unification, with foreigners serving as scapegoats for east German insecurities. As Andreas Staab claims: 'With the continuous decline of other identity markers, ethnicity represented one of the last remaining bastions of self-esteem for East

Germans. Xenophobia and ethnic chauvinism offered ready com-
pensation for widespread feelings of frustration and inferiority.'[12]
The debate over the causes of extremism highlights the two main
currents of thought concerning east German identity during the
post-*Wende* period: the significance of GDR socialisation versus the
importance of prevailing social, political and economic conditions.
Whilst neither influence can be dismissed, the extremism debate witnesses clear proponents of each argument. Christian Pfeiffer, for
example, maintains that the GDR education system, which took
children out of the family home at an early age, followed a strict
daily routine of military-like discipline, order and cleanliness and
required a high degree of conformity, quickly led to the suppression
of creativity and individual expression. This, together with the
GDR's emphasis on collectivism and hatred of the class enemy,
created patterns of behaviour in pupils which made them susceptible to racist attitudes.[13] A number of others also draw conclusions
that suggest agreement with this thesis, finding xenophobic behaviour to result from the failure of the GDR's anti-fascist education,
its over-emphasis on displaying loyalty to the homeland, or its
repressive educative methods.[14]

Such theories, however, meet with resistance from many quarters.
Peter Förster and his colleagues, for example, found that the
upheaval of unification had just as great an impact on young
people's lives as their GDR past, and Elmar Brähler and Horst-
Eberhard Richter reject Pfeiffer's theory on the basis of a study
which revealed that the parent–child bond (supposedly destroyed by
kindergarten education in the GDR) was, in fact, stronger in the east
than in the west.[15] Detlef Oesterreich's study of 16–21 year olds also
concludes that the GDR education system in no way produced
authoritarian personalities, but rather that the material insecurities
led to heightened authoritarian behaviour.[16] Because of the immediate effects of right-wing violence, these conflicting arguments
prove unusually heightened in this debate, but the general principles
of past socialisation versus present conditions colour the broader
debate over national and civic loyalties, as well as separate eastern
and western identities, and prove central to the questions of this
study.

The continuance of separate identities in east and west naturally
depends on the young generation; will they embrace a new patriotism, adopting an active and committed role as citizens of a united

Germany, or will they look rather to the societies of the German past as defining factors of their identity? It is commonly believed that the differences between east and west will gradually decline, and as the journalists Kerstin and Gunnar Decker claim: 'The east Germans are dying out. You can tell by the way that our children are already saying the word "GDR" as if they are saying "Thirty Years War" or "Old Rome". We are history. We don't have a chance. Our children will no longer become east Germans.'[17] To what extent, however, can today's young east Germans grow up unaffected by their divided history and fully embrace their citizenship of united Germany? Does unification in October 1990 represent 'zero hour' for those whose memories have been forged since, or will the collective memory of past regimes be carried forward by future generations, gaining mythical qualities and perpetuating a problematic sense of patriotism?

Frameworks: defining the GDR in the 1980s

In asking the above questions, this book will investigate the loyalties of young people before and after unification in equal measure. Its findings, however, necessarily lie in an understanding of the GDR and its youth policies during the 1980s, when this generation was growing up. With the benefit of hindsight it is tempting to view this period as a downwards spiral leading to 1989, yet the defining events of former decades such as the workers' uprising of 1953 and the building of the Berlin Wall in 1961, or the renegotiation of German–German relations during the period of *Ostpolitik* (politics working towards rapprochement with the East) in the early 1970s, were absent from all but the very end of the GDR's final decade. Indeed, the GDR of the mid-1980s was seen to be a self-confident and established state and, although overshadowed by its richer West German neighbour, its demise did not appear to be on the agenda.[18] In this way, Honecker's visit to Bonn, the capital of the FRG, in 1987, was celebrated in the GDR as confirmation of its equal status with the West German state. This is not to say that the early-to-mid-1980s were devoid of problems, for renewed international hostilities around the turn of the decade provided for a tense atmosphere. The Soviet modernisation of missiles, and consequently NATO's 'twin-track' decision of 1979,[19] for example, took place in the same twenty-month period as the Soviet invasion of Afghanistan and the

elections of staunch anti-communists Margaret Thatcher and
Ronald Reagan, as well as the foundation of the Solidarity movement and the start of workers' strikes in Poland, the suppression of
which caused Reagan to impose economic sanctions on the USSR.
Consequently, the early 1980s were marked by a very real fear of
nuclear war between the superpowers, above all in the GDR, posi-
tioned on the front line of the Cold War.

On the home front, oppositional voices in the GDR were raised
concerning the increasing militarisation of the regime, and peace initiatives gained momentum particularly within the churches. The
increasing evidence of pollution also prompted the emergence of
environmental groups, especially following the nuclear disaster in
Chernobyl in 1986, and the absence of civil freedoms in the GDR
provoked a number of critical voices. Following Gorbachev's
appointment as First Secretary of the Communist Party of the Soviet
Union (CPSU) in March 1985 and his introduction of glasnost and
perestroika, calls for reform in the GDR increased, despite the SED's
dogmatic resistance to these principles. In response, late 1987 and
early 1988 saw a renewed period of repression, during which numerous demonstrators were arrested, censorship increased and pupils
were expelled from schools for criticising the party. Events during
the following year, however, such as electoral fraud, official support
for the violent repression of demonstrations in Tiananmen Square,
and the liberalisation of regimes in Poland and Hungary, saw
increasing calls for a democratic voting system, the right to travel
and freedom of assembly, as well as increasing criticism of the SED.

These developments during the GDR's final years did not,
however, cast doubt on the future existence of the state, and it was
only after the fall of the Wall in November 1989 that unification
became a possibility; prior to this date, few questioned the continuance of the two German states. The GDR's apparent self-confidence
was in no small part due to the stabilisation of German–German
relations during the previous decade, as well as the development of
a more consistent policy on identity. Indeed, in the Basic Treaty of
1972, which represented the culmination of the West German government's *Ostpolitik*, the FRG recognised the inviolability of all
states in Europe, including the GDR, and agreed to the exchange of
permanent representations (rather than fully fledged embassies)
with the GDR. Whilst this move demonstrated the FRG's continued
refusal to recognise separate GDR citizenship, it considerably

increased the legitimacy of the GDR, for it marked the end of the Hallstein Doctrine, designed to prevent international diplomatic recognition of the GDR, and saw a significant increase in the number of states recognising the GDR. Furthermore, both German states became members of the United Nations (UN) in 1973. Within the GDR, *Ostpolitik* triggered a re-evaluation of the concept of the German nation, and the SED embarked on a policy of delimitation, or *Abgrenzung*, in which the party distanced itself from any future possibility of reunification, and instead promoted a separate socialist nation. This laid the foundations for a new concept of GDR identity, and an intensification of patriotic education, which will be discussed in more detail in chapter 1.

The latter half of the GDR period was, without doubt, set apart from the earlier years of Stalinist influence, which saw rapid sociopolitical transformation frequently imposed through repressive means such as party purges and enforced centralisation. Whilst the 1960s were largely characterised by the attempt to catch up with the West, the handover of power from Walter Ulbricht to Erich Honecker in 1971 marked a new era, one which Thomas Lindenberger claims saw a 'real socialist moratorium', allowing GDR citizens more room for negotiation, so long as they did not challenge the authority of the SED.[20] There is little doubt that interaction between state and society in the 1950s was fundamentally different to that of the 1980s, yet attempts to find appropriate paradigms for the GDR, particularly its later years, have proved the subject of much debate since its demise. The classification of the GDR as totalitarian, a model which was frequently used by Western critics to compare fascist and communist regimes during the first half of the Cold War, and which re-emerged with the demise of the GDR, is one which has dominated debate. Of the many variants of totalitarian theory, Carl Friedrich's model proves most influential, outlining six dominant features of totalitarian states: an official ideology, single-party rule, terroristic control, a centrally regulated economy and a monopoly over the media and arms.[21] Whilst each of these can be applied to the GDR, the totalitarian paradigm takes a 'top-down' view of society, concentrating on the aims and structures of the ruling party and its system of control and repression. In doing so, it relies on the aims of the state to denote the regime's nature, rather than describing the actual structures of power, thus failing to capture the complexities and ambiguities of the relationship between state and society which contributed to the relative stability of the later GDR years. Furthermore, the totalitarian model invites the comparison of the GDR with the Third Reich and, whilst the two dictatorships doubtless shared some structural similarities, their fundamentally different ideologies and legacies not only render such a comparison devoid of real substance, but this runs the risk of playing down the severity of Nazi crimes.

Other paradigms have adopted a 'bottom-up' approach, such as the portrayal of the GDR as a 'niche society', a term coined in the early 1980s by the FRG's first permanent representative to the GDR, Günter Gaus.[22] Whilst this model allows for a more differentiated view, highlighting the primacy of private circles outside the 'official' system, it, too, fails to recognise the importance of interaction between the private and the public spheres. Although private niches doubtless played an important role in creating stability and identity, they were neither removed from, nor untouched by, the political sphere. The search for appropriate terminology has thus seen many attempts to encapsulate both the repressive elements of the regime and the complex relations between state and society, with suggestions such as 'welfare dictatorship' (Konrad Jarausch), 'modern dictatorship' (Jürgen Kocka) and 'thoroughly dominated society' (*durchherrschte Gesellschaft*) (Adolf Lüdtke); whilst there is little disagreement that the GDR constituted a dictatorship, the search to qualify its nature has produced much debate. The findings of this book largely support the concept of *Eigen-Sinn*, a sense of one's own interests, as developed by Adolf Lüdtke and Thomas Lindenberger. This notion highlights the importance of interaction between the ruling elite and the masses, in the form of negotiation, bargaining and the pursuit of one's own interests; hence it was not only the state which influenced young people, but also vice versa. The concept of *Eigen-Sinn* thus recognises the grey areas between the artificial black and white divisions of state and society, as well as conformity and dissent, and emphasises the importance of overlap between these areas in maintaining relative stability. As the following chapters will show, this concept proves particularly useful in explaining the influence of GDR socialisation on young people even after unification, for it was above all their personal interaction with the GDR state which has impacted on their post-unification identities. Before examining such interaction, however, it is first necessary to outline the overarching policies and structures which shaped young people's lives during this period.

Growing up under Honecker

From the foundation of the GDR, the SED recognised that no sector of the population was more vital to its future than the young generation, for it was they who were to carry the banner of socialism into the world arena and continue working towards the communist ideal. The SED thus portrayed itself as the guardian of young people that protected and promoted the interests of the state's youth – and it is no coincidence that Erich Honecker and Egon Krenz, the last two General Secretaries of the SED prior to the fall of the Wall, had both previously been at the head of the official youth organisation, the Free German Youth (FDJ). The party's keen interest in the youth sphere, however, was clearly one of self-interest, for it was of existential importance for the socialist state to secure the young generation's loyalty. As the party frequently claimed: 'To have the young is to hold the future.'

In order to win over the youth, the SED developed an all-encompassing youth policy, the primary aim of which was to form a patriotic young vanguard which identified with the socialist state. At the centre of this policy was the concept of the 'socialist personality', which was adopted from Soviet pedagogy in the 1960s and rapidly became a leitmotif within socialist education. This ideal embodied a number of qualities: respect for the collective way of life, commitment to the working class, belief in the socialist, scientific world view as well as Marxism–Leninism, loyal friendship with the Soviet Union and all other socialist countries and, most importantly, pride in the GDR. The creation of 'socialist personalities' naturally demanded large measures of ideological indoctrination, especially during the final decade of the GDR, when new conditions called for a more stringent policy. Young people growing up in the 1980s had not experienced the war or immediate post-war periods, and had played no part in the building of socialism in the 1950s; thus they had few clear reasons to feel indebted to the party, and were in danger of holding a more distanced attitude towards the state than previous generations. Additionally, the growing divide between the living standards of the GDR and the FRG was increasingly undermining the legitimacy of the GDR, and consequently the validity of a GDR identity. As direct comparison of the two German states became inevitable, the GDR was continuously at pains to prove its superiority over West Germany. The party thus strove for complete ideological hegemony in youth work from the earliest of ages and, by the 1980s, numerous educational, societal and pedagogical structures had been developed to infiltrate all areas of young people's lives. Not only were kindergartens, schools and universities recruited for this cause, but also mass organisations, national holidays and ritual ceremonies. Two establishments, however, dominated: the formal education system and the FDJ, which together allowed the state to access nearly all young people twice over.

The 'unified socialist education system', as it was formally known, remained largely unaltered in structure following the Education Law of 1965, and developed in accordance with Marxist principles, advocating the education of all children in state-run institutions. Every child from the age of ten months thus had the right to a place in a crèche, kindergarten or children's home, and all 6–16 year olds were guaranteed an unconditional place in the ten-year 'polytechnic high school' (POS). After completion of the POS, a small number of pupils could progress to the 'extended high school' (EOS), where they would complete the *Abitur* (A-level equivalent), and possibly continue to university. The majority, however, left school at the age of 16 to take up apprenticeships, where they were trained for their future careers. Not only were all levels of education incorporated within this centralised system, but textbooks and teaching aids were published exclusively by the 'Volk und Wissen' publishing house and authorised by the Ministry for Education, securing tight control over all teaching materials. Other than a small number of exceptions, such as special schools for the very gifted, or exemption from all 'obligatory' ten years for the academically weakest of pupils,[23] the ideological training in all educational establishments remained uniform, targeting not the richness of individuality, but rather the compliance of the individual, alongside political stability and ideological unity. Whilst official socialist ideology infiltrated all subject areas, the compulsory civics class for older pupils, *Staatsbürgerkunde*, focused specifically on educating young people in the principles of socialist society. Similarly, students were required to attend a course in the fundamentals of Marxism–Leninism, and the central premise remained clear throughout all stages of education: 'to declare one's support for the German Democratic Republic as one's fatherland at all times.'[24]

Education extended far beyond the bounds of the formal education system, and free-time activities were dominated by the FDJ and its children's branch, the 'Ernst Thälmann' Pioneer Organisation.[25] Founded on 7 March 1946 under the leadership of Erich Honecker, the FDJ was already well established by the time the GDR was officially founded in October 1949; similarly the Pioneer Organisation was formed at an early stage, becoming an association of the FDJ in December 1948. As the only officially sanctioned youth organisations,[26] they monopolised the youth work of the GDR, and the FDJ not only posed as the single representative of all young people's interests, but also carried the title 'helper and reserve of the party'. Both organisations dominated the publication of newspapers and magazines for young people, most notably *Junge Welt* for FDJ members and *Trommel* for Pioneers, but also a large number of other youth publications (all published by 'Junge Welt'), ensuring a uniform ideological influence. Although the majority of FDJ and Pioneer work focused on free-time activities, the organisations never became separated from school life. Indeed, their organisational structures centred around the school, with each class forming the basic membership unit, and as a result 99% of all 6–13 year olds became Pioneers, making it virtually impossible for children to refuse to take part.[27] At the age of 14, transference to the FDJ became an automatic procedure, and whilst this organisation recruited members outside the education system, in factories or in the army, its initial contact with all young people was at school. Whilst membership rates in schools remained near 100%, the overall percentage of 14–25 year olds in the FDJ was considerably lower (at around 70–75% during the 1980s), as young workers participated to a much lesser extent.[28]

The broad aims of the youth organisations were identical to those of the education system, centring around the 'socialist personality' and the propagation of patriotic values. As the handbook for Pioneer leaders stated: '[The FDJ] ensures that its members and all young people prove their worth as socialist patriots and proletarian internationalists, strengthen their socialist fatherland as an inseparable part of the socialist community of states gathered around the Soviet Union, and are prepared to defend peace and socialism at all times.'[29] It is no surprise that the first of the laws of the Thälmann Pioneers read: 'We Thälmann Pioneers love our socialist fatherland, the German Democratic Republic',[30] a principle which underlay its whole range of activities. Whilst many of these were regular after-school clubs and meetings, some activities took place during school holidays, for this was the period during which children were most likely to stray from the influence of the state, and the youth organisations took care never to loosen their hold on young people. The FDJ thus owned a large number of holiday centres throughout the GDR, and controlled the GDR youth travel agent *Jugendtourist*, created in 1975. Whilst generous state subsidies meant that the agency could provide very affordable holidays, whether to other socialist countries or in the GDR, they also ensured that none were free from the influence of official ideology. In this way, all who worked with young people, whether teachers, FDJ leaders or those in charge of youth hostels, were required to show high levels of commitment to the socialist cause, and were just as tightly controlled by the party as the youth itself. All activities were thus carefully structured to allow as little deviance from the socialist norm as possible.

Although the education system and youth organisations formed the two central pillars of youth work in the GDR, numerous other mass organisations were enlisted to act as the 'transmission belts' of SED policy, thereby ensuring the widest possible influence.[31] The most prominent of these for young people was the Society for Sport and Technology (GST). Founded in 1952, its main function was to provide paramilitary training for adults and young people from the age of 14, and to encourage 'love, trust and solidarity with their socialist fatherland, the GDR'.[32] It proved popular for the training it provided in a range of extreme sports, such as parachuting, freefalling and motor sports, and was particularly favoured by young people as it provided them with the opportunity to pass their driving test. Other similar organisations included the German Gymnastics and Sports Association (DTSB) and the German Red Cross (DRK), neither of which targeted young people uniquely, yet aimed to influence citizens from as early an age as possible. The DTSB thus took charge of the majority of sporting activities for children and young people, and as one of the main organisers of the annual 'Week of youth and athletes' it worked in close association with the FDJ, schools and universities. Similarly, the DRK permeated all these institutions, providing first aid courses and medical training primarily for girls, but also for boys who were unfit to do military service. In the cultural sphere, the *Kulturbund* organised literary and artistic competitions for young people, whilst *Urania* encouraged interest in scientific and technological advances, and the Society for German–Soviet Friendship (DSF) arranged international events, encouraging young people to identify with the wider international socialist society. As this plethora of mass organisations demonstrates, all conceivable areas of public life were permeated by state ideology, with the aim of attaining a uniform and controlled public sphere. Their joint influence was most clear during national holiday celebrations, such as 1 May (international workers' day) or 7 October (anniversary of the GDR's founding), when every organisation was mobilised to create amongst the young generation an emotional attachment to their country and publicly to acclaim their commitment to GDR society.

The SED appeared to infiltrate all areas of young people's lives, yet there was one exception: the religious sphere. Churches maintained a degree of autonomy outside the state, and inevitably church youth groups such as the Protestant *Junge Gemeinde* provided competition for the FDJ, especially during its early years. In 1954 the state thus launched the *Jugendweihe*, a secular ceremony dating back to the mid-nineteenth century, in which 14 year olds swore allegiance to the GDR state. With clear parallels to the religious ceremony of confirmation, the initial aim of the *Jugendweihe* was to draw young people away from the churches and recruit them for the socialist cause. However, once the influence of the churches had been curbed by the mid-1960s, the emphasis of the preparatory classes shifted away from the scientific, materialistic world view towards issues of citizenship and, by the 1970s, the development of a GDR consciousness.[33] In the 1980s, 97% of 14 year olds participated, and the *Jugendweihe* had become a ceremony deeply entrenched in the SED's methods of patriotic education, and yet another layer of state influence which enveloped young people's lives.

Researching young behaviours

As demonstrated by the *Jugendweihe*, the SED's methods not only became increasingly sophisticated, but the intensity of propaganda also strengthened in the GDR's later years, reaching its zenith by the 1980s. Images of official occasions, with blue-shirted and flag-waving young people thus presented to the outside world a monolithic and loyal young generation, as promoted by GDR propaganda which commonly spoke of 'the youth', casting each individual into the mould of the 'socialist personality'. In reality, however, the youth sphere was marked by a variety of attitudes and behaviours, as revealed in a number of recent studies of all four decades of the GDR.[34] Surveys carried out by the former Central Institute for Youth Research (ZIJ) in Leipzig, the only authorised organ of research into youth opinion during the 1980s, provide particularly interesting findings in this respect.[35] Despite the restrictive conditions under which their surveys were carried out, and the need to produce reports favourable to the socialist climate, a number of surveys conducted in the late 1980s revealed fissures in the bastion of socialist youth policy. A study on historical consciousness in 1988, for example, found that young people were far from accepting of the official 'progressive' history.[36] Walter Friedrich, director of the institute during its lifetime from 1966 to 1990, also uses data from a number of surveys in order to show how the mentality of young people changed in the 1980s, becoming further removed from the ideals of the state.[37] Others, such as Dorothee Wierling and Jana Lunz, similarly propose that the youth of the 1980s formed a distinct group, different in attitude and behaviour from their parents and grandparents.[38] Whereas Wierling, however, presents the youth of the 1980s as passive in contrast to those of the 1960s, Lunz instead creates a more vibrant picture of the younger generation, revealing a great variety of emerging youth cultures. There is, however, general agreement that despite displaying certain behavioural trends, no single generation is ever homogeneous, and a number of studies have attempted to categorise young people within each generation. Wolfgang Mleczkowski made one of the first attempts in the 1980s, distinguishing between four groups of young people (careerists, followers, self-conformists and activists adjacent to the ruling elite) in order to explain the way this generation functioned.[39] Such findings clearly conflict with both the totalitarian model and the concept of a homogeneous young generation, both of which will also be countered by the findings of this book.

The study of GDR youth has hitherto concentrated largely on the influence of socialisation prior to the *Wende*, and whilst there is no shortage of studies examining the attitudes of young people post-1990, few bridge this divide. One notable exception is a longitudinal study conducted by Peter Förster and Walter Friedrich, who extended a ZIJ study of school pupils in Saxony beginning in 1987, surveying the same group at regular intervals throughout the 1990s.[40] As the only study of its kind, it offers valuable data on the development of young people in east Germany, concerning a wide variety of subjects, such as their hopes and fears, as well as attitudes towards politics, economic development, national and international loyalties. Other research projects concerning attitudes during the 1990s are largely based on quantitative research. Of the surveys concerning this period, the largest and most significant are those sponsored by Shell (comparative east–west studies, dating from 1992, 1997, 2000 and 2002), and those conducted by the German Youth Institute (DJI) (major comparative studies: 1990, 1992, 1997), both of which are committed to tracing the behaviour and attitudes of young people in east and west from 1990. Whilst results from the earlier years reveal a surprising similarity in attitudes between the populations of east and west, the Shell study *Jugend 2000* instead observes an increasing divide, thus supporting the view that Germany's divided history still influences those who have little memory of it.[41] The selection of empirical data from this period is substantial, making it difficult to gain a comprehensive overview, and whilst many studies reveal a gulf between the attitudes of young people in east and west, others claim that this generation is largely united across geographical boundaries.[42] Most do, however, respect Richard Münchmeier's observation that the changing patterns in youth culture today are manifold, and that the term 'youth' refers less to a fixed stage between childhood and adulthood than it used to, instead encompassing a wide range of different types.[43]

Amidst this wealth of literature, not only do very few studies attempt to bridge the 1989–90 caesura, but none performs a detailed examination of the effects of patriotic education, which was so central to the socialist education system, and has consequently been of influence to the formation of post-*Wende* identities. This book thus takes a new approach to the research of east German youth, crossing the traditional 1989–90 boundary and analysing a period of just over twenty years, enabling a detailed examination of the development of patriotic behaviour in young people who have experienced socialisation in the GDR, as well as in those who have little or no memory of it. As a qualitative study, it combines archival research with in-depth interviews, thus departing from the traditional emphasis on either archival research or interview-based studies, whilst incorporating the findings of larger quantitative research projects in order to provide the broader perspective. The period of study from 1979 to 2002, which enables a similar time span both before and after unification, is significant for a variety of reasons. Firstly, 1979 marks the 30th anniversary of the GDR's founding, for which there were numerous national celebrations, most notably the National Youth Festival in June. These events provide a considerable quantity of material of direct relevance to the study of patriotism, as well as an interesting point of comparison with 1989. Secondly, 1979 marks the first full school year in which obligatory military education was carried out in schools, and as a vital component of patriotic education this necessitates detailed examination. Thirdly, the late 1970s and early 1980s mark the revival of Cold War tensions, and in turn the strengthening of patriotic propaganda in the GDR. There is no other decade in GDR history during which patriotism was propagated to such a great extent. The final date of 2002 is significant for the fact that it marks the first year in which school leavers in east Germany had no personal experience of GDR school education, a phenomenon which marks the birth of a new generation.

Given the mass of material available, the majority of primary resources for this study focus on the area of Sachsen-Anhalt, formerly the GDR *Bezirke* (districts) of Halle and Magdeburg. The regional focus enables greater consideration of local identities, this area being chosen for its geographical location and social composition. As a former border region, it provides interesting research opportunities, as contact with West Germany, both before and after unification, has been more intense here. In terms of social and industrial composition, the region also offers great variety, for the south is densely populated and marked by heavy industry, whereas the north is more sparsely populated and agricultural. In this way, it may be seen as largely representative of the GDR. Supplementary material from the central GDR archives in Berlin, as well ZIJ statistics, which were largely taken from the Leipzig area, and national surveys carried out post-1990, place it within a national context.

Chapters 1–5 will adopt a chronological framework, tracing attitudes through the GDR, the *Wende* period and finally unified Germany. Before examining empirical data, however, chapter 1 will discuss the problematic nature of patriotism in twentieth-century Germany, the challenges facing the SED, and its programme of patriotic education in the GDR during the 1980s. Primary materials consulted for the period prior to 1989 include the GDR press, school books, teaching aids and educational journals, but above all party and government files from a variety of archives, primarily the *Stiftung Archiv der Parteien und Massenorganisationen der DDR* (SAPMO) in the *Bundesarchiv* (BArch), the *Stasi* archives, managed by the *Bundesbeauftragte für die Unterlagen des Staatssicherheitsdienstes* (BStU), the *Landeshauptarchiv Magdeburg* (LA Magd) and the archives of the former *Akademie der Pädagogischen Wissenschaften* (APW). These sources, many of which come from official party archives, have been supplemented by twenty interviews conducted in 2001 and 2002 in Magdeburg with individuals born between 1970 and 1974, who thus experienced the GDR education system to the full in the 1980s. As with any oral history project, the material gathered concerns the personal memories of interviewees and cannot be regarded as objective, yet they complement the official nature of the archival material, revealing information that would otherwise be left uncovered. These interviews, alongside a further twenty-three with teenagers born between 1980 and 1984, serve as the primary source for the post-*Wende* period, alongside government reports, newspaper articles and teaching materials. Whilst some of the younger cohort of interviewees have memories of the GDR, these are minimal; they have little direct experience of GDR socialisation, and the majority have experienced nearly all their education in unified Germany. As a result, the comparison of these two generations' patriotic behaviour in post-*Wende* Germany will help to reveal any possible long-term effects of GDR socialisation.

By comparing the older cohort's attitudes and behaviour across the two decades, as well as the two generations' experiences of life as teenagers in each system, this study hopes to ascertain the extent to which rapid social and political change in eastern Germany has caused shifting civic loyalties, and the extent to which these loyalties can also be regulated by the state. Through the study of patriotic behaviour, this project aims to deepen our understanding not only of the downfall of the GDR and the shortcomings of its youth policy, but also of the social development of unified Germany, and the nature of identity formation. On a broader scale, it will help to reveal the way in which patriotic sentiment is formed, thus the extent to which a sense of belonging and loyalty can successfully be imposed from above and the extent to which it is defined in the face of 'the other'. This is of particular relevance at a time marked by globalisation and increased supranational co-operation, for the nature and role of national and regional identities are presently undergoing rapid transformation, faced by an uncertain future. As the following chapters will reveal, however, they are likely to continue to play a vital role in the future development of the German state for a number of years to come.

Notes

1 Jana Hensel, *Zonenkinder* (Reinbek bei Hamburg: Rowohlt, 2002); Claudia Rusch, *Meine freie deutsche Jugend* (Frankfurt am Main: Fischer, 2003).

2 Brigitte Seebacher-Brandt, 'Nation im vereinigten Deutschland', *Aus Politik und Zeitgeschichte (APuZG)*, B42 (1994), 3–9 (p. 8). All translations are my own. On the issue of 'normality' in German history, see Stefan Berger, *The Search for Normality: National Identity and Historical Consciousness in Germany since 1800* (Providence, Oxford: Berghahn, 1997).

3 Following the accepted convention, I will capitalise 'East'/'Eastern' and 'West'/'Western' when referring to the period of division, but not the post-unification period. The hybrid form 'East(ern)' will indicate this geographical area during both periods.

4 Günter Grass, *Deutscher Lastenausgleich: Wider das dumpfe Einheitsgebot: Reden und Gespräche* (Frankfurt am Main: Luchterhand, 1990).

5 Heinrich Jaenecke, 'Wir sind zwei Völker', *Stern*, 33 (2001), 58. Numerous surveys also document the continuing divide between east and west, e.g. *Jugend 2000*, ed. by Deutsche Shell (Opladen: Leske & Budrich, 2000); Elmar Brähler and Horst-Eberhard Richter, 'Deutsche – zehn Jahre nach der Wende', *Aus Politik und Zeitgeschichte (APuZG)*, B45 (1999), 24–31; 'Stolz aufs eigene Leben', *Der Spiegel*, 27 (1995), 40–64.

6 Matthias Matussek, 'Sehnsucht nach dem Totalitären', *Der Spiegel*, 11 (1999), 46–60.

7 Marc Alan Howard, 'Die Ostdeutschen als ethnische Gruppe? Zum Verständnis der neuen Teilung des geeinten Deutschland', *Berliner Debatte INITIAL*, 6/4–5 (1995), 119–31 (p. 125).

8 Helmut Meier, *Geschichtsbewußtsein und historische Identität in der DDR*, hefte zur ddr-geschichte 31 (Berlin Forscher- und Diskussionskreis DDR-Geschichte, 1996), pp. 39–40.

9 Cited by Kerstin und Gunnar Decker, *Gefühlsausbrüche oder Ewig pubertiert der Ostdeutsche* (Berlin: Das Neue Berlin, 2000), p. 21.

10 Lothar Probst, 'Ost-West-Differenzen und das republikanische Defizit der deutschen Einheit', *APuZG*, B41–42 (1998), 3–8.

11 See 'Distanz, Enttäuschung, Haß', *Der Spiegel*, 34 (1992), 30–7.

12 Andreas Staab, *National Identity in Eastern Germany: Inner Unification or Continued Separation?* (Westport, CT: Praeger, 1998), p. 159.

13 Christian Pfeiffer, 'Anleitung zum Haß', *Der Spiegel*, 12 (1999), 60–6.

14 E.g. Bernd-Reiner Fischer, 'Das Bildungs- und Erziehungssystem der DDR – Funktion, Inhalte, Instrumentalisierung, Freiräume', in *Materialien der Enquete-Kommission 'Aufarbeitung von Geschichte und Folgen der SED-Diktatur in Deutschland'*, vol. III.2, ed. by Deutscher Bundestag (Baden-Baden: Nomos, 1995), pp. 852–75; Harry Waibel, 'Jugendliche Rechtsextremisten in der DDR und die Reaktionen der FDJ', in *'Links und links und Schritt gehalten . . .', Die FDJ: Konzepte – Abläufe – Grenzen*, ed. by Helga Gotschlich (Berlin: Metropol, 1994), pp. 276–89; Hans-Joachim Maaz, *Der Gefühlsstau: Ein Psychogramm der DDR* (Munich: Knaur, 1992).

15 Peter Förster *et al.*, *Jugend Ost: Zwischen Hoffnung und Gewalt* (Opladen: Leske & Budrich, 1993); Brähler and Richter, 'Deutsche – zehn Jahre nach der Wende'.

16 Detlef Oesterreich, *Autoritäre Persönlichkeit und Gesellschaftsordnung: Der Stellenwert psychischer Faktoren für politische Einstellungen – eine empirische Untersuchung von Jugendlichen in Ost und West* (Weinheim, Munich: Juventa, 1993).

17 Decker, *Gefühlsausbrüche*, p. 9.

18 Henry Krisch, *The German Democratic Republic: the Search for Identity* (Boulder and London: Westview Press, 1985), p. 173.

19 The twin-track decision was made in 1979, and involved the modernisation of medium-range nuclear missiles in Western Europe, with simultaneous negotiations to reduce such weapons on both sides.

20 Thomas Lindenberger, 'Herrschaft und Eigen-Sinn in der Diktatur. Das Alltagsleben der DDR und sein Platz in der Erinnerungskultur des vereinten Deutschlands', *APuZG*, B40 (2000), 5–12 (p. 12).

21 See Cory Ross, *The East German Dictatorship: Problems and Perspectives in the Interpretation of the GDR* (London: Arnold, 2002), pp. 20–5.

22 Günter Gaus, *Wo Deutschland liegt: Eine Ortsbestimmung* (Hamburg: Hoffmann und Campe, 1983).

23 See Fischer, 'Das Bildungs- und Erziehungssystem der DDR', p. 859.

24 *Beiträge zur staatsbürgerlichen Erziehung älterer Schüler*, ed. by Hans-Georg Hoffmann *et al.* (Berlin: Volk und Wissen, 1968), p. 10.

25 Ernst Thälmann was the leader of the communist party during much of the Weimar Republic. Arrested by the Gestapo in 1933, and killed at Buchenwald concentration camp in 1944, he became the GDR's best known anti-fascist martyr.

26 Although church youth groups existed, they never enjoyed comparable status to the official organisations as a result of state repression.

27 'Pionierorganisation "Ernst Thälmann"', in *DDR Handbuch*, ed. by Bundesministerium für innerdeutsche Beziehungen (Cologne: Wissenschaft und Politik, 1985), p. 984.

28 Dorle Zilch, *Millionen unter der blauen Fahne* (Rostock: Norddeutscher Hochschulschriften, 1994).

29 *Wie Ernst Thälmann treu und kühn: Handbuch für Freundschaftspionierleiter* (Berlin: Kinderbuchverlag, 1985), p. 16.

30 *Ibid.*, p. 14.

31 Lenin was the first to use the term 'transmission belt', with reference to workers' unions; it is now widely applied to mass organisations in the GDR. See Rainer Eckert, 'Zur Rolle der Massenorganisationen im Alltag der DDR-Bevölkerung', in *Materialien der Enquete-Kommission*, vol. II.2, pp. 1243–300.

32 *Wörterbuch zur sozialistischen Jugendpolitik* (Berlin: Dietz, 1975), p. 88.

33 See Anna Saunders, 'The Socialist and Post-socialist *Jugendweihe*: Symbol of an Evolving East(ern) German Identity', *Focus on German Studies*, 9 (2002), 43–60.

34 E.g. Alan McDougall, *Youth Politics in East Germany: The Free German Youth Movement 1946–1968* (Oxford: Oxford University Press, 2004); Marc-Dietrich Ohse, *Jugend nach dem Mauerbau: Anpassung, Protest und Eigensinn* (Berlin: Ch. Links Verlag, 2003); Jeannette Madárasz, *Conflict and Compromise in East Germany, 1971–1989: A Precarious Stability* (Basingstoke: Palgrave, 2003).

35 See Walter Friedrich, Peter Förster and Kurt Starke (eds), *Das Zentralinstitut für Jugendforschung Leipzig 1966–1990: Geschichte, Methoden, Erkenntnisse* (Berlin: edition ost, 1999).

36 SAPMO-BArch, DC4/304, Wilfried Schubarth, 'Zum Geschichtsbewußtsein von Jugendlichen der DDR' (Leipzig: ZIJ, March 1988).

37 Walter Friedrich, 'Mentalitätswandlungen der Jugend in der DDR', *APuZG*, B16–17 (1990), 25–37.

38 Dorothee Wierling, 'The Hitler Youth Generation in the GDR: Insecurities, Ambitions and Dilemmas', in *Dictatorship as Experience*, ed. by Konrad H. Jarausch (New York, Oxford: Berghahn, 1999), pp. 307–24; Jana Lunz, 'Zwischen Aufbau und Aufgabe', in *Fortschritt, Norm und Eigensinn: Erkundungen im Alltag der DDR*, Dokumentationszentrum Alltagskultur der DDR e.V. (Berlin: Ch. Links, 1999), pp. 277–93.

39 Wolfgang Mleczkowski, '"Der Staat sind wir nicht." Probleme der politischen Gegenkultur Jugendlicher in der DDR', in *Jugendprobleme im geteilten Deutschland*, ed. by Siegfried Baske and Horst Rögner-Francke (Berlin: Duncker & Humblot, 1986), pp. 51–71.

40 Förster *et al.*, *Jugend Ost*; Förster, 'Die 25jährigen auf dem langen Weg in das vereinte Deutschland', *APuZG*, B43–44 (1999), 20–31, and '"Es war nicht alles falsch, was wir früher über den Kapitalismus gelernt haben." Empirische Ergebnisse einer Längsschnittstudie zum Weg junger Ostdeutscher vom DDR-Bürger zum Bundesbürger', *Deutschland Archiv* (*DA*), 34/2 (2001), 197–218.

41 The last Shell study relevant to this period, *Jugend 2002*, does not focus on east–west differences.

42 E.g. Claus Leggewie, *die 89er: Portrait einer Generation* (Hamburg: Hoffmann und Campe, 1995); Klaus Janke and Stefan Niehues, *Echt abgedreht: Die Jugend der 90er Jahre* (Munich: Beck, 1995).

43 Richard Münchmeier, '"Entstrukturierung" der Jugendphase', *APuZG*, B31 (1999), 3–13.

1

The parameters of patriotism

In securing and further strengthening the alliance between the Soviet Union and the other states of the socialist community, [the working class and all working people] are promoting the development of the socialist German nation in the GDR . . . The socialist patriotism of the working class and all working people is revolutionary. (Academy of Pedagogical Sciences of the GDR, 1978)[1]

We in Germany – today we say this with pride in our country, self-critically but also self-confidently patriotic. We want to modernise and we want to stick together. And we want to embrace our new role in Europe and in the world. As a normal nation. (Franz Müntefering, General Secretary of the SPD, 2002)[2]

As the above quotations demonstrate, not only do the criteria for defining 'normality' change with time, but so too do those for concepts such as 'nation', 'state', 'nationalism' and 'patriotism'. Several generations of scholars have attempted to provide definitions for such terms, all noting the 'notoriously difficult and unsatisfactory' nature of their complexity.[3] Moreover, the discussion of these concepts relating to Germany is complicated by the frequent reshaping of twentieth-century German states and their nation(s). Yet without terminological clarity, the examination of identities during this period remains confused, and whilst the boundaries between the 'nation' and the 'state' are frequently blurred, their distinction is of primordial importance to our understanding of patriotism. This chapter will thus begin with a brief discussion of the identifying features of these concepts, before turning to the specific parameters of patriotism in post-war Germany, and the GDR's patriotic programme of the 1980s.

Nation and state

Friedrich Meinecke's differentiation between the *Staatsnation* (nation state) and the *Kulturnation* (cultural nation) in 1908 has had a lasting influence on scholarship, for the distinction between the political and the cultural, or the civic and the ethnic, remains essential. The state is thus commonly associated with political and civic elements, and was notably described by Max Weber as an agency within society which possesses the monopoly of legitimate violence.[4] Although this image may be somewhat outdated today, the emphasis on the state as an order-enforcing agency is widely accepted, and as Anthony D. Smith claims: '[The state] refers exclusively to public institutions, differentiated from, and autonomous of, other social institutions and exercising a monopoly of coercion and extraction within a given territory.'[5] In contrast, the nation contains a broader and more abstract range of identifying features, including cultural and ethnic elements, language, common values and traditions, as well as religious, physical and material interests. Whilst any combination of such elements may constitute a nation, it is commonly recognised that these are bound together by a spiritual or moral principle, whereby two members of the same nation will recognise themselves as such through their common convictions, loyalties and solidarities.[6] Benedict Anderson's definition of the nation as an 'imagined community' draws on this concept, and is undoubtedly the most dominant of all interpretations today. As he explains, the nation is imagined, because the members of even the smallest of nations will never know or meet each other, yet 'in the minds of each lives the image of their communion'.[7] It is also imagined as a community because the nation is perceived as a deep comradeship, despite the existence of real inequality or exploitation.

The cultural and political elements of modern states have become so closely allied that the terms 'nation' and 'state' are often used synonymously, whether or not they are merged into what is commonly labelled a 'nation state'.[8] It is, however, the boundary between the two which frequently gives rise to the principle of nationalism, which, in Ernest Gellner's words, 'holds that the political and national unit should be congruent'.[9] Some critics believe that this political definition is too limiting, failing to do justice, for example, to the 'nationalism' of football fans which may not be political in nature.[10] Support of the nation evidently need not be accompanied by political demands, and it is ultimately a matter of terminology as to whether or not this is described as nationalistic. For the purposes of this study, Gellner's widely accepted definition will be adopted, in order to provide a clear delineation of these terms. National loyalties, which may simply be cultural in nature, thus need not be national*ist* in their demands.

Where, then, does this discussion leave patriotism? In contrast to the above concepts, patriotism has been the subject of much less scholarly work over recent decades, yet forms the focus of this book because of its predominance in the propaganda of the GDR. It was frequently appealed to in socialist regimes, as it called for the collective loyalty of their citizens, yet avoided the use of the term 'nationalism', which was dismissed by Marx as class-based and bourgeois in nature. Instead, patriotism, meaning 'love of the *patria*' or 'fatherland', was not seen to advocate a specific political agenda. As a principle, however, it is closely related to the world of politics, for it is allied to the concept of the state, and many commentators emphasise the importance of a civic element in patriotic sentiment, describing it as 'civic nationalism', 'civic loyalty' or a 'civic religion'.[11] Hobsbawm more specifically refers to 'state-based patriotism', underlining that the original revolutionary–popular idea of patriotism was state-based rather than nationalist in nature, as patriots in the French Revolution were 'those who showed the love of their country by wishing to renew it by reform or revolution. And the *patrie* to which their loyalty lay, was the exact opposite of an existential, pre-existing unit, but a nation created by the political choice of its members.'[12] Rogers Brubaker also distinguishes between civic and ethnic elements in his study of French and German citizenship, showing that in France, citizenship became defined as a territorial community based on *ius soli* (territorial jurisdiction), whereas in Germany it was based rather on *ius sanguinis* (principle of descent).[13] Hence, as he argues, the state preceded the nation in France, yet the nation preceded the state in Germany. Patriotism as a civic concept therefore involves loyalty to one's citizenship based on the principle of *ius soli*, and demands the defence of, as well as the exercise of, civic rights, rather than any emphasis on ethnic roots.

This civic emphasis has led many to follow Dolf Sternberger in assigning democratic roots to patriotism, associating it with values such as equality, humanism and individualism, whilst nationalism is regarded as more essentialist in nature, bearing the ethnic banner and carrying in its wake dogmatism, dominance and exclusion.[14] Such a distinction between patriotism and nationalism is widespread and, whilst others employ different labels, such as Peter Schmidt's use of 'unconditional loyalty' (nationalism) and 'critical loyalty' (patriotism), the emphasis remains the same: one is 'safe' to encourage, yet the other potentially poses a danger.[15] Johannes Rau made this distinction in his speech of thanks following his election as Federal President in May 1999: 'I never want to be a nationalist, but rather a patriot. A patriot is someone who loves his fatherland, a nationalist is someone who despises the fatherlands of others.'[16] The difference apparently lies between 'good patriotism' and 'bad nationalism', a distinction which, according to Stefan Berger, is 'fatally flawed', since 'no concept of national identity can exist without such dissociations and exclusions'.[17] There do, indeed, appear to be a number of problems with this distinction. Firstly, the boundaries between these two concepts frequently become blurred and, as Hobsbawm states:

> The very act of democratizing politics, i.e. of turning subjects into citizens, tends to produce a populist consciousness which, seen in some lights, is hard to distinguish from a national, even a chauvinist, patriotism – for if 'the country' is in some way 'mine', then it is more readily seen as preferable to those of foreigners, especially if these lack the rights and freedom of the true citizen.[18]

Secondly, patriotism can also become a potentially threatening concept within the state, for the emphasis on universal rights can lead to the neglect of societal divisions caused by class, race or gender. In this way a patriot may reveal very limited characteristics, insisting 'that a cumulative tradition of unity continues to preside over the deepest divisions of his community'.[19] Thirdly, states may attempt to reinforce patriotism with the sentiments and symbols of an 'imagined community', sometimes going so far as to invent traditions or even nations for this purpose, and thus adopting qualities that could be labelled as 'nationalist'. As the following section will reveal, the GDR was a prime example of a state which attempted to 'create' its own nation.

The distinction between 'good patriotism' and 'bad nationalism' is clearly unhelpful, as patriotism can be limiting if abused, and 'bad patriotism' can exist just as equally as 'good nationalism'. However, the distinction between the civic and ethnic bases of patriotism and nationalism remains important, especially for this study. Patriotism thus primarily denotes loyalty to the civic institutions of the state, and whilst this does not exclude loyalty to the nation and national values, it does not demand the unity of the state and nation; it should not be dismissed as, or confused with, nationalist sentiment.

Germany: problematic patriotisms

The basis of patriotism can clearly vary greatly from country to country, defined by different political, social and cultural traditions. It is, however, also subject to constant reinterpretation in accordance with different historical periods, and the historical development of a state is of central importance to the evolution of patriotic sentiment. Indeed, it is widely recognised that citizens of countries with deep historical roots are more likely to have consistent patriotic feelings than those in countries with a fragile past. Where a strong shared sense of legacy and destiny exists, the forging of identity in the present will thus be more easily facilitated.[20] As a result, patriotism is often the by-product of a stable political process, and states that enjoy territorial, political and economic stability, such as Switzerland, rarely feel the need actively to develop patriotism, for it will grow unaided. If, however, internal divisions or external pressures exist, the cultivation of patriotism may become vital in order to create an aura of unity, a strategy called upon by Vladimir Putin in Russia shortly after his election as President.[21]

It is no surprise that Germany's fragile past, which witnessed five main systems of state in the twentieth century alone, has given rise to a tentative patriotism. Whilst the most recent German debates concerning concepts such as patriotism, nationalism and the nation have been fuelled by unification, the National Socialist past still proves a major stumbling block for the expression of all forms of national identity, for the extreme perversion of patriotic and nationalistic sentiment during this period jeopardised its existence for future generations. Indeed, the late 1960s witnessed the uprising of young West Germans against their parents' generation in rejection of their roots, a phenomenon which Lothar Probst labels 'negative nationalism',[22] and still today there is far less enthusiasm for national symbols in Germany than in neighbouring countries. In light of the 'normalisation' debate, some critics see this reticence to be detrimental and even dangerous; Martin Walser, for example, pleads his fellow citizens to allow the 'nation' back into public consciousness, ascribing the development of right-wing extremism to 'the neglect of national sentiment, of which we are all guilty'.[23] Yet it is not only the National Socialist past that has proved problematic to the expression of patriotism, but also the division of Germany in 1949, viewed by many left-wing Germans to be the just punishment for crimes committed in the name of the German nation. Division naturally challenged the notion of the 'German nation': was it to be defined by essentialist elements such as language, customs, common cultural and historical heritage, or rather in a constructionist fashion, through politics and social structure?[24] Whilst there were two German states, it was not clear whether there were also two German nations.

The FRG maintained the notion of one Germany throughout division, and recognising only one German citizenship, it claimed to speak on behalf of the repressed masses in the East. However, alternative post-national forms of identity were rapidly adopted in the West in order to replace the tarnished nation with other foci of pride. The late 1950s thus witnessed the rise of 'DM-nationalism', rooted in the economic growth and stability of the FRG. Whilst this principle has remained an important source of pride, it became increasingly rejected as a conservative form of identity in the late 1960s. Instead, the concept of constitutional patriotism gained strength, and as claimed by Richard von Weizsäcker: 'Patriotism has, however, regained a focus for its orientation: in the constitution as a responsibility.'[25] The idea of constitutional patriotism originated with Dolf Sternberger, who intended to use the West German Basic Law to promote the concept of the fatherland and free it from shame, thus rejuvenating patriotic feeling and creating a new vehicle with which to show attachment to the German nation.[26] However, it was popularised in the 1980s by Jürgen Habermas as a patriotism which would be 'free of the fatherland', thus one in which the constitution would replace the nation.[27] This was indicative of the popular desire to distance oneself from the nation, and to seek alternative forms of identity elsewhere. As a result, regional and even supranational loyalties have gained importance, in many ways substituting the value of the nation, for with relatively untarnished legacies, these communities offer collective identities free of guilt, shame and confusion. As Thomas Oberender commented: 'It is pleasant living in Germany today, as Germany is rarely to be found within Germany any more.'[28] Through the development of 'nation substitutes' in the FRG, collective identity became increasingly orientated away from the national past, and towards the civic, economic and regional foci of the present.

In contrast, the idea of the nation remained a respectable focus of pride in the GDR.[29] This was achieved by a process of redefinition, and from 1949 the GDR presented itself as the only true state of the German people, and the embodiment of 'good' socialist traditions. Until the 1960s, the GDR's official aim remained unification on its own ideological terms, and socialism was presented as synonymous with the 'national' (all-German) interest. Following the building of the Berlin Wall in 1961, however, and an increasing sense of permanent division, the official line changed, claiming that the German nation found itself at different stages of development within the two German states: united in the GDR, yet class-divided in the FRG, and the 1968 constitution thus described the GDR as 'a socialist state of the German nation'.[30] By the early 1970s, however, and in reaction to *Ostpolitik*, official policy changed again in order to enable full recognition of the GDR as a sovereign state, and consequently the goal of unification on socialist terms was abandoned. As part of the policy of delimitation, the 'German' nation was redefined as the 'socialist' nation of the GDR, presented in the revised constitution of 1974 as 'a socialist state of workers and peasants'.[31] From this point onwards the SED openly propagated the idea of two German nations, even going so far as to replace the adjective *deutsch* (German) with *DDR* (GDR) in official literature.[32]

The redefinition of the 'nation' according to class, not ethnicity, was clearly an attempt to bypass the problematic 'German' fatherland, and to create a new nation in which pride, not shame, could be dominant.[33] In accordance with this policy, patriotism also adopted a new guise as 'socialist patriotism', pertaining uniquely to the working class, and thus transcending national borders. As it was officially defined: 'Socialist patriotism is not only expressed through devotion and loyalty to the immediate homeland, but also to the whole socialist world system, and through pride in its achievements and its superiority over capitalism, as well as through solidarity with the working classes of all countries in the battle against imperialism.'[34] Hatred of the imperialist enemy consequently became an integral part of socialist patriotism, which was inculcated into the population from an early age. In constructing a nation that was defined by its present structure rather than essential elements of its past, the SED's strategy was not entirely dissimilar to that of 'nation substitution' in the FRG: both attempted to escape the essentially ethnic definition of the historic German nation.

One difference, however, remained important, for the GDR laid claim to specific historical roots in order to build the foundations of the socialist nation. As with the concept of patriotism, official history was manipulated to suit the needs of the state, emphasising working-class history and the struggle of 'progressive' socialist forces versus reactionary forces. In this way, the GDR was presented as a logical progression from the communist resistance movement, and Germans responsible for the evils of National Socialism were conveniently considered capitalists, who supposedly lived in 'imperialist' West Germany. Anti-fascism thus became the cornerstone of GDR legitimacy, effectively freeing the socialist nation and its people from the notion of a guilty past. The contrast between West Germany, where the nation remained a guilt-ridden concept and taboo subject, and East Germany, where a newly fashioned nation was installed as the very monument of patriotic pride, demonstrates just how far apart the two Germanies had grown by 1989.

The GDR's patriotic programme

In the wake of *Ostpolitik* and delimitation, the concept of the GDR nation naturally became a central component of patriotic education during the late 1970s and 1980s, infiltrating all areas of young people's lives. A patriotic programme thus developed which aimed to promote a strong GDR consciousness amongst the young generation, appealing to both heart and mind. The dissemination of such values became highly centralised, and the attempt to involve young people emotionally was deemed particularly important, for this increased the chances of raising a generation that was socially and politically engaged. As one teacher claimed of a history lesson: 'If I do not reach the emotions of pupils here, I cannot regard this lesson to be successful.'[35] The use of language in educational materials was consequently of prime importance, and the standard reference to '*our* GDR' aimed to make young people feel emotionally closer to their country. Margot Honecker, Minister for Education, highlighted the importance of language,

summing up the essence of GDR education policy with the following words on the art of formulating questions: 'We must do
more, even in asking questions, to make our viewpoint stronger,
and to challenge the position of the person we are talking to. The
question "What do you think of the GDR?" . . . is too open, and
presents too little [ideological] position.'[36] The same attitude was
evident in pedagogical structures, which favoured traditional
teaching methods such as lecturing and textbook-based learning,
thus ensuring uniformity and tight control, and allowing minimal
time for free discussion. When pupils' opinions were sought, they
were expected to produce the 'correct' answers according to socialist ideology, and whilst in full-time education, young people were
allowed little opportunity to stray from the accepted socialist
norms of the GDR state.

The patriotic programme was clearly channelled through centralised structures and uniform pedagogical aims, yet what specific
values were to be disseminated? Five distinct thematic areas
recurred in educational materials, each of which aimed to promote
patriotic values and provoke an emotional response to the GDR.
The following sections examine each theme in turn, revealing the
desired nature of patriotic sentiment in the GDR and the qualities
which young people were expected to develop.

Historical consciousness

The deployment of history for the purpose of state legitimisation is
a method which can be traced back as far as the history it evokes.
The GDR was no exception, and the desire to create amongst young
people a secure historical consciousness was high on the patriotic
agenda, for it was believed that young people who saw themselves
as part of a longer tradition would carry it into the future with
greater commitment. History was thus considered more than a
simple relic of the past and, in accordance with Marxist theory,
young people were to see themselves as actors in history rather than
onlookers. The wearing of the FDJ uniform was symbolic of this
attitude, for the blue shirt was worn in the service of modern-day
socialism, yet also represented the continuance of a tradition of
socialist youth movements. By bringing history into the future, propaganda clearly aimed to create loyalty to the wider sphere of socialism, and the principal aims of history teaching were twofold: firstly
to secure in young people a conviction of socialist ideology as the

basis of the GDR state, and secondly to instil in them confidence in the legitimacy of the regime.[37]

The first aim was the most fundamental, and followed the Marxist view of history as a continuous class struggle which would ultimately result in the victory of socialism over capitalism. This naturally involved highly selective education materials, as demonstrated by a report from the Ministry for Education in 1984: 'As far as the history of our brother nations is concerned, a course on the history of the Soviet Union would be conceivable. A course on the history of Poland would not be advisable, as their own history there has not yet been conclusively reappraised.'[38] Events such as the founding of the GDR and the building of the Berlin Wall thus frequently featured in school books, whereas other more contentious events, most notably the uprising of 17 June 1953 and the GDR's role in the Prague Spring, were either neglected or studied merely in terms of counter-revolutionary revolts. In this way, the GDR could present itself as the culmination of all 'progressive' elements of German history, and thus as superior to the FRG.

In order to demonstrate its legitimacy, the second aim of historical propaganda, the GDR claimed to have made a clear break with the history of National Socialist Germany, and promoted itself as the heir of the anti-fascist and communist resistance movements during the war. As one FDJ report stated: 'It remains the daily duty of parents, school, veterans, the FDJ and its Pioneer organisation to instil the anti-fascist spirit deep into every young heart from generation to generation, and to constantly renew it. This is the responsibility of each generation for the next.'[39] Communist war veterans were thus invited to numerous FDJ meetings, and the former concentration camp at Buchenwald became one of the most visited sites by school pupils, where they learned not only about the evils of National Socialism, but also about the heroism of the anti-fascist and communist resistance movement. Furthermore, martyrs for the cause, such as Karl Liebknecht and Ernst Thälmann, were promoted as historical role models, their names becoming enmeshed into the landscape of the GDR, with eponymous streets, schools, factories and numerous other public buildings. Anti-fascism clearly became installed at the heart of GDR legitimacy.

Whilst these two aims remained primary throughout the history of the GDR, a number of changes took place during the early 1980s in order to reinforce the historical roots of the SED's construct of the GDR nation. As outlined by the party, such changes involved a broadening of the GDR's heritage: 'In strengthening our national consciousness, we are including the whole of German history. In doing so we are returning to its beginnings and not restricting ourselves to the present geographical area of the GDR. New conditions for the examination of history have developed.'[40] These 'new conditions' were primarily the GDR's relations with the FRG, for not only were they strained during the Cold War tensions of the early 1980s, but increasing numbers of East Germans were turning their vision Westwards, rather than putting their energies into the development of socialism. The widening of the GDR's historical heritage was thus an attempt to expand the foundations of GDR consciousness, and to create a broader basis for the development of patriotism, incorporating German traditions outside the immediate 'progressive' history of the working classes. Seen within the context of Cold War rivalry, this was evidently part of a German competition for legitimacy, in which both East and West attempted to bolster their respective collective identities. Such changes famously witnessed the reinstatement of the equestrian statue of Frederick the Great on Unter den Linden in Berlin in 1980 and the staging of large-scale celebrations in 1983 to mark the five hundredth anniversary of Luther's birth, as well as the revision of historical characters such as Bismarck and Luther in textbooks and teaching materials.

As the 1980s drew to a close, one other area of German history was increasingly brought into the public consciousness: the Holocaust. This had previously been overshadowed by the prominence given to the anti-fascist resistance movement, yet by the late 1980s, widespread access to western television, together with the approaching fiftieth anniversary of *Kristallnacht*,[41] meant that Jewish history was no longer easy to ignore. As a result, 1988 witnessed two important events in the attempt to redress the balance: firstly, a memorial day on 9 November to mark the anniversary of *Kristallnacht*, and secondly, the announcement that the synagogue on Oranienburger Straße in East Berlin would be rebuilt as a memorial to the Holocaust. These changes clearly all aimed to increase the legitimacy of the GDR, as they placed the socialist nation within the whole of German history, preventing the West from regarding it as 'an illegitimate "accident of history" '.[42] At the same time, the distinction between 'good' and 'bad' history was still retained in the differentiation between the GDR's 'Erbe', or 'legacy' (the whole of the historical past) and its 'Tradition' (the 'progressive' historical past), thus enabling the GDR to maintain its moral superiority over the West.[43]

Alongside the widening of the GDR's historical heritage, the 1980s also witnessed greater efforts to further penetrate the historical consciousness of young people. The revised *Jugendweihe* programme of the early 1980s, for example, allowed for greater historical emphasis, and the new school history curriculum in 1988–89 foregrounded above all German history. In many ways this curriculum revision represented the culmination of the SED's policy to intensify historical propaganda: 'The historical foundations of an active party-based relationship to the socialist fatherland, a close attachment to the GDR, played a fundamental role . . . in the process of drawing up new syllabi. The aim was to impart a basic knowledge of all stages of the GDR's historic development in a more solid and comprehensive fashion.'[44] Despite changes in policy, historical propaganda was consistently employed to create attachment to the GDR state, and remained central to patriotic propaganda throughout its forty-year history, above all during its final decade.

Militarism

In order to protect the carefully constructed GDR nation, military defence formed the second component of patriotic education. This was considered one of the highest forms of patriotic activity, and was enshrined in the Youth Code as both the right and the bounden duty of young people.[45] Pride in the fatherland was thus regarded as a prerequisite for military engagement, as highlighted by the Defence Minister, Heinz Hoffmann: 'The most important thing is not whether a boy can walk along a narrow plank with two buckets. It is rather that from his first school day, this boy grows up thinking: I am a citizen of the socialist state of the German nation, and I am willing to defend this socialist state with my life.'[46] The National People's Army (NVA) consequently played a prominent role in youth work, and young people were confronted with military education from the youngest of ages: kindergarten children learned socialist fighting songs, made Christmas cards for soldiers posted on the border and visited local barracks. A report written by the Ministry for Education in 1981 demonstrates how far this was taken: 'It would be possible to develop more toys to stimulate NVA role play (e.g. caps, epaulettes with military ranks, flasks, map cases, signalling stick, etc.), as well as modern military vehicles, which would enrich pedagogical work concerning the patriotic education of children.'[47] Children of school age would take part first in the annual 'Snowflake' pioneer manoeuvres, which were supported by the NVA, before progressing to military activities coordinated by the FDJ and GST, most notably the annual 'Hans-Beimler competitions',[48] as well as 'youth spartakiads' and large-scale FDJ parades on national holidays. Within the classroom, the late 1970s saw a significant development with the introduction of the *Wehrunterricht*, formal military classes, from September 1978. This was an obligatory subject for years 9 and 10 of the POS, and was accompanied by a voluntary military training camp for boys, or a compulsory course in civilian defence for girls and the remainder of boys. These necessitated a high degree of discipline and required all participants to wear uniform for the duration of the course. From 1981, the *Wehrunterricht* became an obligatory course for all *Abitur* students, and beyond school, apprentices and university students were also required to complete military training. Furthermore, militarism was reflected in the strict discipline that was expected of pupils of all ages, with roll-call and military drill being regular features of the FDJ and school life.

The justification for such military dominance in education was the need to secure peace and the army was presented purely in defensive terms. As a result, peace was never absent from military propaganda and was frequently linked to the concept of socialist solidarity. At the eleventh SED party congress in 1986, for example, it was declared that 'military service in socialism is peace service', an idea that featured as a leitmotif in military education throughout the final years of the GDR.[49] Through this role a certain romanticism was lent to the army, and not only were soldiers presented as child-loving and caring individuals who fought for the instatement of worldly justice, but training camps were to encourage elements such as cooking and singing around the campfire.[50] Indeed, the imagery of comradeship in arms was to be manipulated to the full, above all to entice young men to sign up for periods of military service longer than the mandatory eighteen months. This motive was implicit in many areas of youth work, from sporting activities to the *Jugendweihe*, and pressure on boys to commit to the armed forces at an early age was considerable. From year 7, for example, teachers were instructed to single out children who showed particular interest or talent in military affairs and report them to the local schools' inspection service.[51] Parents were also warned that if their sons failed to 'volunteer' for military camp, their final school marks might suffer. Such pressure only increased during the 1980s, and attempts to instil military prowess into young people continued to reach new heights; as Defence Minister Keßler announced in 1987, 'in future more must be done to deepen the love of the socialist fatherland amongst our youth'.[52]

There were three reasons for this intensification. Firstly, a dramatic fall in the birth rate in the mid-1970s resulted in a shortage of boys due to enter the NVA in the early 1990s.[53] The situation was considered urgent by the late 1980s, and in Magdeburg it was estimated that by 1990 every second young male would be obliged to commit to at least three years' service.[54] Secondly, amidst the renewal of Cold War tensions in the late 1970s and early 1980s, the SED justified the introduction of the *Wehrunterricht* by claiming that it was simply reacting to western militarism: 'Our measures are . . . an effective response to the heightened preparation of school children for military service in the FRG, who have already been manipulated in the spirit of militarism for years.'[55] Thirdly, the SED felt the need to counter increasing numbers of young people who were being attracted to church-based peace initiatives. Many pupils, for example, were found to be wearing the 'Swords into ploughshares' logo in 1982 even though it was banned by the party, and the credo 'Make peace without weapons' found support amongst a relatively large number of young people. The principal difference between this peace movement and that of the state related to military dominance, for these unofficial circles regularly objected to the production and sale of 'war toys', compulsory military education and public demonstrations of military power. Initially efforts were made to counter such opposition with FDJ slogans and campaigns such as 'Make peace against NATO-weapons' and 'Peace must be armed', but as the pressure increased, the youth organisation was forced to remodel itself along more inventive lines. Thus in 1982 the popular music festival 'Rock for Peace' was created in order to win over young people for the state's peace policies and more youthful slogans were propagated, such as 'Better active than radioactive' and '*Sonne statt Reagan*' ('sun not rain/Reagan' – a play on the German word for rain, *Regen*).

By the 1980s, young people simply could not avoid being caught in this propaganda war of peace and militarism, which became an integral part of GDR socialism and patriotic commitment. The route to the NVA could hardly have been more comprehensively mapped out for young people, and as one parents' guide aptly summarised: 'They [the children] see military equipment and vehicles on the streets, on TV and in the cinema, and almost develop a natural interest in them. The army belongs to our environment.'[56]

The hostile enemy

In order to underline the necessity of military propaganda, dissemination of the hostile image of the enemy proved essential. According to official ideology, patriotic love of one's country and loyalty to the socialist cause necessitated the vehement hatred of all which lay in its path, namely the Western world of imperialism: 'Instilling a deep love of the German Democratic Republic and of socialism into the young generation also means teaching them to hate imperialism.'[57] By casting imperialism as the aggressor set to destroy socialism, it was believed that the emotions of young people would be stirred, and that they would, in turn, defend the state against potential sources of opposition.

In the attempt to create contempt for the West, the SED propagated the image of an immoral Western world dogged by crime, exploitation and violence. This frequently involved the 'interpretation' of original sources for the benefit of young people, and as one *Jugendweihe* document stated: 'It is our duty to use all opportunities in the *Jugendweihe* programme to condemn American imperialism and its allies, and to expose the fact that when Reagan speaks of peace, he means and practises war, destruction and murder.'[58] Although all powerful capitalist states came under attack, the FRG received the most vitriolic treatment, for it was not only geographically closest to the GDR, but its shared culture, language and history, as well as family ties, meant that it claimed a potentially large emotional hold over young East Germans. As a result, schoolbooks never failed to draw attention to unemployment figures in the FRG, its crime rate or the large number of homeless people living on Western streets; and issues concerning young people, such as drugs problems, were naturally given pride of place in order to heighten their impact. On the rare occasions that holiday trips were organised to West Germany, the most unusual sites would thus be visited in order to impress such images on young people. The itinerary for a group that visited Saarbrücken in 1986, for example, included not only a retraining centre for young unemployed people but an area on the outskirts of the city plagued by homelessness and a huge high-rise inner city area where the majority of the inhabitants were unemployed and lived in squalor.[59]

This propaganda was coupled together with the stringent censorship of Western influences in youth work, for the party suspected that Western forces concentrated their efforts on this vulnerable sector of the population, particularly through music and sporting propaganda, as well as through churches and unofficial youth groups. In 1983, for instance, it was feared that Western provocateurs were attempting to weaken patriotic education by creating an 'inner opposition' amongst young people in Halle, encouraging them to demand political pluralism and more comprehensive personal freedoms.[60] In view of such fears, correspondence between the FRG and the GDR was subjected to rigorous controls and checks, and West Germans were kept out of the GDR during important political events, such as the National Youth Festival of 1979, when 1,542 West Berliners were refused entry into East Berlin.[61] Whilst it was relatively easy to restrict the movement of people and even written literature, however, it was impossible to control the airwaves on which Western radio and television programmes were broadcast. By the 1980s, the widespread availability of modern technology thus posed a serious threat to the validity of official propaganda and patriotic education. Indeed, Stasi files and GDR youth surveys revealed a growing number of young viewers of West German television; in 1981 it was estimated that 80% of all 14–16 year olds in *Bezirk* Halle watched Western television on a regular basis.[62] Aware that it could do little to counter this trend, the party increasingly emphasised anti-Western propaganda in formal education and free-time activities, above all presenting the West as the 'enemy of youth', in the hope that this would prevent young people's loyalties from turning Westwards.

Proletarian internationalism

The SED was acutely aware of the potential dangers of encouraging the vehement hatred of the imperialist enemy alongside a pronounced patriotism, and called upon a strong sense of proletarian internationalism in order to neutralise the possibility of nationalist overtones: 'We must pay full attention that the education of pupils to love their socialist fatherland protects them from behaving

arrogantly towards other peoples and nations.'[63] Rather than conflicting with the concept of socialist patriotism, proletarian internationalism was thus regarded as its indispensable partner, and
represented the unity of the working classes across the globe in the
battle against capitalist exploitation and repression.

Proletarian internationalism was most frequently manifested
through the expression of friendship between the GDR and other
socialist states, first and foremost the Soviet Union. This special relationship was concretised in numerous slogans, such as 'The Soviet
Union is our best friend' and 'To learn from the Soviet Union means
to learn to triumph'. Russian lessons in schools thus became an
obvious medium for the transmission of internationalist values, for
not only did they include language teaching, but also education in
the culture and society of the Soviet Union. Many GDR schools
were twinned with schools in the Soviet bloc, allowing pupils to
write to young people in other socialist countries, compare experiences and take part in exchange programmes. Twinning arrange-
ments between the GDR youth organisations and their Soviet
counterparts, 'Komsomol' and the Pioneer Organisation 'Vladimir
Ilyich Lenin' were equally common, involving the exchange of
letters, songs, poems and other artefacts. Furthermore, international
sporting events such as the 'Friendship' athletics competition which
took place under the umbrella of the FDJ allowed young people to
develop friendships with others in the socialist world, and to deepen
their knowledge of life in those countries. The DSF, to which all
Jugendweihe participants were automatically admitted, was also an
important organisation in this sphere, promoting cultural events
such as film screenings, literature readings and Soviet-style evenings
in order to educate the population in Soviet traditions. Whether or
not young people took part in such activities, all pupils and FDJ
members were required to show active support for the solidarity
movement, above all by engaging in regular fund-raising campaigns
and youth projects to provide aid for Third World countries.

Contact with representatives of other socialist countries invariably adopted a formal character, yet young people were nevertheless
presented with many opportunities to familiarise themselves with
the different cultures and traditions of the international socialist
community. This was all the more essential during the arms race of
the early 1980s, when the ideological divide between East and West
was at its most intense, and the need to promote a patriotism

founded in the principles of socialist ideology was greater than ever. As in other areas of the patriotic agenda, proletarian internationalism attained heightened relevance during the 1980s.

Pride in the GDR present

All four of the above themes worked towards one common goal: the creation of an emotional attachment amongst young people to the country in which they lived and its socialist ideology. This was no clearer than in the final component of patriotic education, which was the most immediate of all: to produce in young people pride in the achievements of contemporary society, in terms of political, social and industrial developments, as well as natural, sporting and cultural assets. This was evidently linked to all other themes, for young people who took pride in the present were more likely to be active for the military, represent their country in international festivals, or take an eager interest in the past.

One way of creating pride in the present was to encourage young people to feel eternally grateful towards their state. Consequently, subjects such as *Staatsbürgerkunde* stressed the state's provisions for young people, and extra-curricular activities taught children about the workings of society, with *Jugendweihe* groups visiting local factories, and Pioneer groups receiving guided tours of their town hall. Newspaper articles, such as those in the *Junge Welt* series 'Typically GDR', also attempted to foreground the GDR's achievements and its commitment to young people, stressing the high number of young members of parliament, the large quantity of new housing, or the latest technological achievements.[64] It is no surprise that the social and economic achievements of the GDR which were promoted, such as job security, health care, education and equality of pay, were all positive inversions of the negative phenomena found in the West, most notably unemployment and inequality.

Other elements, such as the promotion of the GDR's natural beauty through camping trips and outdoor activities, or the emphasis on cultural and sporting events, were also central in encouraging an emotional bond with the fatherland. As a result, the broader cultural sphere became highly politicised. One of the central functions of rock music, for example, was to support the socialist order and promote the patriotic cause: 'Rock music is suitable for propagating the beauties of life in peace and socialism, for strengthening one's courage for life, for creating pride in achievements, for promoting civic behaviour and activity.'[65] Furthermore, 60% of the music played by discos and radio stations was to come from the GDR or other socialist countries, thus ensuring optimal effect. In a similar way, sporting role models for young people were chosen not only for their achievements, but also their political loyalty. One such example was the cyclist Gustav Adolf Schur, affectionately nick-named 'Täve', whose popularity was frequently played upon in order to influence young people. A textbook for year 3, for example, recounted how the West German police would not allow him to wear a T-shirt sporting the GDR emblem during a race in the FRG, so he decided to sew an emblem onto his shorts instead. Although he was still prevented from racing at the last minute, this was con-sidered to be a victory over the West German police, and 'Täve' was proclaimed a socialist hero.[66] As demonstrated here, great weight was laid on the importance of GDR national symbolism, and school lessons ensured that children learned the symbolic meaning of the flag and the historical roots to the national anthem. General knowl-edge concerning the GDR, its *Bezirke* and its cultural traditions was also strongly encouraged. However, as one schools' report stated: 'The formal knowledge of pupils does not help us; the knowledge that they have acquired must be reflected in the behaviour of each and every one of them.'[67] Young people were thus expected to uphold the law and order of the GDR through responsible citizen-ship, and actively engage in promoting the ideals and values of socialist society. This was particularly encouraged in two ways: firstly through diligence and hard work, and secondly through active political commitment.

As a 'state of workers and peasants', the GDR foregrounded the importance of identity through work in the socialist state: 'The first duty towards the fatherland is constant industriousness. Patriotism *without* skilfulness and efficiency in one's job is an empty and hollow word.'[68] A positive attitude towards work not only strength-ened the economy and furthered the achievements of the state, thus securing a more stable and prosperous future, but also demon-strated commitment to all that the state had hitherto accomplished. The emphasis on work began early: diligence and respect for the working people constituted two of the Pioneers' ten mottos, and cer-tificates were awarded for hard work in primary school. From year 7, the subject 'Introduction to Socialist Production' (EsP) formed a compulsory part of the curriculum, and by the age of 14, pupils were required to spend three hours per week working in factories or on farms. Outside school, initiatives such as the *Messe der Meister von Morgen* (MMM), an annual trade fair designed to promote the advances of young people in industry, encouraged innovation on a more competitive level. Every young individual was thus expected to contribute to the collective through industrious work, thereby helping society approach the goal of communism and continuing the historic mission of the working class.

Commitment to political activity was considered equally vital to the patriotic cause: 'The patriotic behaviour of young GDR citizens is expressed in their *active participation in political life, in their political activity*, in school and in public.'[69] In order to create an enthusiastic young vanguard, political participation was thus encouraged from the earliest of ages: kindergarten children were expected to wave flags on national holidays, Pioneers to participate in 'pioneer afternoons' and elect their class representatives and FDJ members to attend regular meetings and ultimately join the SED. Additionally, annual FDJ projects such as the *Friedensaufgebot* (a 'summons' and call for peace) of 1983 also encouraged active political participation. Many of these were associated with the protection of the environment, and ranged from collecting newspaper and glass for recycling, to taking care of woodland and restoring memorials in town centres. The aims here were clear: firstly to create in young people an attachment to their natural surroundings, and secondly to assure that this attachment had firm political foundations. As the SED believed, it was political commitment that transformed pride from a two-dimensional concept into the desired form of socialist patriotism, or according to one *Jugendweihe* book: 'In this sense the German Democratic Republic is not only the homeland, but also the socialist fatherland.'[70]

Conclusion

Against a background of GDR-specific characteristics, the state attempted to play off the evils of the imperialist world against the assets of socialism, in order to create what was often referred to as 'socialism in the colours of the GDR'. Five distinct elements of patriotic education combined to encourage the formation of a patriotic youth, and whilst each varied in intensity and weight during different periods of the GDR, three clear trends can be identified during the 1980s. Firstly, the SED's goal remained one of uniformity, casting all young people into the mould of the 'socialist personality' and the 'socialist patriot'. Through the education system, mass organisations, national holidays and ritual ceremonies, it aimed for complete ideological hegemony in all areas of youth work, aiming to create *one* youth, loyal and committed. Secondly, the changing nature of the GDR's patriotic programme reflected the important influence of international events on the development of SED policy. *Ostpolitik*, the arms race of the early 1980s and developments in other socialist regimes, as well as the growing attraction of the FRG, were all significant in shaping the education of young people. Whilst the GDR state remained the focus of patriotic sentiment, it was shaped as much by outside influences as it was from within. The third trend was undoubtedly one of intensification, largely resulting from international changes and growing competition with the FRG, but also due to the changing demographics of a society that was producing fewer children. Whether exemplified in the growing pressure on boys to undertake longer military service, the ever-more elaborate national parades, or the increasingly desperate attempts to draw young people away from the churches, the campaign to foreground the fatherland in all five areas of patriotic education was never more prominent than during the late 1980s.

The high membership rates of the FDJ, the demonstrations of apparent loyalty at national anniversaries and the widespread acceptance of the *Jugendweihe* all appeared to reveal the relative success of the GDR's patriotic programme. Indeed, just four months before the fall of the Berlin Wall, Erich Honecker laid testament to the loyalty of young people at the National Youth Festival of 1989: 'Such a youth provides good prospects for the republic. We are succeeding in raising generation upon generation in the spirit of the party. As our society grows, so too does our party.'[71] The intensification of patriotic education, however, revealed a lack of satisfaction with the status quo, for newer and more sophisticated methods were continually being sought with which to influence young people. Indeed, 1989 was marked by calls to reinstate the socialist fatherland at the heart of all youth work, and Margot Honecker declared that 'a true patriotic education' was needed to counter the ever-increasing Western influences.[72] Despite public praise of a loyal youth, these campaigns rather suggested that previous attempts to foreground the fatherland had proved insufficient, and that the goal of a single committed youth was still far off. To what extent did young people thus accept or reject this propaganda? Did the SED's efforts to influence young people from early childhood have a long-term impact? Can patriotism be effectively imposed from above, or does it rather develop in reaction to a variety of other influences? These are the central questions to be addressed in chapter 2, through the examination of young people's patriotic attitudes and behaviour during the 1980s.

Notes

1 DIPF/BBF/Archiv: Sign.: 15.891, 'Die Erziehung der Jugend zur Liebe zum sozialistischen Vaterland . . .', Jan 1978, pp. 3–4.
2 Franz Müntefering, 'Nation, Patriotismus, Demokratische Kultur', www.spd.de/servlet/PB/cmd/print/index.html?id=1015831&project= SPD.de, accessed on 15 Oct 2003.
3 Ernest Gellner, *Nations and Nationalism* (Oxford: Blackwell, 1983), p. 7.
4 Max Weber, *Wirtschaft und Gesellschaft: Grundriss der Sozialökonomik*, vol. 1, 3rd edn (Tübingen: Mohr, 1947), pp. 29–30.
5 Anthony D. Smith, *National Identity* (London: Penguin, 1991), p. 14.
6 Gellner, *Nations and Nationalism*, p. 7.
7 Benedict Anderson, *Imagined Communities* (London, New York: Verso, 1991), pp. 6–7.
8 This is, however, a confusing term which does not reflect the complexity of the term 'nation'. United Germany, for example, is often referred to as a 'nation state', yet this fails to account for the fact that Austria shares much of the same national heritage as Germany, or that the Sorbs, living in south eastern Germany, may not feel they are part of the same 'imagined community' as Germans.
9 Gellner, *Nations and Nationalism*, p. 1.
10 Craig Calhoun, *Nationalism* (Buckingham: Open University Press, 1997), p. 11.
11 See, for example, Eric Hobsbawm, *Nations and Nationalism since 1780* (Cambridge: Cambridge University Press, 1992), p. 85; David McCrone, *The Sociology of Nationalism* (London, New York: Routledge, 2003), p. 9; Peter Alter, *Nationalism*, 2nd edn (London: Arnold, 1994), p. 2.
12 Eric Hobsbawm, *Nations and Nationalism since 1780*, p. 87.
13 Rogers Brubaker, *Citizenship and Nationhood in France and Germany* (Cambridge, MA: Harvard University Press, 1992).

14 Dolf Sternberger, *Verfassungspatriotismus*, Schriften X (Frankfurt am Main: Insel, 1990).

15 Peter Schmidt, 'Nationale Identität, Nationalismus und Patriotismus in einer Panelstudie 1993, 1995 und 1996', in *Werte und nationale Identität im vereinten Deutschland: Erklärungsansätze der Umfrageforschung*, ed. by Heiner Meulemann (Opladen: Leske & Budrich, 1998), pp. 269–81. For other examples, see Stefan Berger, *The Search for Normality: National Identity and Historical Consciousness in Germany since 1800* (Providence, Oxford: Berghahn, 1997), pp. 209–10.

16 'Ansprache an die Bundesversammlung', 23 May 1999, in Johannes Rau, *Reden und Interviews*, vol. 1.1 (Berlin: Presse- und Informationsamt der Bundesregierung, Oct 2000), pp. 25–7 (p. 26).

17 Berger, *The Search for Normality*, p. 255.

18 Hobsbawm, *Nations and Nationalism since 1780*, p. 88.

19 J.H. Grainger, *Patriotism: The Making and Unmaking of British National Identity*, vol. 1 (London: Routledge, 1989), p. 26.

20 Mary Fulbrook, *German National Identity after the Holocaust* (Cambridge: Polity Press, 1999), p. 17.

21 Aleksandr Dugin, 'Putin's task is to create a stable political regime in Russia', *Versiya*, 31 May 2000, http://eurasia.com.ru/versia3105.html, accessed on 19 Sep 2003.

22 Lothar Probst, 'Ost-West-Differenzen und das republikanische Defizit der deutschen Einheit', *APuZG*, B41–42 (1998).

23 Martin Walser, 'Deutsche Sorgen', *Der Spiegel*, 26 (1993), 40–7 (p. 43).

24 For essentialist and constructionist theory, see Fulbrook, *German National Identity after the Holocaust*, p. 8.

25 Richard von Weizsäcker *et al.*, *Nachdenken über Deutschland* (Munich: Bertelsmann, 1988), p. 12.

26 Sternberger, *Verfassungspatriotismus*, pp. 17–31.

27 Jürgen Habermas, *Autonomy and Solidarity: Interviews with Jürgen Habermas*, 2nd edn, ed. by Peter Dews (London, New York: Verso, 1992), pp. 237–43.

28 Thomas Oberender, 'Vom "D" zum "de" ', in *Kursbuch: Das gelobte Land*, vol. 141, Sep 2000, p. 91.

29 For a detailed analysis of the concept of the nation in the GDR, see Joanna McKay, *The Official Concept of the Nation in the Former GDR* (Aldershot: Ashgate, 1998).

30 'Verfassung der DDR, 1968', art. 1, in *Die deutschen Verfassungen des 19. und 20. Jahrhunderts*, 14th edn, ed. by Horst Hildebrandt (Paderborn: Schöningh, 1992), p. 236.

31 'Verfassung der DDR, 1974', art. 1, in *ibid*.

32 With a few remaining anomalies, most notably *Deutsche Reichsbahn*, *Freier Deutscher Gewerkschaftsbund*, *Freie Deutsche Jugend* and *Sozialistische Einheitspartei Deutschlands*.

33 An ethnic element was not entirely abandoned, for the distinction between GDR citizenship and German nationality was maintained until 1989, yet nationality was always secondary in importance to citizenship.

34 *Kulturpolitisches Wörterbuch* (Berlin: Dietz, 1978), p. 551.

35 Harri Siegmund, 'Einheit von Rationalem und Emotionalem bei der Herausbildung politisch-ideologischer Überzeugung im Geschichtsunterricht', in *Fortschrittberichte und Studien: Erkenntnisse und Erfahrungen zur politisch-ideologischen Erziehung älterer Schüler* (Berlin: APW, 1984), pp. 39–43 (p. 40).

36 SAPMO-BArch, DY30/IV2/2.039/237, 'Notiz über ein Gespräch mit Genossin Margot Honecker am 9 Nov 1988', Eberhard Aurich, p. 109.

37 *Lehrplan der zehnklassigen allgemeinbildenden Oberstufe: Geschichte, Klassen 5 bis 10* (Berlin: Volk und Wissen, 1988), p. 4.

38 BArch, DR2/A.3872, 'Niederschrift über die Problemberatung am 18.12.1984 . . .', p. 15.

39 SAPMO-BArch, DY24/14301, 'Die Jugend der DDR, der 50. Jahrestag des Ausbruchs des zweiten Weltkrieges . . ., Sep 1989, pp. 5–6.

40 SAPMO-BArch, DY30/IVB2/14/82, 'Beschäftigung mit der Geschichte', no date [1982?], p. 66.

41 *Kristallnacht* was the massive pogrom directed against Jews in Germany and Austria on 9 November 1938.

42 *Die SED und das kulturelle Erbe*, ed. by Akademie für Gesellschaftswissenschaften (Berlin: Dietz, 1988), p. 508.

43 See Friedemann Neuhaus, *Geschichte im Umbruch: Geschichtspolitik, Geschichtsunterricht und Geschichtsbewußtsein in der DDR und den neuen Bundesländern 1983–1993* (Frankfurt am Main: Lang, 1998), pp. 69–70.

44 DIPF/BBF/Archiv: Sign.: 11.106/Ib, 'Standpunktmaterial – Herausbildung des Geschichtsbewußtseins . . .', 27 Jan 1989, pp. 6–7.

45 *Jugendgesetz der DDR*, (Berlin: Staatsverlag der DDR, 1974), art. 24, p. 33.

46 Cited in Peter Eisenmann, 'Die vermilitarisierte Jugend in der DDR', in *Jugendprobleme im geteilten Deutschland*, ed. by Siegfried Baske and Horst Rögner-Franke (Berlin: Duncker & Humblot, 1986), pp. 73–87 (p. 86).

47 BArch, DR2/A8898, 'Orientierung zur Erhöhung des Niveaus der patriotischen Erziehung in den Kindergärten', Feb 1981, p. 4.

48 Hans Beimler was an anti-fascist hero killed in the Spanish Civil War. This particular choice of name to designate a paramilitary competition

was clearly chosen to reinforce the underpinning idea of anti-fascist legitimacy within the GDR.

49 *Protokolle des XI. Parteitages der Sozialistischen Einheitspartei Deutschlands* (Berlin: Dietz, 1986), p. 92.

50 SAPMO-BArch, DY24/9624, Horst Dübner (FDJ First Secretary, *Bezirk* Halle) in letter to Egon Krenz, 11 July 1979, p. 161.

51 Uwe Blacknik, 'Wehrerziehung in der Schule', in *Materialien der Enquete-Kommission*, vol. III.1, pp. 277–88 (p. 278).

52 Cited in 'DDR-Führung mit politischer Haltung von Jugendlichen unzufrieden', *Der Tagesspiegel*, 12 Jun 1987.

53 SAPMO-BArch, DY30/JIV2/2/2220, 'Konsequenzen aus der demographischen Entwicklung d. DDR . . .', p. 69.

54 LA Magd, -LHA-, Rep. P13, IV/D-2/12/617, 'Bericht über Ergebnisse, Probleme und Aufgaben der militärischen Nachwuchssicherung . . .', no date [1980?].

55 SAPMO-BArch, DY30/IVB2/14/51, 'Zum Vorgehen bezüglich der Einführung des Wehrunterrichts . . .', p. 12.

56 Helmut Stolz, *Wie soll dein Kind sein?* (Berlin: Volk und Wissen, 1988), p. 38.

57 *Methodik des Sportunterrichts*, 4th edn (Berlin: Volk und Wissen, 1979), p. 65.

58 SAPMO-BArch, DY21/18, 'Tagung des Zentralen Ausschusses für Jugendweihe am 8. Nov 1983', p. 176.

59 SAPMO-BArch, DY30/IV2/2.039/243, Letter from Egon Krenz to Erich Honecker, 15 Dec 1986, pp. 194–5.

60 BStU, BV-Halle, Sach AKG/131, 'Analyse der politisch-operativen Lage unter jugendlichen Personenkreisen', 10 Feb 1984, p. 3.

61 BStU, Z4140, 'Information über durchgeführte Maßnahmen zur Gewährleistung der Sicherheit und Ordnung . . .', 6 Jun 1979, p. 14.

62 BStU, BV-Halle, Sach AKG/433, 'VVS Hle 049 – 123/81', p. 17.

63 DIPF/BBF/Archiv: Sign.: 15.891, 'Die Erziehung der Jugend . . .', APW, Jan 1978, p. 23.

64 E.g. 'Typisch DDR', *Junge Welt* (*JW*), 26 June 1989.

65 SAPMO-BArch, DY30/vorl.SED/39004, 'Standpunkt zur Entwicklung der Rockmusik . . .', May 1984, p. 5.

66 *Heimatkunde 3: Lehrbuch für Klasse 3*, 5th edn (Berlin: Volk und Wissen, 1982), p. 88.

67 LA Magd.-LHA-, Rep.P13, IV/D-2/9.02/549, 'Einschätzung des Unterrichts in den Fächern Staatsbürgerkunde und Geschichte', 16 Oct 1979, p. 4.

68 Adolf Diesterweg (pedagogical theorist, 1790–1866), cited in Stolz, *Wie soll dein Kind sein?*, p. 39. Emphasis in original.

69 DIPF/BBF/Archiv: Sign.: 15.891, 'Die Erziehung der Jugend', APW, Jan 1978, p. 10. Emphasis in original.
70 *Vom Sinn unseres Lebens*, 5th edn (Berlin: Neues Leben, 1987), p. 143.
71 SAPMO-BArch, DY30/IV2/2.036/8, 'Ausführungen des Genossen Erich Honecker zur Einschätzung des Nationalen Jugendfestivals . . .', 5 Jun 1979, p. 65.
72 Michael Mara, ' "Vaterlandserziehung" soll gegen westliche Einflüsse wappnen', *Der Tagesspiegel*, 11 April 1989.

2

Young people of the 1980s: a generation of loyal patriots?

The young generation of today, which has been born into socialism and grown up under its influence, sees and self-confidently exploits its achievements on a daily basis. With full confidence in the party of the working class, the words and actions of this generation show that socialism will always exist on German soil and will continue to develop well. (Eberhard Aurich, First Secretary of the FDJ, June 1989)[1]

Speaking at the last Pedagogical Congress of the GDR, Eberhard Aurich typically demonstrated how the regime liked to believe its own propaganda, extolling the virtues of its young generation, and proclaiming the effective nature of its patriotic programme. On the one hand, the elaborate FDJ parades on national holidays confirmed this image of a loyal youth; on the other, however, the events of the autumn of 1989 illustrated a radically different group of young people, many of whom demonstrated against the GDR state or fled its borders. As the journalist Josef Joffe observes, these events suggested that 'no GDR state consciousness, no identification with the Honecker regime had developed'.[2] Whilst clearly lying at opposite poles, Aurich and Joffe both fail to recognise the complexity of the actions of the masses: the large corpus of young people who silently rejected SED propaganda, and the tens of thousands who remained in their country, adopting the slogan 'We are staying here!'. The question of loyalty in the GDR is highly complex, and demands more than the simple affirmation or negation of a GDR identity; only by treading between these extremes can the nature and diversity of identity formation be fully explored. This chapter will thus undertake a differentiated examination of youth identity in the GDR, assessing the extent to which young people in the 1980s accepted and rejected the five areas of the SED's patriotic programme identified in chapter 1, and the way in which patriotic behaviour evolved during this decade in the face of intensified propaganda.

The foundations of identity: historical consciousness

Because of the broadening of the GDR's historical heritage in the early 1980s, and subsequent curriculum revisions, the historical consciousness of young people was closely monitored by the ZIJ, the Ministry for Education and the APW. One of the most significant ZIJ surveys, carried out in March 1989, found that young people's interest in GDR history correlated strongly with their sense of attachment to the state, thus confirming the SED's theoretical understanding of historical consciousness.[3] To what extent, however, did the young generation of the 1980s show interest in GDR and German history? Did its consistent presence and heightened importance in educational materials ignite their enthusiasm, or rather dull their sensitivity to the subject? Wilfried Schubarth suggests that young people were presented with only two options concerning historical education in the GDR: 'As an independent, impartial and multi-faceted interaction with history was barely possible, there basically only remained the alternatives of accepting or rejecting the proposed view of history.'[4] This section reveals, however, that the young generation's historical consciousness proved considerably more complex, frequently combining the acceptance of some elements of SED propaganda with the rejection of others, thus providing for many shades of grey in young people's knowledge, interest and emotional involvement in history.[5]

Historical interests and knowledge

Official statistics revealed a considerable interest in history, with over 20,000 FDJ discussion groups choosing to study the history of the GDR during the academic year of 1988–89, almost one in five in the region of Magdeburg.[6] Yet the real interests of young people often lay elsewhere, for history was largely considered the lesser evil of the available options for such groups, proving more attractive than subjects such as Marxist–Leninist theory. When ranked alongside other interests, history thus appeared much less popular, lagging behind areas such as nature, sports and technology and, by 1988, only 12% of young people were reported to declare a strong interest in history.[7] This was reflected in a number of surveys and tests, which found that pupils' knowledge of GDR history was sketchy in most areas other than specific key events, such as the uprising of 17 June 1953 and the building of the Wall in 1961, which had been the subject of more intense propaganda.[8] Furthermore, there was little evidence to suggest that young people's ability to regurgitate a number of important dates reflected the desired ideological effect or promoted any sense of patriotism. A 'control test' carried out in *Staatsbürgerkunde* in 1983, for example, revealed that whilst 95% of pupils in year 8 could name the exact date of the founding of the GDR, only 67% could state why, according to socialist ideology, this had been necessary.[9]

There were three principal reasons for this lack of interest in official history and subsequent deficit of knowledge. Firstly, dry teaching methods and the constant emphasis on overtly political themes were responsible, and one pupil commented: 'I cannot claim that I find history uninteresting . . . But there is too much talk of objectives, economic plans and evil imperialism.'[10] Indeed, evidence suggests that when more varied teaching materials were used, such as television documentaries or historical recordings, pupils showed greater interest and could relate better to their history.[11] Secondly, history instruction in the GDR concentrated on a select number of major historical events rather than analysing social developments.[12] When asked to give key words concerning 'GDR history', the majority of young people in one ZIJ survey thus named dates such as 7 October 1949 and 13 August 1961, or figures such as Grotewohl, Pieck, Ulbricht and Honecker. In contrast, the historical development of the social welfare system, childcare and education were usually mentioned in last place, if at all.[13] Ironically these are the elements that many east Germans genuinely valued in society, and look back on today with nostalgia (see chapter 4), thus revealing where their real attachment lay. In the majority of cases, however, official GDR history was perceived to be a string of party congresses, a list of heroic anti-fascist figures and a portfolio of examples demonstrating the superiority of socialism over capitalism; it is little surprise that interest was low. Thirdly, the heightened emphasis given to historical material frequently proved counter-productive. It seems surprising, for example, that a history examination at seven high schools in Magdeburg in 1985 should have revealed a lack of knowledge concerning the role of Ernst Thälmann in the Weimar

Republic, when this historical figure permeated more history books and youth activities than any other.[14] This was, however, precisely where the problem lay. The elementary repetition of material, and its treatment in the full range of forums, from history lessons and FDJ meetings through to *Jugendweihe* classes and preparations for anniversary celebrations, meant that young people often became over-saturated, causing them to interact with the subject only to the bare minimum.[15] Freya Klier confirmed this trend in her survey of 200 pupils on historical events and personalities: 'Historical events had been reduced to key words (17 June – workers' uprising, Prague Spring – invasion of Soviet troops into Prague . . ., wasn't that 1968?) – behind which there was emptiness, no How, no Why.'[16] Similarly, the constant repetition of terms such as 'anti-fascism', 'socialism' and 'imperialism' rendered them devoid of any true meaning for young people, who simply reproduced them without a second thought.

By the end of the 1980s, the aversion to official GDR history was reported to have reached serious proportions, endangering the development of a GDR patriotism: young people were developing a stronger interest in the history of other countries, and by 1989, interest in FRG history was, on average, higher than that of the GDR.[17] Perhaps the only area of official history to engender any genuine interest was that of regional history, which was frequently promoted due to its immediacy and relevance for young people. Whilst this proved particularly popular amongst girls, it was also ranked much higher than other areas of history by all sectors of youth,[18] and many reports commented on the effective nature of local history in arousing historical interest amongst young people. The Heimat festival at the FDJ Whitsun Meeting in May 1989, for example, was regarded to be one of the meeting's most successful events, with folk songs and dance, local traditions and customs creating much interest amongst young participants.[19] The tedium of textbook teaching was evidently absent here, yet so too was the clear ideological focus required by the party, thus the success of such activities in creating a bond with the socialist fatherland, rather than simply the more 'apolitical' Heimat, was questionable.

The majority of areas in which enthusiasm was evident, however, clearly strayed from the mould of official GDR history. The period of National Socialism, for example, increasingly aroused interest, especially towards the end of the 1980s, when more differentiated material became available to young people.[20] A *Junge Welt* article on the Hitler–Stalin Pact of 1939, published shortly before the fall of the Wall, thus found great resonance amongst its readers, many of whom had no prior knowledge of this agreement.[21] Interest was, indeed, often high in areas where there was a clear deficit of knowledge, or where party propaganda distorted the facts; it is no surprise that once Gorbachev's reforms had permitted the disclosure of information concerning Stalin's crimes, 79% of students claimed to be interested in events in the Soviet Union under Stalin, yet a mere 11% felt well informed on this subject.[22] This imbalance suggests that the state's deliberate negligence to instruct young people in certain areas only instilled in them a heightened curiosity in the subject. As was reported towards the end of the GDR, this trend saw a renewed interest in questions of GDR history, arising from 'a search for a realistic, differentiated portrayal of history which cannot be found in most history books, or only in highly simplified form'.[23] Whilst this reflected genuine interest in the GDR past, it rarely corresponded to the requirements of socialist patriotism.

Trends concerning historical knowledge and interests were not, however, uniform throughout the different sectors of the GDR's youth, and ZIJ studies revealed that two principal groups of young people existed. The first consisted primarily of apprentices and pupils under the age of 16, amongst whom a general lack of historical knowledge was evident. The second group, however, showed much greater knowledge, and consisted mainly of students, *Abitur* pupils and young members of the intelligentsia. Whilst the difference was clearly founded in education, this was not necessarily a reflection of the education itself, but rather of the political commitment of these young people. Those who were hoping to attain places in higher education, for example, were much more likely to show loyalty to the system and were driven by personal motivation to learn about the history of the GDR. Variation could also be witnessed amongst different generations, for a progressive decline of interest in official GDR history could be seen amongst all sectors of young people in the 1980s, the same period during which historical propaganda was intensified.[24] Comparative statistics from 1987 and 1988 reveal the rapidity of the change towards the end of the decade, for the number of students and apprentices declaring an interest in GDR history fell noticeably during this single year.[25] This trend was countered by growing interest in the history of the

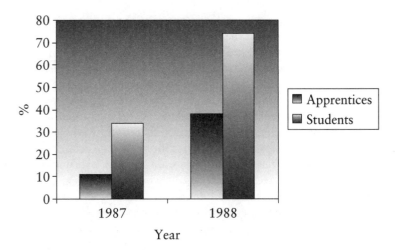

Figure 1 Interest in Soviet history, 1987 and 1988
(percentage answering 'strongly/very strongly' to the question 'How
strongly are you interested in the history of the Soviet Union?')

Source: BArch, DC4/305, 'Zum Geschichtsbewußtsein von Jugendlichen der
DDR', [1] Mar 1989, p. 34.

FRG, which had been steadily creeping forwards over the years,
and above all in that of the USSR, which rose sharply following
Gorbachev's rise to power in 1985 (see figure 1). It seemed that the
intensification of the history syllabus was thus having the contrary
effect to that which was desired, and by the end of the decade, there
is little doubt that interest in history was developing in clear conflict
with the aims of the SED and its patriotic programme.

Emotional involvement in history
Trends concerning the historical knowledge and interest of young
people help show where their allegiances lay, yet do not necessarily
reveal the extent to which they accepted or rejected the ideological
basis of historical propaganda. Their emotional attachment to the
GDR's historical roots is thus important in revealing the extent to
which they saw themselves as the future guardians of socialist tradition and as socialist patriots.

Within the sphere of GDR history, the SED's attempts to draw the
link between the past, present and future frequently fell on deaf ears,
for many young people were found to show ambivalence towards

the work of their grandparents' generation in the building of social-ism, taking the state of affairs in the 1980s for granted.[26] Con-sequently, history played little role in providing orientation in their lives, a trend which became increasingly widespread – an average of 78% of young people in 1978 fully agreed that the founding of the GDR formed a 'turning point' in the history of the people, whereas this was true of only 46% ten years later.[27] This lack of emotional attachment was no clearer than in the rejection of the FDJ blue shirt, which supposedly represented the traditions of the socialist youth movement, yet was rarely worn with pride. Instead, as a number of interviewees recollected, this frequently lay crumpled in the bottom of pupils' schoolbags, only to be worn for the absolute minimum period of time.[28] Some even went so far as to create an 'attachment' of a blue collar and red neckerchief that could be placed around the neckline of a jumper, so as to speed up the whole procedure. The uniform was considered to be dated, unfashionable and uncomfort-able, and its historical meaning was simply irrelevant to the huge majority of young people, who were more concerned with keeping up to date with fashion on the other side of the Wall.

In contrast to official GDR history, one would expect National Socialist history, which aroused above average levels of interest, to have greatly affected the emotions of young East Germans. However, even here a certain distance and pragmatism was evident, as the huge majority of young people were found to believe that the GDR had succeeded in ridding society of all fascist roots, and thus saw this part of history to be of little relevance to the present day.[29] This pragmatism manifested itself in a number of ways. Firstly, many young people treated the Third Reich much as any other period, evaluating its positive and negative sides,[30] and reactions to this period appear to have been emotionally little different to those concerning the founding phase of the GDR. Many, for example, mentioned elements of the Nazi regime such as industrial and sci-entific advances, but few seemed aware of the fact that these were made in highly unethical environments. Until the late 1980s, when the Holocaust and Jewish history gained importance, many young people remained ignorant of Judaism,[31] a reflection of the fact that only 2–5% of schoolbooks on this period covered the persecution of the Jews, and none used the terms 'Holocaust', 'Shoa' or 'Genocide'.[32] Young people in the GDR were also found to exp-erience few feelings of shame or guilt concerning the Holocaust, a phenomenon which provided striking contrast to the West. A group of young people from Hessen, for example, who joined a group of East German youth in a visit to Buchenwald in the mid-1980s, noted their differences: 'GDR youth see themselves as belonging to the tradition of the anti-fascist resistance movement . . . They do not want to have anything to do with the atrocities of fascism, and they do not feel responsible for them . . . Western youth do feel jointly responsible for the disaster of the Third Reich, although they do not, of course, share the blame.'[33] Young East Germans were, thus, more likely to see Germans as victims than aggressors, and showed a clear willingness to forgive the older generation who had co-operated with the Nazi regime.[34] The question of individual guilt was avoided in the same way that ethical questions were rarely asked and a lack of emotional involvement with this period was the norm. Although young people's reactions to the Third Reich and the building of socialism in the 1950s were not dissimilar, one important difference did exist: whereas the lack of emotion concerning the building of socialism resulted from a rejection of SED propaganda, that concerning the Third Reich came about as a result of propaganda. The party's portrayal of the GDR as the embodiment of anti-fascism thus appeared to have gained some influence amongst young people, who did not see themselves to be part of this period of German history.

One further question relating to the emotional sphere was the identification of young people with historical role models. These were promoted as an accessible means of creating identity with past events, and were typically communist or anti-fascist martyrs, killed in service of the anti-fascist and socialist cause, such as Ernst Thälmann, Karl Liebknecht and Rosa Luxemburg. Yet very few young people claimed to have any historical role models[35] and some schools even reported the vandalism of displays dedicated to such historical figures.[36] Once again, teaching methods were partly to blame, with pupils frequently reaching a level of over-saturation in this area, especially where popularised figures such as Ernst Thälmann were concerned. On the other hand, however, young people were more inclined to adopt role models from the present, such as pop stars (often from the West), sporting heroes, and occasionally politicians, as was the case with Gorbachev. Ironically, the one historical figure who did develop some kind of model status was Hitler.[37] It should be stressed that this could be witnessed amongst

only a very small minority group of skinheads and neofascists, yet
the party was aware of the 'Hitler-cult' to such an extent that,
fearing the eruption of ugly scenes, it issued strict orders to prevent
any planned celebrations on the anniversary of Hitler's 100th birthday on 20 April 1989.[38] Rather than being able to reap the benefits
of its policy of historical role models, the party was instead forced
to employ methods which would prevent it from being abused
amongst highly nationalist and unpatriotic circles.

The SED clearly failed in all but a minority of cases to create
amongst young people the desired emotional attachment to their
historical roots, and thus a stable basis for the development of patriotic behaviour. History was, however, successfully mobilised by the
emerging opposition movement during the 1980s in order to win
over the young generation. In February 1982, for example, Rainer
Eppelmann launched his Berlin Appeal to coincide with the thirty-
seventh anniversary of the bombing of Dresden, a historical event
which he used effectively to drum up support for this appeal for
peace. In a similar way, in 1988 the opposition movement used the
remembrance day of the murders of Karl Liebknecht and Rosa
Luxemburg for their own purposes, quoting Rosa Luxemburg's
controversial phrase 'Freedom is always freedom for one who
thinks differently'. By using this day and its historical connotations,
demonstrators were able to display their discontent, whilst still
showing support for the socialist ideal, and a number of schools
recorded incidents supporting the demonstration, in the form of
political graffiti as well as verbal and written declarations of
support.[39] As these examples demonstrate, it clearly was possible to
transport history into the present, bring it alive in the minds of
young people and employ it effectively for a political cause.
Crucially, however, and in contrast to the SED's attempts to mobilise
history for the patriotic cause, it was not forcibly imposed from
above.

'Peace must be armed!': protecting the fatherland

Reform movements such as Eppelmann's Berlin Appeal, which often
called on historical circumstances to back their cause, did so
frequently with a common aim: to oppose the state's military nature,
which was central to the socialist nation situated on the front line of
the Cold War. To what extent, however, was the young generation

influenced by such movements on the one hand, and the comprehensive structures of military education on the other? The findings of this section reveal that attitudes towards military training and the NVA not only varied with age, but also according to young people's perceived status in society, and in clear contrast to the popular image of a homogenised youth, military education provoked a wide range of behaviours and attitudes.[40]

From kindergarten to NVA

With military education beginning in early childhood, the SED liked to believe that young people would develop an organic interest in military affairs, and reports concerning kindergarten education noted the success of NVA games and military toys.[41] Whilst 4 and 5 year olds knew no different, and enthusiastically 'played soldiers', resistance sometimes came from a small number of parents and relatives, many of whom wrote petitions (*Eingaben*) against militarism in kindergartens, a form of protest which was allowed by the authorities. Some were outspoken in their objections and active in the church peace movement and although no formal changes to the system were achieved before 1989, their influence had some notable effect, for reports observed that a number of kindergarten teachers showed 'a certain reticence concerning the importance of the NVA, possibly even an underestimation of this side of patriotic education'.[42] By primary school age, some children were themselves influenced by parental attitudes, and numerous incidents revealed how the will of parents came into direct conflict with school life. Katharina H., for example, was prevented from doing her music homework in year 4 by her father, who disagreed with the military content of the song she was to learn.[43] Although the majority of children of this age continued to participate without objection, evidence suggests that a minority were beginning, of their own accord, to reject military structures. In January 1983, for instance, the Protestant weekly magazine *Der Sonntag* published a poem written by a group of children about their dream town, which included not only friendly people, green leafy areas, clean rivers and good shops, but also the desire to abolish both war and the army. As a result, this issue of the magazine was swiftly withdrawn, for despite the children's desire for peace, the rejection of the army was considered unpatriotic and unacceptable by the state, especially when coming from its youngest citizens.[44]

The point at which most young people consciously began to consider military education was at the age of 14, when the *Wehrunterricht* was introduced. Whilst few pupils looked forward to such classes, only a very small minority actively protested against them, and of the 303 petitions that were sent to the central authorities by 1980, only a handful were written by young people themselves, and a mere 0.07% refused to take part in the first year of classes in 1978–79.[45] In fact, by the early 1980s, the number of boys who volunteered to attend military camp had reached such a level that demand could not be satisfied. In Halle, for example, 91.6% of male pupils in 1983 were reported to have been willing to attend, whilst there was space for only 72.2%.[46] It is unlikely, however, that patriotic feelings gave rise to the large numbers of 'volunteers', for those who refused to comply were put under considerable pressure by teachers and risked facing discrimination in their future schooling. Additionally, the alternative course in civil defence, which was primarily for girls and consisted of first aid and civilian defence methods, proved to be a particularly unattractive proposition for the majority of 15–16 year old male adolescents. Numbers attending military camps thus remained strong but reports from the early to mid-1980s recorded an increase in boys refusing to handle weapons.[47] It is no surprise that this coincided with the founding period of a number of unofficial peace groups led by the churches and that regions with strong religious affiliations, frequently in more rural areas, witnessed greater resistance towards military structures.[48] The numbers involved, however, remained small, with the national average of boys refusing to shoot remaining under 0.05% until 1989,[49] and the success of the peace movement remained limited here.

Clearly the huge majority of young people continued to comply with the SED and, of all activities, shooting was frequently reported to have engendered the most enthusiasm. There are few indications that 15 year olds saw the use of weapons to be problematic,[50] and in view of the everyday 'normality' of military structures the *Wehrunterricht* was simply accepted without serious reflection. As one young man remembered: 'I didn't really think about . . . why tanks were still driving around, that's just how it was.'[51] As demonstrated here, the acceptance of military structures did not necessarily indicate enthusiasm for any ideological content, and the chance to spend time away from home with one's friends was far more appealing than the accompanying ideology. The memories of one teenager were typical: 'There were loads of boys, and it was more like holiday camp – we had fun, and whatever was taught there simply passed us by.'[52] Even those who stayed at home for the course in civil defence welcomed the break from the everyday routine of school life, claiming that it was 'better than school', and many interviewees recollected being unable to take the course seriously, as the materials provided were not only inadequate, but would have been highly ineffective in the case of nuclear war.[53] The courses were thus welcomed for their novelty, and enthusiasm for military structures was rarely founded in ideological reasons, contributing little towards patriotic commitment to the socialist fatherland.

Evidence clearly suggests that scepticism towards military service grew with age and increasing exposure to military education. A survey of young men undergoing paramilitary training in the GST, for instance, found that training had an adverse affect on their views and that their primary expectation was physical fitness, a quality which involved no ideological requirements or patriotic commitment.[54] More notably, however, instances of active protest against military structures were noted amongst older pupils, often inspired by events at the Carl-von-Ossietzky school in Berlin in the autumn of 1988.[55] Here four pupils studying for their *Abitur* were expelled, and two others sent to different schools for initiating an anti-military campaign and organising a petition which called for the abolition of military parades at the GDR's national anniversary celebrations. They mustered the support of thirty-seven signatories before the petition was banned – a large number given the risks involved and the fact that these were *Abitur* pupils, generally deemed to be more ideologically conformist.[56] As the party was all too aware, even the loyalty of 'reliable' pupils could not always be counted on, and as young men approached the age of military service, they appeared ever more set against it.

Despite growing scepticism, over a third of all boys volunteered to serve longer than the basic eighteen months right until the end of the GDR. This willingness especially increased amongst those wanting to gain a place in higher education: whilst 47.5% of university applicants in Magdeburg and 54.8% in Halle volunteered for three years or more in 1983, the figures had reached 63.3% and 74.3%, respectively, by 1986.[57] Although such statistics suggest an element of success in the SED's drive to recruit more young men following the fall in the birth rate, motivations once again proved largely personal, and rarely denoted a patriotic stance. The prime motivation for longer service was without doubt the desire to gain a place in further education and the pressure exerted on young men, parents and girlfriends was often too great to resist, with many unwillingly agreeing to three years' service.[58] In contrast, the quotas for posts longer than three years, thus those which demanded true levels of patriotic commitment, became increasingly difficult to fill, and had fallen well below the target figures by the late 1980s.[59] Furthermore, the number of conscientious objectors and *Bausoldaten* (those choosing to serve without weapons) increased dramatically during the 1980s,[60] and the rise of pacifist thinking during this decade provided considerable cause for concern for both the SED and the FDJ.[61]

The reasons for young men's unwillingness to serve more than the mandatory eighteen months (if at all) were threefold. Firstly, those with strong religious convictions invariably upheld a pacifist stance, thus rejecting the use of weapons or complying only to the necessary minimum. This was particularly evident amongst Jehovah's Witnesses and Seventh Day Adventists, both of which formed very small communities, but produced the largest number of conscientious objectors and *Bausoldaten*.[62] Secondly, the reluctance of young men to leave friends and family significantly shaped their views, with girlfriends and parents proving so influential that functionaries considered carrying out special work with them in order to secure a reliable intake for military service.[63] Many were also unwilling to leave their home town or village,[64] thus demonstrating that regional loyalties often ranked higher than loyalty to the GDR and, as seen with historical consciousness, the frequently 'apolitical' nature of regional attachment effectively won over 'political' loyalty to the state. Thirdly, the international situation, and particularly the threat of atomic war, was frequently used to dismiss the need for military service, with many believing that 'if the worst-case scenario happens, then it's too late anyway'.[65] This is not to say that young people were unconcerned by the eventuality of war; on the contrary, the international situation significantly contributed to the rise in pacifism. This was further enhanced by détente in the later 1980s, for greater co-operation with the West only deepened young people's scepticism towards the necessity of military defence. As one report claimed with reference to military service: 'Many pupils are not immediately willing to recognise the term "duty of honour" without reservations (such as "two German armies", "order to shoot at the border", "Germans shooting at Germans", etc.).'[66] Many young men thus argued that they could serve the GDR through better ways than military service, such as in industrial or agricultural production and, in doing so, they cleverly used the party's own formulations to present plausible and more acceptable reasons for rejecting longer service.

Once young men reached the army, few found that experience of the NVA improved their attitudes, and reports noted a lack of military pride amongst both soldiers and their relatives.[67] Indeed, those who had completed military service were regularly found to have discouraged younger friends and relatives from signing up for longer than eighteen months,[68] which suggests that experiences in the NVA often weakened already doubtful loyalties, rather than strengthening any fundamental belief in GDR socialism. *Bausoldaten* also found army life discouraging, and the experiences of many not only led them to a more whole-hearted renunciation of militarism but often to a rejection of the GDR state, with some claiming to have experienced a 'deeply offending institution' which served as a 'basis for hostility towards the state'.[69] Their views were likely to be biased, owing to their pacifist stance and the fact that they were often unfairly treated by army officials who viewed them as shirkers, yet the proportion of *Bausoldaten* whose main motivation was pacifism rather than religious conviction increased, demonstrating a growing core of opposition to military propaganda.[70] By 1988, former *Bausoldaten* had established twelve regional groups across the GDR, in order to exert anti-military pressure on the government,[71] and increasing acceptance of their status amongst the population at large during the 1980s, especially the younger generation, suggested that their anti-militarism found sympathy amongst wider circles. Reports in the late 1980s thus not only displayed growing concern at the lack of boys being recruited, but also at the widespread nature of pacifist views; once again it seemed that the SED's propaganda had proved largely ineffective.

From conformists to critics

Despite the increasing rejection of military propaganda with time and age, a range of attitudes and behaviours can be identified within these broader trends, once again revealing that young people formed a far from monolithic mass. Four distinct sets of attitudes can be identified amongst teenagers in response to military education, each of which aids our understanding of this young generation's relationship to their state.

Firstly, a small group of loyal supporters existed who entered into military education with full enthusiasm, undertook the longer military service and sometimes opted for a military career. Such young people were, however, hard to come by, as opportunism, rather than genuine enthusiasm, was frequently the cause of apparently loyal behaviour. Yet evidence suggests that a small group of enthusiasts did voluntarily declare their military commitment, for some young people entered into the full programme of GST events, later becoming young leaders and instructors themselves, thereby far exceeding the levels of commitment required to secure social mobility. Their reasons ranged from the highly ideological stance, such as 'I am ready to fight for our socialist GDR in the event of capitalist and imperialist aggression',[72] to the more regional attitude: 'I don't want my home town, which was reduced to rubble by Anglo-American bombers on 16 January 1945, to be destroyed again.'[73] In both cases, the overriding desire was to protect the achievements of the GDR and to prevent aggressive Western forces from penetrating the country. Whilst such comments often demonstrated that young people had simply learned the right formulations, those which were backed up with active commitment showed that SED propaganda had gained influence amongst some, and that genuine military enthusiasm often reflected a patriotic stance.

At the opposite end of the spectrum from loyal supporters were those who openly rejected the party's military propaganda, along with GDR society in general. This group was divided into two contrasting subgroups: right-wing skinheads and pacifist punks. The first, skinheads, embraced military life as one of their most important principles, and were, in many ways, ideal candidates for the NVA, placing importance on discipline, physical fitness and a healthy lifestyle. Some skinhead groups thus organised paramilitary weekend training camps, and attempts were even made to recruit members through GST groups. Their enthusiasm was not, however, compatible with GDR militarism, for it seriously conflicted with socialist ideology: they subscribed to a Hitler cult, idolised the *Schutzstaffel (SS)* as their military model, collected Nazi memorabilia and wore clothing that resembled Western military uniforms.

Ironically, those who were the most fanatical about militarism also held the most inimical attitudes towards the state, and as one skinhead stated: 'We stand for a unified Germany. The whole of the left, it makes you sick in this damn state.'[74] The military consciousness desired by the SED in young people was primarily defined by ideology, and military enthusiasm alone clearly did not denote support for the GDR.

The second subgroup was as anti-military as the first was pro-military. Punks provided colourful contrast to the appearance of skinheads and stood for everything the right-wing extremists rejected: anarchism, pacifism, non-conformity and individualism. Considering themselves social outcasts, these young people also protested against socialist society and refused to co-operate with the accepted social norms. The refrain of one punk song best demonstrated this attitude: 'Refusing to do military service, not paying taxes, painting walls, not going to work, refusing to do military service, ignoring laws . . .'[75] They thus renounced military education and propaganda not only because of their pacifist beliefs, but also in outright rejection of the GDR and its social structures. Despite the conflicting ideologies and appearances of skinheads and punks, both can thus clearly be described as 'anti-patriotic', for their extreme reactions to military propaganda reflected a clear rejection of the GDR state.

Both the above categories represented only a small sector of GDR youth; the majority of young people instead constituted a third group, adopting the lowest level of commitment possible in order to facilitate a relatively comfortable life in the GDR. Whilst some felt the need to complete three years' service in order to gain entry to university, all young men in this group struck a compromise, publicly declaring agreement with the system, whilst privately taking little on board. In doing so, they all 'worked the system' for their own benefit, a form of conduct which was lamented in many a report: 'In general there is an understanding for, and agreement with, the need for military defence . . . However, where personal decisions are concerned, there is hesitation and reticence.'[76] A certain helplessness could be perceived amongst this group, for they believed they were unable to change anything, and thus made no attempt to do so. In this way, many became adept at using the international state of affairs to support their position, using possible nuclear war or détente as arguments for the irrelevance of military

defence. Indeed, apathy marked this group even during the heightened international tensions of the early 1980s.[77] Ironically, the
state's efforts to intensify military education in the 1980s simply
enhanced this apathy, and many retreated into the private sphere,
increasingly regarding personal comforts, familiar surroundings
and girlfriends to be more important than the concept of service to
the state. A letter sent from the trainee officer Peter L. to the
Ministry for Education in 1985 lucidly illustrated these problems.
Having helped to train 15 and 16 year old boys at a military camp,
he was horrified at the extreme lack of interest, with many arriving
on the first day claiming that 'the day we go home will be the best
day',[78] before even having had a chance to sample camp life.
Attached to Peter L.'s letter was a set of maps which he had asked
his class to produce in a double lesson: only two out of the entire
class were correctly completed, the rest ranging from half-hearted
attempts to a lack of any noticeable effort; at least four papers consisted only of cartoons and graffiti. He concluded that participation
must be truly voluntary, as the more pressure that was exerted on
boys, the less they were willing to participate. Apathy was not necessarily a response to the principle of military education itself, but
rather to the way in which it was enforced by the state, once again
demonstrating the counter-productive nature of the SED's patriotic
programme.

   The majority of young people fell into the above category, yet a
considerable number formed a fourth group, whose stance also
emerged in reaction to the state's military policies. Rather than
regarding their position to be helpless, however, they believed they
could make a difference: by protesting against militarism, and
embracing commitment to a peace which would be free of military
influence. Whilst many described themselves as pacifists, they dif-
fered from punks as they refused to opt out of the system, aiming
instead to change it from within. Most demonstrations were organised by young Christians, keen to oppose the FDJ's calls for 'armed'
peace with slogans such as 'Destroy your image of the enemy' and
'Dare to trust – so that we can live',[79] and in doing so often giving
up any hopes of further education. Although the majority of such
demonstrations were connected to the churches, not all those
involved held strong religious beliefs, for churches were attracting
growing numbers of young people precisely because of their desire
to promote a 'peace' that the state would not tolerate. Indeed, many

were provoked into action by the state's overbearing display of militarism; pupils at the Carl-von-Ossietzky school, for instance, explained that it was not the existence of the army that disturbed them, but rather the nature of military propaganda: 'We need our NVA, but we are against the display of weapons and power.'[80] By the late 1980s, similar objections even came from members of the army, who claimed that new international conditions called for a different approach, demonstrating just how far such discontent had spread.[81]

Whilst dissatisfaction and active protest marked out this fourth group, their chosen forms of opposition varied greatly. Protest ranged from the support of campaigners, a phenomenon that was experienced in the far-reaching expression of sympathy for the pupils expelled from the Carl-von-Ossietzky school, to the organisation of large-scale initiatives and demonstrations, such as the attempt in 1982 to sabotage the GDR's national anniversary celebrations with cardboard tanks painted with flowers.[82] The most long-term protest, initiated in 1981, was the campaign for a community 'peace service' as a real alternative to military service (although *Bausoldaten* were not required to use weapons, they were still employed by the NVA), which made use of slogans such as 'Swords into ploughshares' and 'Ready to help, not fight'.[83] Whilst protesters of all kinds had to expect possible and sometimes severe punishment, this group's rejection of militarism did not necessarily mean that they rejected the GDR and all it stood for. The majority in fact declared their firm intent to remain in the GDR, as exemplified by eight young men who wrote to Honecker protesting against the military regime, all but one of whom wished to continue living in the GDR.[84] One of them summarised the feelings of many: 'R. emphasised that he is in favour of socialism, and that the future of humankind cannot be found in imperialism. However, the realities of life in the GDR make it difficult for him to be in favour of this socialism.'[85] The real aim of such protesters was thus to make others think more critically, rather than to create a hatred for the GDR: 'Through our work we hope to help shake up the consciousness of the people, and make them receptive to the problems of the GDR – without wanting to question socialism itself.'[86] This suggests that criticism of militarism not only resulted from young people's concern for the future of the GDR but that it was also a response to the large number of apathetic conformists who were upholding the system rather than attempting to change it for the better.

As these four categories reveal, the renunciation of militarism did
not always mean a direct renunciation of the GDR and the socialist
system (or vice versa). What it did mean, however, was a rejection
of the state's methods, for the more the state attempted to create a
military youth, the more the youth resisted in one form or another.
As one young man claimed: 'It's always about duty, duty, duty . . .
Why always threaten with military service? People are overfed with
this propaganda. More attention should be paid to their feelings.
The discussion is not being led in the right direction.'[87] Such pressure clearly pushed some young people into 'hostile' and 'unpatriotic' circles and, whilst many demonstrations began in specific
protest against militarism, they frequently ended in protest against
the SED, whose rigid control of events won them no supporters.
Although the principle of military defence itself did not necessarily
discourage loyalty to the GDR, the enforced militarism of the SED
certainly did, and succeeded only in pushing an increasing number
of young people, who displayed potential loyalty to a central
element of socialist patriotism, one step nearer to its periphery.

'Educating hatred': young people and the 'imperialist' West

Young people's reticence towards military affairs in the 1980s was
evidently influenced by the international situation, particularly
détente and attempts to disarm. Yet the evils of the 'imperialist' West
had been losing definition in the eyes of young people for some time,
especially in view of widely accessible West German television and
radio, which became increasingly relied upon thanks to the unreli-
able and inefficient processing of news in the GDR. As a result, not
only were traditional forms of youth journalism, such as *Junge Welt*,
losing out to Western competition, but also more modern forms of
media, such as the once popular youth radio station DT64.[88] To
what extent, however, did the increasing influence of the West shape
the actions and views of young people in the 1980s, and how did
this affect their loyalties to the socialist fatherland? Did the very
presence of the 'other' German state undermine the SED's attempts
to create a GDR patriotism? This section firstly examines the ways
in which young people showed their attraction to Western values,
before turning to the allegedly 'negative' effects of Western influence
on young people, and the special relationship between the FRG and
the GDR.

East looks West: a cultural attraction

The increasing use of Western media, combined with growing despondency towards the GDR's official youth activities, saw a shift in young people's cultural interests. Whilst Western trends had always attracted the interest of Eastern youth, GDR singers and writers found themselves competing against an ever-growing core of popular Western artists. Officials noted an increase in 'trashy and smutty literature' that was crossing the border from West to East, and West German writers such as Heinrich Böll and Günter Grass gained increasingly wide circulation.[89] Former GDR intellectuals, such as the songwriter Wolf Biermann and the author Reiner Kunze, also saw their popularity rise once they had left the GDR, as many showed defiant solidarity with their situation. The growing appeal of the Western cultural sphere was, however, most evident in the area of rock music, where the political motives of performers were of paramount interest to the party. In order to curb this influence, and following a dispute between the West German band BAP and the GDR authorities, West German groups were banned from performing in East Germany in 1984.[90] The annual (from 1985 biennial) event 'Rock for Peace' was consequently promoted as a 'national exhibition of GDR rock music',[91] and tailored to young people's needs, yet the popularity of Western bands could not be dampened. Indeed, East German stages did not remain free of Western groups for long, once again hosting names as famous as Bob Dylan by late 1987.

This change of policy was largely a reaction to events in June 1987 near the Brandenburg Gate, where, in celebration of Berlin's 750th anniversary, top musicians such as David Bowie, the Eurythmics and Genesis gave open-air concerts on three successive evenings outside the Reichstag in West Berlin. During the three evenings, over 6,000 young East Germans gathered on the Eastern side of the Wall to catch the sounds carried over by the wind, and the atmosphere became progressively disruptive, with demands to pull down the Wall and abolish the police, alongside cries of support for Gorbachev and calls for human rights.[92] The result was 158 arrests and a large question mark over the GDR's policy on rock music, for Western rock groups had not only gained the support of the GDR's youth, but had also called into question the political loyalty, and ultimately the patriotism, of this generation. The SED's response was swift and, realising its weak position, it decided to allow Western artists to perform in the GDR once again. This new policy was most evident in June 1988, when a planned repeat of the West Berlin festival compelled the GDR to organise its own three-day open-air festival in East Berlin, an event which was significantly described as 'an urgent political necessity'.[93] The famous Western names of Joe Cocker and Bruce Springsteen attracted significant numbers of young East Germans, and Springsteen's performance alone produced the largest rock concert in GDR history. It appeared that the state had gained a victory, for that year only 2,000 people gathered at the Brandenburg Gate to hear the Western concert, and disruptions were minimal.[94] The validity of this victory, however, remains dubious, for the state was only able to counter Western influence through the very harnessing of Western music. In this way, the failure of the SED to resist the popularity of Western performers and to create a GDR identity through rock music could hardly have been more dramatic.

A similar trend emerged in relation to the Western fashion industry, which was also avidly followed by the majority of young East Germans, yet disapproved of by the SED. Long hair for young men, ripped jeans and Doc Marten boots, which the SED believed reflected a lack of discipline, thus proved highly popular, as well as the wearing of Western logos and emblems from NATO states.[95] Many young people also adopted token elements of punk and skinhead fashion, a trend which became an increasingly popular way of directing mild protest towards the state, without adhering to the ideologies of these groups. The party clearly saw the need to regain some control and, with the aim of quelling this trend, one educational report from 1988 suggested the mass production of such fashion items, in order to remove their oppositional character.[96] Whilst this suggestion came too late to be implemented, it demonstrates a familiar pattern, for in order to prevent young people from displaying attraction to the Western world, and thus their dissatisfaction with the GDR, the party felt it necessary to adopt elements of Western culture itself, thereby betraying its attempts to inculcate specific GDR forms. This displays the complex nature of the relationship between the GDR state and its people, and demonstrates the blurred boundaries between the two: despite the state's attempt to impose rigid patriotic norms on the young generation, it found that young people's pursuit of their own interests could not be ignored. Whilst the youth was largely required to comply with the state, the state was also forced, at times, to comply with the youth in order to maintain both its status and a credible patriotic programme.

The imperialist West: root of all rebellion?

By the 1980s, signs of increasing tobacco and alcohol consumption, rowdiness and a rising crime rate began to concern GDR officials.[97] Pupils were caught on school trips drinking alcohol and sniffing liquids, and numerous cases of vandalism were put down to the inebriated state of young protagonists.[98] The number of political provocations in schools also increased, more than doubling between 1987 and 1988.[99] In the eyes of the SED it was logical that such behaviour stemmed from the West, where levels of crime and drug abuse were notably higher than in the East.[100] Furthermore, the SED claimed that the West was developing new techniques in the late 1980s, ranging from the production of specific youth television programmes to the sending of messages attached to helium balloons, all of which aimed to spread rumours of an 'identity crisis' amongst young people in the GDR and build them up as a 'potential source of conflict'.[101] The accuracy of such claims, however, along with the pretension that all negative behaviour stemmed from the 'imperialist' West was dubious, yet they provided fuel for the SED's campaign against the West and conveniently allowed the party to disclaim all responsibility for its own youth problems. To what extent, however, was the party justified in doing so? Did social behaviour which contravened the norms of socialist patriotism not also grow from within society?

Whilst the Western world clearly influenced young people's lives, archival evidence suggests that disruptive and provocative behaviour found its roots largely within GDR society, where boredom and frustration with monotonous routines and uninspiring FDJ activities were growing. As one Stasi report noted: 'Many problems which affect young people are, in their eyes, neglected, and cannot be compensated for with discos or FDJ celebrations. According to them, life in the GDR is secure and unburdened by social problems, but otherwise uninteresting and associated with a certain lack of enthusiasm.'[102] Given the lack of alternatives to the FDJ, those who rejected official activities were left to their own devices outside school time, often seeking out lenient bar owners who would serve underage customers. Such places became regular meeting places which attracted increasing numbers of young people and subsequently developed a reputation for drunk and rowdy behaviour.[103] Others, however, sought out environments in which they felt they had control over their activities; a number of teenagers, for example, visited so-called 'black discos', where the choice of music met their tastes, rather than the SED's requirements, whilst others created independent interest groups of their own, often connected to football:

> Various young people have formed 'fan clubs' – in breach of the existing regulations – some with fantastical names and flags . . . It is particularly these groups which are often responsible for lighting fireworks on football pitches, organising negative political chants and provoking arguments between supporters of different teams.[104]

The search for identity within such groups created micro-centres of political activity, many of which grew into networks of punks, skinheads, goths and other similar groupings throughout the GDR. Although modelled on Western culture, these groups largely gained membership as a result of frustration with GDR society, rather than incitement from the West.

Of all such groups, the emergence of neofascist tendencies in the GDR was most directly attributed to the West, for the possibility that nationalist activity could ever have grown out of anti-fascist GDR society was deemed impossible: 'there is neither an ideological nor a socio-economic basis for neonazism in the GDR.'[105] Yet by late 1988, skinheads and neonazis were estimated to number between 1,000 and 1,500, and the number of young offenders put on trial for such crimes more than tripled from 44 in 1988 to 144 in 1989, many of which were connected to the celebration of Hitler's 100th birthday.[106] There were certainly indications that the West influenced the actions of skinheads and neonazis in the GDR, for West German neonazi magazines and fashion accessories found their way into the East, through either personal contacts in the FRG or the black market. The nature of some incidents also displayed the influence of outside forces, such as racist violence towards Turks at the World Cup qualifier match between the GDR and Turkey in Magdeburg in April 1989.[107] With negligible numbers of Turks living in the GDR, it is probable that such behaviour found inspiration in the West, where anti-Turkish attitudes were already rife amongst certain groups.

The presence of the 'other' Germany clearly did help to undermine some elements of the SED's patriotic programme, yet sources of inspiration for neofascism could also be found in the GDR. Although young people and also their parents were too young to have experienced German fascism, their grandparents' generation still had vivid memories of the Third Reich and were often a source of anecdotes, photographs and memorabilia. Young people in the 1980s thus still had some personal contact with this era, and those who were curious to learn more had little difficulty in accessing literature or other items of interest that often lay forgotten amongst personal belongings.[108] Skinheads and neonazis also found motivation from contemporary society, for in contrast to similar groups in the West, their identity was often built around a clear rejection and negation of the state in which they lived. For many, the attraction of fascism lay as much in its damaging effect on the GDR state as in its ideological basis and, by demonstrating fundamental disagreement with the founding principles of the state, thereby rejecting the ideological basis of GDR patriotism, they found a powerful weapon with which to oppose the regime. As a Stasi report observed: 'They have found the sensitive spot in this society, which is antifascist. They have found out what hurts this society . . . – and that is exactly what they are doing.'[109] In this way, many skinheads rejected the tenet that they were driven by Western forces, for this in itself robbed them of their autonomy and their identity.[110]

Alongside skinheads, punks were estimated to number approximately 1,000 across the GDR by 1981, with as many as 10,000 sympathisers.[111] Similar to skinheads, they modelled their appearance on West German and British groups, accessing fashion commodities and music via the West. They also followed the broad ideological beliefs of Western groups, supporting anti-fascism, anarchy and, as seen with military service, withdrawing from organised society. Yet they, too, developed an identity which was specific to the environment in which they lived. This was largely in reaction to the SED's interpretation of socialism, for in contrast to skinheads it was not the principle of socialism that they rejected, but rather the way in which it was realised in the GDR. Their criticism of society most notably pointed towards the SED's dominant control and desire for uniformity, as demonstrated in the refrain of one punk song: 'Norm, norm, norm, you were born to be a norm/If you don't conform here you're forlorn.'[112] Punks thus found a number of ways to attack the

state, most notably in their unconventional lifestyles and appearances, which seriously conflicted with the socialist ideal of obedient,
orderly citizens. Many also wore badges proclaiming slogans such
as 'hate' or 'no future', both of which negated the SED's ideals of
peace and the visionary appeal of a socialist future. Other forms of
protest were more provocative, ranging from anti-SED graffiti to
politically charged concerts; one banner that was paraded by punks
in the streets of Quedlinburg typically read: 'It was Jews get out,
then Turks get out, and in the GDR it's Punks get out.'[113] By creating for themselves a specific identity in reaction to socialist society,
GDR punks thus distanced themselves in equal measure from their
Western counterparts and the SED's patriotic propaganda.

Numerous other minority groups existed, such as heavy metal
fans ('Heavys'), goths ('Grufties'), 'New Romantiks', 'Poppers',
'Funkies' and 'Tramper'. Whilst many of these accepted some
aspects of socialist society, they ultimately all rejected the SED
regime, demonstrating their opposition through clothing, music and
unacceptable social behaviour. The importance of this oppositional
element, rather than the specific ideology of each group, was
demonstrated by the constant flow of movement between groups,
even between those as ideologically different as skinheads and
punks. The common aim was to reject established society, and to
create for oneself an identity which was distinct from the monolithic
FDJ culture; one young goth's choice of identity typically rested on
the fact that 'goths are more shocking'.[114] Even where a loose affil-
iation with such groups was grounded in fashion rather than ideology, this was still a form of showing discontent with the state.
Indeed, although the core of activists from all these groups was
small (estimated to be 0.9% of young people in Halle in 1984[115]), it
exerted a wider influence on young people who sought an outlet for
their frustrations. As one skinhead sympathiser said: 'I don't want
a new Hitler or anything, I don't want that. Just a state that's like
any other normal state.'[116] These groups, often referred to as 'sub-
cultures', would thus be more accurately described as 'anti-cul-
tures', for they formed in clear opposition to the accepted youth
culture of the FDJ and the patriotic propaganda of the SED.
Continued attempts to shield these young people from Western
culture, however, were to have little effect, for such groups were
only likely to fall in number or membership once a valid alternative
to official youth work had been created.

In view of the deficit of alternative youth activities, churches strengthened their youth work during the 1980s, with Protestant churches introducing 'open' youth work, designed to attract any young people who found themselves on the edge of society. As a result, many became meeting places for members of minority groups such as punks and goths, as well as others who sought a focus of activity outside the FDJ, and in Magdeburg it was estimated in 1984 that only 10% of participants at large-scale church events were religious.[117] It is no surprise that the growing influence of the churches was also believed to result from stronger ties between East and West, particularly in light of a growing number of partnerships between student groups in the 1980s. Protestant student circles in Göttingen, Gießen, Hildesheim, Kassel and Konstanz, for example, made regular contact with their counterparts in Halle, Eisleben, Merseburg, Naumburg and Köthen,[118] as did Protestant youth workers in Düsseldorf and Magdeburg.[119] As young people were typically over-represented at major church events, the party feared resistance from these quarters, above all in the creation of an 'inner opposition'.[120] Its fears that the West proved influential were not unfounded, for many such meetings, which discussed issues such as the environment, peace and 'alternative' lifestyles, often used the FRG flag symbolically, or quoted and circulated Western literature; some groups were even funded by Western sources.

The agenda of these groups, however, maintained an unequivocally Eastern character and, whilst their purpose was to oppose the GDR regime (particularly its armed peace policies and over-emphasis on militarism), this was generally in the interests of preserving the GDR rather than causing its destruction. As one student claimed, the over-riding aim was to create a more democratic GDR, in which 'tolerance, trust and a willingness to change one's ideas' may grow.[121] The dual origins of one of the most successful slogans for peace, 'Swords into ploughshares', demonstrates the East German character of such campaigning: not only did it claim biblical roots, quoted in Isaiah 2.4 and Micah 4.3, but it also symbolised the historic mission of socialism to maintain peace, for it was concretised in a New York statue, given to the United Nations by the Soviet Union as a gift and expression of peace. The choice of slogan and the production of badges worn by young supporters was clearly not a result of Western influence, and impetus came largely from within GDR society, growing from the discontent of GDR citizens concerning not only the state's peace policies but also the education system and the restriction of basic human rights. The primary aim was to change the society in which they lived, and whilst aid and encouragement came from the West, this was in no way the main source of inspiration.[122] As with the extreme minority groups, their motivation – and, indeed, their identity – lay as much in the rejection of the SED's patriotic norms as in the attraction of the West.

The West German relative: the FRG through the eyes of young people

Whilst the SED guarded against the influence of all Western capitalist nations, it was without doubt that of the FRG which made the party most nervous, for its geographical, linguistic and cultural proximity to the GDR inevitably gave rise to a special relationship between these states. Highly representative of imperialist ideology in schoolbooks and official propaganda, the FRG was, however, also the home of relatives and family histories, thus somewhat compromising the image of the Western 'enemy'. The youth's relationship to the FRG was thus complex and, although the fashions, music and literature of the FRG proved highly attractive, it was division rather than unity that was perceived to be the norm for this generation, and consequently the large majority regarded the FRG to be a foreign country like any other.[123] Moreover, young people also appeared to hold a certain pride in their Eastern distinctiveness, reportedly rejecting remarks made by Kohl about 'the open German question' in 1987.[124] In this way, the very presence of the FRG sometimes gave rise to a type of defensive pride, and many objected to the FRG's claim to speak on behalf of all Germans.[125] Indeed, despite clear material differences, the desire to show that one was in every other way equal to, or better than, the average FRG citizen was widespread, pre-dating the *Trotzidentität* which was observed during and after the *Wende* (see chapters 3 and 4). As one report found: 'At organised, but also private meetings, the presumptuous, patronising and arrogant manner of FRG citizens is very often met with disapproval, and a spontaneous pride in the GDR emerges (with comments about "Bundis" and "West Germans").'[126] Similarly, the occasion of Honecker's visit to Bonn in 1987 and the FRG's public recognition of GDR sovereignty were reported to trigger feelings of pride amongst numerous FDJ members.[127] It was clearly important that the GDR should not be seen as the FRG's poor relative, but rather as an independent state with its own credentials and worthy of equal status.

Despite this air of competitiveness, young people also viewed the FRG in a more favourable light than they did other Western states. Indeed, numerous reports noted, with frustration, the youth's tendency to play down the aggressive and exploitative nature of imperialism in the FRG, compared to the USA, Britain and France.[128] Although many feared war, and above all the USA's course of armament in the early 1980s, few cast the FRG into the same mould, rather finding it difficult to regard the West German state as their enemy.[129] Even the *Bundeswehr*, traditionally symbolic of imperialist aggression, rarely aroused strong negative feelings amongst young people.[130] Political events and personalities in the FRG, particularly during the late 1970s and early 1980s, played an important role in influencing young people's views in the GDR. The decision to present the notoriously right-wing Franz-Josef Strauß as the CDU/CSU's candidate for chancellor in the elections of 1980, for example, created widespread concern, and triggered a wave of sympathy for the Social Democratic Party of Germany (SPD) and Helmut Schmidt, whose meeting with Honecker in 1981 met with widespread approval.[131] The SPD also gained the support of many young people following Willy Brandt's visit to Moscow in 1981, and the increasing co-operation of the 1980s created amongst young people the perception that the FRG was a country to be worked with rather than fought against. This was particularly evident in 1987 following Honecker's visit to Bonn, which confirmed for many the growing feeling that the FRG was no longer the embodiment of the 'enemy'.[132] Indeed, young people asked deliberately awkward questions concerning the nature of the FRG regime:

- If they are suffering, why don't the workers of the FRG become revolutionary and vote communist?
- Why aren't impoverished and unemployed FRG citizens standing at the border wanting to come into the GDR?[133]

The doubts of young people became increasingly vocal, causing the FDJ in Magdeburg to provide special training for functionaries to help them deal with such questions and, by the late 1980s, young people's understanding of FRG imperialism rarely matched up to the party's expectations. Many also felt that the party's constant

defamation of the West German state overshadowed more important issues, and resulted only in sapping valuable energy and
resources away from the home front and neglecting positive developments within the GDR.[134] Not only was the West thus drawing
young people away from the grasp of the SED, but it ironically also
appeared to be drawing SED resources away from the GDR.

During the final years of the GDR, reports noted that a significant
number of young people felt their identity to be 'German' rather
than specifically 'East German', and perceptions of the 'fatherland'
increasingly incorporated both Germanies.[135] As a ZIJ study found
in April 1989, half of all young people regarded the GDR to be their
'fatherland', yet over a third found Germany as a whole to embody
this entity.[136] Whilst older generations, who remembered Germany
prior to division, could be expected to retain some emotional attachment to a united Germany, this youngest generation had no such
personal connection, and had been raised post-*Abgrenzung*. Indeed,
one would expect the proportion of young people who identified
with the GDR to increase consistently with time, yet surveys from
the 1970s suggest that levels of identification were higher then than
in the mid-to-late 1980s.[137] The SED's attempts to build on the
apparent support of the 1970s appeared to be counter-productive,
for subsequent surveys revealed that this weakening identity with
the GDR was accompanied by a growing emotional attachment to
the West.[138] Whilst the presence of the FRG posed an obstacle to the
validity of GDR patriotism from its outset, the SED's careful plans
to 'educate hatred' did little to convince young people of the evils of
West Germany, and not only failed but in many ways backfired.

Proletarian internationalism: the politics of solidarity

It was believed that anti-imperialist propaganda was complemented
by the values of proletarian internationalism, which guarded against
the dangers of nationalism and promoted two central components
of GDR patriotism: the unity of the working classes and the anti-
fascist cause. FDJ leaders indeed appeared confident that the SED
was raising a young generation of committed internationalists, and
regarded the GDR to be the very model of proletarian internationalism and the embodiment of anti-fascism: 'the societal roots of
fascism and anti-Semitism, racial discrimination and xenophobia
have been eradicated in the socialist German republic, once and for

all.'[139] Yet to what extent did official propaganda on the one hand, and genuine encounters with foreigners on the other, influence young people's understanding of international solidarity? Which proved most influential in the formation, or rejection, of patriotic sentiment?

Socialist solidarity in the public and private spheres

International events organised for young people were often approached with interest and enthusiasm, for they provided a variation from the usual pattern of school classes and FDJ meetings. In 1985, for example, the fortieth anniversary of the end of the Second World War gave rise to many joint GDR–Soviet commemorations, during which meetings between FDJ and Komsomol members were described as 'particularly cordial', and seen to reflect genuine personal commitment.[140] Young GDR citizens were also given the opportunity to travel abroad with the FDJ, either to attend international socialist festivals, or participate in holidays organised by *Jugendtourist*. Although these trips usually involved group travel, the chance to experience a different culture and make friends abroad often helped counter unfavourable preconceptions or misjudgements concerning foreigners, and a number of reports noted a change in young people's attitudes following foreign visits.[141] Where foreign travel was not viable, young people still appeared to show public concern and support for the international socialist community. This was particularly evident in the provision of aid for Polish citizens following the uprisings of 1980, and by December 1982 the FDJ in *Bezirk* Halle had sent 254,186 parcels to Polish children, along with a donation of 362,074 Marks.[142] Campaigns to raise money for those further afield in Third World countries proved similarly popular, with young people reported to be 'passionately committed' in their resolve to aid those less fortunate than themselves.[143] The young generation thus appeared willing to support the international community through official initiatives and events, and where encounters between foreigners and GDR citizens were organised, a friendly and co-operative atmosphere generally reigned.

Outside the formalised rituals and events which littered the socialist calendar, however, direct contact with foreigners remained minimal, for the number of foreign workers in the GDR only just surpassed 1%, the majority of whom were temporary residents.[144] One need not search long in files to reveal that everyday attitudes

Table 1 Pupils' views of other nationalities, 1968 and 1988
(responses to the question: 'How do you assess the populations of
different nations according to the following characteristics?' 1 = very
strong characteristic / 7 = very weak)

		Cuba	Vietnam	Soviet Union	USA
Reliable	1968	2.34	1.79	1.53	3.35
	1988	3.41	2.94	2.59	3.16
Intelligent	1968	2.64	2.36	1.42	2.24
	1988	3.25	2.82	2.47	2.20
Friendly	1968	2.06	2.05	2.06	2.93
	1988	3.59	3.05	2.90	2.67
Modern	1968	2.79	2.90	1.39	2.25
	1988	3.56	3.27	2.41	1.66

Source: Walter Friedrich and Wilfried Schubarth, 'Ausländerfeindliche und
rechtsextreme Orientierungen bei ostdeutschen Jugendlichen', *DA*, 24/10 (1991),
1052–65 (p. 1059).

and private encounters with foreigners did not always correspond
to the official image. This became increasingly evident throughout
the 1980s, as noted by Walter Friedrich in 1988: 'Respect, friendship, solidarity and helpfulness towards certain peoples/races have
recently been less forthcoming; in contrast a more critical, pejora-
tive, even hostile attitude has gained ground.'[145] Indeed, there
appeared to be an increasing lack of tolerance for certain national
characteristics and customs and, as demonstrated in table 1, pupils'
stereotypes of foreigners changed considerably between 1968 and
1988. Whilst Cubans, Vietnamese and Soviet citizens were seen to
be much more reliable, intelligent and friendly than Americans in
1968, the tables had dramatically turned by 1988, revealing young
people's increasing attraction to the West and their decreasing
respect for other socialist countries. The growing intolerance of
these nationalities was commonly expressed in small-scale incidents
in the 1980s such as graffiti, name-calling or the vandalism of
foreign flags. On a larger scale, 1986 witnessed the first known
attack in the GDR on a residence for foreigners in Halle, and violence against foreigners became increasingly common at football
matches between the GDR and other socialist countries.[146]

Negative attitudes towards foreigners were clearly nationally
selective, and those nationalities and cultures which were present
in sizeable groups in the GDR appeared to be more negatively

stereotyped than others. The largest group of foreigners living in the GDR were Soviet soldiers and their families and, although GDR citizens had more frequent contact with Soviets than other nationalities, their clear military presence did little to aid their integration into GDR society. Housed together in barracks or residential areas reserved for families, they were often regarded with suspicion by local residents, many of whom complained about the 'untidy' and 'dirty' nature of the surrounding area. More significantly, however, the Soviet army was commonly still regarded to be a post-1945 occupying force which had failed to leave the GDR, and much of the anti-Soviet sentiment in the 1980s constituted resentment towards their continued military presence. Negative attitudes were also passed down to children from their parents and grandparents, who had experienced the raping and looting by Soviet soldiers immediately after the end of the war. Whilst there were few reports of violence towards Soviet citizens in the GDR, a strong undercurrent of anti-Soviet attitudes was primarily demonstrated through derogatory graffiti, offensive songs and terms of abuse.[147] In one cinema in Magdeburg, a group of young people even applauded during a historic military film, when a Nazi general refused to answer a Soviet officer because of his inferior status.[148] Such extreme reactions were not widespread, yet the positive effects of education in forging a GDR–Soviet bond appeared minimal, with many reports complaining that youth activities failed to engage young people.[149] Indeed, comparative studies reveal that in the late GDR trust in the Soviet Union increased with age, with the young generation holding the least sympathetic image of Soviet citizens.[150] This was particularly prominent amongst school pupils, and by 1988 only 8% claimed to feel close to the Soviet Union, the huge majority (73%) feeling no or hardly any sense of emotional proximity.[151]

The appointment of Gorbachev in 1985 presented the SED with a potential opportunity to halt such trends and strengthen both a sense of GDR identity and partnership with the Soviet Union. As perestroika and glasnost took hold, so too did Gorbachev's popularity amongst young people; Russian classes became popular and Soviet politics became a new focus of intense interest. By 1989, 95% of students in Halle supported Gorbachev's policies,[152] and through him young people hoped for a new lease of life for the GDR. The SED, however, failed to grasp this new optimism and continued to promote the traditional historic model of the Soviet Union, whilst quietly ignoring Gorbachev's new policies. As a result, Gorbachev and the Soviet Union became two very separate entities in the minds of young people, and many used Gorbachev's policies to embarrass the government, wearing 'Gorbi' stickers and perestroika T-shirts, or reciting excerpts from the Soviet press to provoke teachers and party officials, who often had few credible responses.[153] The message the party sent to young citizens was highly confusing, if not hypocritical, and during the public holiday celebrations on 1 May 1989, pictures of Gorbachev were ripped down by officials, whilst nearby speeches praised the 'steadfast brotherly bond with the Soviet Union'.[154] In sticking to its unwavering course, the SED simply further polarised young people's loyalties, for on the one hand their support of Gorbachev's new policies grew stronger, yet on the other hand, their prejudices towards Soviets living in the GDR, who represented the old order, also strengthened. Once again the SED's attempts to impose a set of beliefs on young people achieved the exact opposite.

Polish citizens also often experienced negative attitudes in the GDR, largely for historical reasons, and once again the tensions of recent history coloured private encounters, even after the passing of forty years. Despite the parcels and large sums of money which FDJ members helped sent to Poland in the early 1980s, many young people held highly prejudiced views of the Polish people: 'Judgements have, . . . in part, tended to amount to a display of nationalist arrogance, such as: "The Poles should first learn to work properly, before they make such demands", "Taking the best from us and the Soviet Union without doing anything oneself can only be to the cost of others".'[155] Files thus revealed a number of incidents where conflicts between GDR and Polish youths degenerated into verbally and physically violent behaviour, in which the arrogance of young East Germans was countered by terms of abuse such as 'Nazi swine' or 'German sod'.[156] The circulation of Polish jokes reportedly also increased during the early 1980s,[157] and although many young people took part in formal displays of solidarity, it was evident that little genuine sympathy was felt.

Whilst prejudices towards Soviets and Poles often originated in historical tensions, foreigners whose homelands had little historical contact with Germany also experienced racial tensions in the GDR. Young Mozambicans and Angolans, for example, who arrived to work in Hettstedt, *Bezirk* Halle, in 1987 did not always find themselves welcome, and as the Stasi reported: 'Since they have been here, conflicts of varying proportions have arisen between themselves and GDR citizens, above all young people.'[158] These disputes originated largely in the boredom of the young (mainly male) Africans, whose free-time activities in the GDR were limited, and who provided competition for local young men over girls. Their possession of Western goods also caused jealousy amongst GDR youths, who had little access to such items. Similar tensions could be witnessed in Staßfurt, where the 'School of Friendship' was opened in 1982, dedicated to the education of approximately 900 young Mozambicans. Here problems mounted as soon as the pupils were old enough to leave the school grounds unattended, for fights at bars and discos between local youths and young Mozambicans became regular, and the African pupils experienced verbal abuse as well as being barred from some venues. Events took a more serious turn in September 1987, when one Mozambican drowned after being pushed off a bridge by a young East German.[159] The Stasi showed considerable concern that such frictions would extend to other nationalities in the area,[160] and not without reason; Vietnamese citizens in *Bezirk* Magdeburg, for example, faced similar racial tensions in the 1980s, despite their relatively peaceful co-existence during the previous two decades.[161]

As the above examples reveal, the policy of proletarian internationalism failed to fulfil the function of securing a patriotism that was free from chauvinist and apparently nationalist thought. The party, however, consistently downplayed incidents of violence and abuse as rowdiness committed by 'negative-decadent' youth: 'Anti-imperialist solidarity remains as strong as ever. Occurrences of racism, xenophobia, chauvinism remain an absolute exception. Occurrences of dispute between GDR youth and youth from friendly nation states in smaller places (e.g. in discos) are characterised less by national conflicts, but normal youthful rivalry.'[162] It seems, however, that many incidents extended beyond the bounds of 'normal' youthfulness, and aggression was often a reaction to specific phenomena, such as historical tensions or material circumstances. Were signs of a nationalist sentiment thus emerging amongst young people, or did such trends arise as a result of discontent with life in the GDR? Was xenophobia endemic within the GDR regime, as Christian Pfeiffer has suggested, or did it permeate its borders from Western sources, as the SED believed?

The roots of national rivalries

The official relationship that was propagated between the GDR and other socialist states was central in determining the attitudes of its young citizens, even if it failed to incite their enthusiasm. Most influential was the GDR's self-image as 'big brother', helping other less fortunate nations in their battle for socialist freedom, and thus by implication presenting itself as superior to these states. In this way, young GDR citizens travelling abroad were encouraged to act as ambassadors of GDR culture. The FDJ brochure 'Holidays with friends' for young people visiting Poland, for example, contained as much information about GDR culture as Polish culture, which young people could dutifully present to their Polish hosts.[163] It was thus implied that GDR citizens had more to teach other socialist nations than to learn from them, clearly insinuating their superiority. This impression was often further highlighted by visits to these countries, where technical provisions were even sparser than in the GDR, and the state of the buildings and streets more dilapidated. As seen with West Germany, young people's attitudes towards their own state were not only shaped by forces within the GDR, but also by international comparisons.

The status of foreigners living in the GDR also reflected this implied inferiority, for they were housed together in foreigners' residences where they were subject to strict regulations. Vietnamese citizens living in *Bezirk* Magdeburg, for example, were allowed visitors only between 5 p.m. and 10 p.m.; entry into their living quarters was controlled by GDR officials and all female workers were required to take the contraceptive pill, as pregnancy would ensure their passage home.[164] Similarly, the 'School of Friendship' in Staßfurt provided all Mozambican pupils and teachers with living quarters, as well as medical care and sports facilities, gardens, playgrounds, and even a shop.[165] As a result, there was no real need for them to mix with the population at large, and GDR citizens remained largely ignorant of their guests' cultural origins. The integration of foreign workers and pupils into the local community was clearly not actively encouraged, and as late as 1990 60% of East Germans claimed never to have had personal contact with foreigners.[166] The forced nature of proletarian internationalism did little to help this situation, for participation in international FDJ events or campaigns was often far from voluntary, thus creating resentment amongst young people who felt they had better use for their free time. The tedious over-emphasis on socialist solidarity and the large range of forums in which it was addressed also meant that young people frequently reached saturation point, rarely internalising the regime's values.[167] Consequently their ignorance and lack of understanding became stronger, sometimes paving the way for aggressive and abusive behaviour towards foreigners, who were often perceived as threatening. Whilst many young people publicly committed themselves to proletarian internationalism for personal gain, in order to secure a holiday place or simply pay lip service to the party line, official policy and propaganda in this area not only failed to create the desired effect within the personal sphere, but often proved counter-productive and ultimately damaging to the concept of socialist patriotism.

Contact with foreign workers in the GDR was thus often limited to brief encounters in public places such as shops, bars or discos, where jealousy towards foreigners who wore Western clothing and young males who flirted with East German girls often degenerated into abuse. Tensions were often caused by material considerations, above all the perception that foreigners received favourable treatment and special facilities. The envy of locals in Staßfurt at the construction of the 'School of Friendship' in 1982, for example, was considerable, many feeling that this display of solidarity with Mozambique was too far-fetched. One father even stated that he would paint his son black, in order to smuggle him into the school, claiming 'there he will get everything that I've been trying to get him for years'.[168] Parents' frustrations with material shortcomings and the alleged privileges of foreigners were undoubtedly passed down to children in the same way that historical resentments lived longer than the memory of such history, thus colouring children's judgements before they themselves became conscious consumers. Locals were also angered by foreigners' tendency to buy up large quantities of goods in shops. This was caused by the fact that their wages could not be converted into foreign currency and were of no value in their home countries, so many resorted to sending large amounts of material goods to their families back home. Because of the acute shortages in the GDR, East Germans inevitably often complained that this constant 'hamstering' deprived them of their own products.[169] Furthermore, there appeared to be an imbalance which provoked angry questions such as: 'How come the Soviets can buy up everything in our shops . . ., yet our GDR citizens can't get into Soviet stores?'[170] The official treatment of foreigners neither helped their integration into society nor encouraged the sympathy of GDR citizens, yet it was often the failing economic situation in the GDR, particularly evident in material shortages and inadequate facilities, which provided concrete grounds for young people's complaints.[171]

Official claims that the GDR provided no basis for xenophobic attitudes clearly held little truth, as did the argument that tensions were caused uniquely by Western influences. The young generation, however, became skilled at playing the party's game, and during the course of interviews between superiors and young people who were responsible for xenophobic abuse or graffiti, protagonists often revealed that they had found inspiration from West German radio and television.[172] Whilst these may well have influenced the choice of vocabulary used in graffiti or verbal abuse, the above examples demonstrate a very GDR-specific background to tensions, rather than a more generic racism that the SED claimed to be widespread in the West. Young people, however, realised that by blaming their misdemeanours on Western influences, they not only gave the party a plausible and acceptable reason for their actions, but also found a way of taking only partial responsibility for their crimes.

The party's claim that apparently racial tensions were simply examples of 'normal youthful rivalry' also held little water. Yet the situation of young people in the 1980s should not be ignored, for archival evidence suggests an increasing lack of orientation during this decade, and a growing sense of frustration and helplessness. Whereas the 1970s were widely regarded to be a period of comparative stability, with surveys revealing relative loyalty to the socialist system, identification with the ideals of socialism and the GDR rapidly declined during the following decade.[173] In addition, generational change began to take place at an accelerated pace, unsettling the hitherto more stable patterns of society. A youth report sent to Egon Krenz in 1987 thus claimed: 'these changes can no longer be encapsulated by the "classical notion of generations" (i.e. approximately 20 years apart). Today the mentality/characteristics of the youth, their moods, interests, demands, habits, patterns of thought and behaviour, change dramatically after 5 to 10 years.'[174] This trend was the result of a number of political and social changes: the very real fear of nuclear war caused by renewed Cold War tensions in the early 1980s, an increasingly aged Politburo that was rapidly losing touch with the GDR's youth, a lack of public role models to which to aspire, a widening divide between reality and propaganda and the need to develop a 'divided personality' (i.e. public and private faces) in society. Many young people consequently felt robbed of a stable identity and perceived the cultural diversity of foreigners to be threatening, rather than beneficial or enriching.[175] Furthermore, many young people felt frustrated at being misunderstood, finding that any attempts to bring about positive change were rebuffed by officials who feared disruption to the system. It is no surprise that reports testified to an increasing lack of motivation amongst young people both at school and at work,[176] for although the SED regime continued to serve their basic needs, it did little to encourage in them confidence or hope in an inspiring and fruitful future. In contrast, the temporary nature of most foreigners' stay in the GDR meant that they would eventually start a new life elsewhere, and local residents, particularly young people starting out in life, felt that foreigners were able to milk the GDR for all it was worth yet escape the longer-term negative effects. Having received an advanced level of education in the GDR, for example, a number of foreigners would reap benefits in their home countries that the average GDR citizen could never hope for; some even went to work in non-socialist countries, a move that was considered to be a serious breach of contract by many in the GDR.[177] Until young East Germans could feel content with their own lives, whether materially or emotionally, it seemed unlikely that they would develop a complete acceptance of foreigners living in the GDR, and thus fully embrace the values of proletarian internationalism.

Attitudes towards foreigners clearly adopted a GDR-specific nature, resulting from the SED's stringent policies concerning foreign workers and students, and the insufficiencies of GDR society. Negative attitudes thus rarely appeared to be based on racist grounds, but were rather a reaction to the conditions of the 1980s. In this way, the SED was correct in its assertion that proletarian internationalism and socialist patriotism formed an inseparable partnership. Whilst the party called on one in the attempt to bolster the other, however, it was in practice the lack of patriotic sentiment that brought about a rejection of proletarian solidarity.

Rooted in the present? Pride in the achievements of the GDR

Whilst the SED concentrated much of its patriotic propaganda on channelling foreign influences in the desired direction, young people's attitudes towards present-day circumstances in the GDR were most immediate in shaping their loyalty to the state. Propaganda and newspaper reports that emphasised the standard of life in the GDR, its achievements and its 'progressive' outlook, were thus considered essential, above all towards the end of the GDR, when ever-more citizens were applying to leave the country. This section will examine the extent to which young people took pride in the 'here and now' of the GDR, asking whether their behaviour and attitudes were shaped by SED patriotic propaganda or, rather, by other social, economic or political factors.

Emotional identity in the present: sports, culture and the natural environment

Sports, culture and the natural environment were all mobilised to promote emotional attachment to the GDR, from which it was believed that political activity and engaged citizenship would draw inspiration. With a number of internationally acclaimed sporting figures such as the cyclist Gustav Adolf Schur and ice-skater Katarina Witt, sport was an obvious sphere for the promotion of patriotism, and opportunities to meet sporting heroes were received with enthusiasm by teenagers.[178] However, young people did not rank sport highly in a survey concerning civic identity, placing it after numerous personal and political elements (such as family and friends, secure job prospects, peace policies and social equality) for its relevance in forming a GDR identity, thus leading the study to warn that sports 'do not even affect politically motivated people'.[179] Support for certain sports, such as football, clearly underlined this warning, for more young people were found to support the West German national football team than that of the GDR, and 70–80% of regional teams supported by young people came from the FRG.[180] Furthermore, rowdy behaviour began to mark numerous football matches in the 1980s, which was often initiated by opposing minority groups. As one skinhead recalled: 'we went to the BFC [Berlin Football Club Dynamo], simply because the club's hated everywhere, because the chairman is Erich Mielke, from the State Security . . . And there's often aggro with other fans there, especially with Magdeburg. Magdeburg has a hard core of left-wing radicals.'[181] Whilst many such fans were barred from official political events, football matches gave them an opportunity to air their discontent, and in this way the role of sport as a vehicle for patriotic pride was turned on its head, used by some as a forum for opposition.

In the cultural sphere, similar patterns were seen in young people's attraction to Western writers, artists and singers. Their appeal was, however, only strengthened by the lack of attractive GDR alternatives, largely resulting from strict state controls. This was especially true for rock music and, although a number of songs which overtly supported the principles of socialism still proved popular, the willingness to write political songs declined during the 1980s. It was noted, for example, that in comparison to international projects such as 'Live Aid' and the 'Red Wedge' in Britain, or 'Artists in action' in the FRG, musicians in the GDR were neglecting their political duties.[182] This was partly in response to the number of fans who objected to the political overloading of rock music, yet the restrictive atmosphere in which musicians were required to write and perform also drove some away. The band 'Magdeburg', for example, applied to leave the GDR in 1982 following a string of repressive measures concerning its name (originally 'Klosterbrüder', or 'monks', deemed unacceptable by the SED), the scruffy appearance of its singer and limited travel opportunities.[183] As a result of an enforced image change, the band's fans dwindled in number, and it felt unable to continue in the East. Even the most politically engaged musicians began to find party pressure unbearable, as demonstrated by the flight of Burkhard Lasch, an influential songwriter and member of the SED who was active on cultural committees, in 1987. Once again, the GDR's strict controls ultimately proved counter-productive and, as a study from 1988 found, young people's top twenty titles barely featured any GDR groups, a trend which had become increasingly common throughout the 1980s.[184] The SED's constant attempts to influence popular music in the GDR did little to encourage enthusiasm amongst either musicians or young people. Whilst strict controls drove the former to frustration, often to the point of fleeing the GDR, the measured political content of songs bored the latter, inciting them to seek alternative 'unofficial' cultural entertainment and tread beyond the bounds of patriotic behaviour.

In contrast, emotional attachment to the natural environment appeared strong, for campaigns which foregrounded the protection of the local environment often produced impressive results, inspiring large-scale recycling projects or tree-planting operations in towns and cities. Whilst such activities aroused particular enthusiasm and commitment in rural areas, where the range of activities was more limited,[185] it should be noted that the promise of financial reward (however minimal) for the collection of paper and glass often proved to be the prime incentive for young people's activity, rather than any real environmental or political concern. Furthermore, the attraction of outdoor activities such as the planting of trees or the care of local ponds often had little to do with political commitment, but rather the enjoyment of being away from the predictable and repetitive nature of classroom teaching.[186] There was clearly a failure to link emotional regional loyalties with political state loyalties, and as one teenager claimed: 'My Heimat is wherever it is quietest. In the village. I am more for nature. I am not bothered whether this is in capitalism or in socialism.'[187] Similarly, a ZIJ study revealed that considerably more young people found identity in their immediate vicinity than in the GDR state, and the SED's attempts to root patriotic sentiment firmly within socialist ideology had clearly been lost on many.[188]

Young people's concern for the future of the environment was, however, heightened by the Chernobyl disaster, alongside notable evidence of water and air pollution in the 1980s. Whilst the SED was keen to use their renewed commitment to its advantage and highlighted the state's environmental policies in its youth work, the stark reality of increasing pollution only undermined such efforts. Young people, it was reported, 'mostly express surprise at the considerable activity of the GDR in the area of environmental protection, but often doubt whether so much is really being done',[189] and evidence of far superior environmental protection schemes in the FRG only led young citizens to further doubt the commitment of their government.[190] Church discussion groups and meetings on environmental themes that focused on ways to improve environmental protection, but also highlighted the critical situation in the GDR, thus proved popular amongst the young generation, causing the FDJ considerable concern and forcing it to recognise its 'insufficient success' in countering adverse views concerning environmental pollution.[191]

Whilst evidence suggests that young people felt emotionally close to their local environs, this emerged primarily as a territorial attachment with few, or even oppositional, political foundations. Although the SED recognised the value of this attachment for the development of patriotic sentiment, the party was unable to mobilise the young generation successfully in the face of growing environmental problems and influence from the West and the churches. Young people remained sceptical towards state policy, and it was the 'Heimat', rather than the socialist fatherland, which remained the focus of emotional attachment.

Young people and the economy: work, technical achievements and material pride

Living standards during the 1980s were better than ever before, and young people were the first to benefit fully from the hard labour and technological advances of previous decades. The socialist state was also able to offer considerable social benefits to its population and, as reports and surveys from the late 1980s show, young people ranked the guarantee of employment, along with other social security policies, such as free health care, low rents and good childcare facilities very highly in their assessment of the GDR.[192] It fell to young people to further these achievements for the future of the state, yet many took this situation for granted, considering hard work to be a necessary evil rather than a voluntary pledge of loyalty. Indeed, it seemed that the SED had failed to create the link in young people's minds between individual effort and collective benefit, and the inadequate personal commitment of pupils was frequently lamented by teachers.[193] Subjects such as *Staatsbürgerkunde* were thus commonly considered little more than a means to achieve individual gain, namely securing a place in further education, beyond which their value was scorned by many. Moreover, the knowledge that employment was guaranteed and that one's life would follow a prescribed path often led to complacency; young people who had never known anything different were rarely encouraged to push themselves harder, for as many claimed: 'It is comfortable living in the GDR.'[194] The needs of the collective thus frequently became neglected, and many displayed increasingly hedonistic characteristics, reportedly developing a tendency towards 'one-sided thinking to the benefit of the individual'.[195] Rather than drawing young people out of this complacency, the numerous awards and prizes created by the SED to recognise high achievement, such as the 'Certificate for good learning', often had the opposite effect, regularly becoming the focus of ridicule and vandalism amongst pupils.[196] Their superfluous nature thus failed to create real distinction, diminishing the value of real achievement and doing little to encourage dedication to the socialist cause.

A similar pattern could be seen in the field of science and technology, the advances of which were promoted in youth work above all during the 1980s. Whilst this field enthused many young people, particularly at the MMM trade fair, where over a million young participants presented innovative ideas and creations every year,[197] the GDR concentrated much of its propaganda on ground-breaking developments that hit the headlines, rather than on smaller everyday advances. Sigmund Jähn, for example, the first German to go into space in 1978, became an overnight hero in the GDR and an exemplary figure used repeatedly in youth work. Although such large-scale technological achievements often succeeded in firing the imagination of young people, there was little feeling that they reflected the reality of life in the GDR, and were often regarded with scepticism, denounced as pure propaganda or 'rejected as boasting'.[198] This attitude was foregrounded by the fact that the GDR lagged far behind the West in this field, and comparison between the two created shame rather than pride in the GDR; reports noting feelings of inferiority amongst young people in this area could not fail to recognise the failure of GDR policy.[199] Experiences of everyday life in the GDR, particularly amongst those working in industry or agriculture, only further highlighted the scarcity of modern equipment and technology in the socialist state. Young workers, for example, complained about the difficulties in obtaining spare parts for machinery, and outdated equipment slowed productivity, thus reducing efficiency.[200] One pupil's description of the GDR as a technological 'dwarf' was exemplary of the common lack of pride in this area,[201] and however extensively the SED attempted to propagate the GDR's 'great' achievements they would always be undermined by the harsh reality of life under socialism.

The reality of consumer goods shortages in the GDR, however, formed the most frequent cause of frustration amongst young people, with approximately half their criticisms of the GDR falling in the area of production and consumer problems.[202] Common complaints in this area concerned supply and demand, for shortages not only created long queues or waiting lists for desirable goods, but many items were simply not available. Fashionable clothing and electronic items such as hi-fi systems and personal stereos were rarely in adequate supply to satisfy young people; even more basic items such as meat, milk and fruit proved insufficient, and the frequent 'hamstering' of scarce goods only underlined the constant fears of shortages which permeated the population. Moreover, the high subsidy of basic foodstuffs invariably led to wastage, yet so-called 'luxury' items were often too expensive for the masses. The clothing market was of particular concern for young people, who were keen to appear as fashionable as possible, yet found their needs poorly served. By the late 1980s the party was making efforts to resolve this problem with projects such as the FDJ initiative 'Consumer goods production – by youth, for youth' and the 'Young fashion collection "GDR 40" ', which aimed to produce large numbers of desirable items to be modelled and sold at the Whitsun FDJ Meeting in May 1989.[203] The party, however, misjudged the severity of the shortages, failing to secure adequate supplies of popular garments, and thus simply provoking further discontent.[204] It was clearly in the interests of the party to placate the youth on this point for, as we have seen, clothing was becoming an increasingly popular way of directing protest against the state. As with other consumer goods, however, it was not simply the shortage of fashionable clothing that caused discontent amongst young people, but the high prices and dubious quality of such items. As a result, young people not only sensed that their needs were being ignored, but they felt increasingly cheated and exploited by a system which supposedly protected their interests. It is no surprise that complaints over lavish displays of state power, such as the 750th anniversary of Berlin in 1987, provoked angry calls for a more modest affair, allowing workers to 'have more for their money'.[205] The fact that such events frequently took place in East Berlin only aggravated the resentment of those living in the regions, especially in more rural areas, who felt that the capital and other large cities received better supplies and resources.[206] Whilst recommendations in education advocated the development of pride in the GDR's capital,[207] the state's practical distribution policies instead created resentment amongst those outside Berlin and, once again, young people's priorities did not match those of the state and often came into direct conflict with patriotic policy.

It seemed that little could be done to win over a young generation that was becoming increasingly materialistic and dissatisfied with GDR provisions. Their growing frustration was not, however, to be taken lightly, for the early 1980s saw the emergence of a significant phenomenon relating to attempts to recruit young SED members. In addition to the 'standard' reasons for refusing party membership

(such as lack of time and maturity), young people began to link consumer issues directly to their political commitment, with comments
such as: 'Only when the shops are full again will I become a candidate for the SED', or 'I don't agree with the policies on supply and
pricing. As a member of the party I would have to justify this situation, and I can't.'[208] Not only did the reality of shortages, unfair distribution, exorbitant prices and lack of quality prevent young
people from developing pride in the GDR economy, but they created
outright rejection of the party. The SED's patriotic programme
could have little effect if it was not backed up by the status quo in
the GDR, for the contours of daily life within the personal sphere
were clearly more influential in shaping young people's loyalties
than the larger ideological concepts.

Political participation

Although problems in the economic sphere produced scepticism and
distance towards the political system, FDJ membership increased
during the 1980s, attaining approximately 75% of all 14–25 year
olds,[209] *Jugendweihe* participation rates surpassed 97% nationwide,
and in some areas 99%,[210] and the number of FDJ members taking
part in the annual cycle of FDJ study groups increased from 50%
to nearly 75% between 1973 and 1987.[211] Furthermore, young
workers were found to be more politically active than the average
GDR citizen, with 43% holding a position in a mass organisation
compared to the average of 25%.[212] Alongside such figures, however,
growing signs of apathy and disinterest were evident, and increasing
participation was accompanied by declining enthusiasm. The same
report that noted an increase in participation in FDJ study groups,
for example, also found that the proportion of young people who
participated without commitment had doubled.[213] Even students,
traditionally the most loyal sector of young people, showed waning
enthusiasm, and as demonstrated in figure 2, their identification with
both the SED and the FDJ decreased dramatically between 1977 and
1989. Many left election assemblies early, refused to wear the FDJ
shirt or simply missed meetings without explanation, and considerable numbers complained that political events were excessive in
number, reducing the amount of free time they could spend with
friends and family. Political discussions at meetings were frequently
hesitant, and many members simply brushed over political themes,
subscribing to the so-called 'Aha-effect' of agreeing with what was

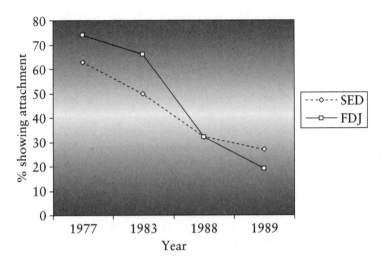

Figure 2 Attachment to the SED and FDJ amongst students, 1977–89 (percentage responding 'strongly/very strongly' to the statement 'I feel strongly attached to the SED / FDJ')

Source: BArch, DC4/469, 'Student 1989', ZIJ, Aug 1989, p. 48.

said, apparently without second thought – largely through lack of interest and to speed up discussions.[214] Interviewees' recollections of political events and festivals such as 1 May or 7 October also revealed the apolitical nature of their participation, many taking part for the first few minutes so that their presence could be noted, before disappearing with their friends. Whilst such events were seen as a tiresome duty, however, the public holiday was also welcomed as an opportunity to enjoy the company of friends and family in the private sphere, and as Katharina remembered: 'when it was over, that was when the real celebrations began. And then the 1 May was no longer the 1 May.'[215] Similarly, the *Jugendweihe* became valued as a family celebration and a coming-of-age ritual, yet lost all political meaning as a celebration of state loyalty. In this way, events which were formally dedicated to the celebration of patriotic values regularly became utilised to suit young people's private needs, consequently inverting the intentions of the SED.

Alongside this political apathy, evidence also reveals an increasing tendency towards active resistance; one need only examine Stasi files in the lead-up to any large-scale political event in order to gauge the concern, and sometimes paranoia, of officials. In 1979, for example, prior to the National Youth Festival in Berlin, 486 'negative-decadent' youths were arrested, and a further 10,200 barred from Berlin during the festival.[216] Even smaller regional festivals were subject to similar precautions and, although many events were largely free of political unrest, the paranoia of the Stasi was not unfounded, for small-scale discontent was frequently displayed at public events long before the demonstrations of 1989. The follow-ing report of the GDR's thirtieth anniversary celebrations in Magdeburg was not unusual: 'Disrespect for state and social symbols was displayed predominantly through the ripping or removal of flags from their holders. The tendency to burn or cut up GDR flags and flags of the working class is increasingly emerging.'[217] Unfortunately for the SED, the GDR flag lent itself particularly well to vandalism, for the removal of the central emblem transformed it into the flag of the FRG, thus creating a particularly politically contentious form of protest. Whilst such vandalism was often carried out under the influ-ence of alcohol, and may have represented little more than youthful over-exuberance, the fact that the flag was one of the most frequent targets demonstrated the GDR's failure to create in its youth an emo-tional attachment to the symbols of the state. Disrespect for other symbols, such as the FDJ blue shirt, further highlighted the under-developed emotional attachment to the state and its institutions, and although refusal to wear the shirt was often a fashion statement or a sign of apathy, some incidents involving the burning of shirts showed clear opposition to the regime.[218]

The SED was fighting a losing battle throughout the 1980s; on the one hand the masses sank only further into apathy, yet on the other an increasingly rebellious minority was seeking negative attention. As any study of youth behaviour will note, apathy and rebellion are highly typical of this age group within industrialised societies. The GDR was clearly no exception yet, as noted above, the young gen-eration in East Germany actually engaged in higher levels of politi-cal activity than their elders. Clearly compulsion was an important factor here, but low levels of genuine political enthusiasm appeared symptomatic of GDR society as a whole, not least because of the dry presentation of politics. As one pupil wrote of a *Jugendweihe* class in the mid-1980s: 'A few days ago, a man came to visit us, and spoke about the difference between capitalism and socialism. God it was boring. It was worse than most lessons.'[219] Not only did the ideological emphasis of activities do little to engage young citizens, but the language used was frequently outdated and distant, and terms such as 'bulwark', 'bastion' and 'programme for combat' did little to engender emotional attachment to the political cause. Similarly, the term 'FDJ work' failed to promote activities as fun and interesting, and the tedious repetition of concepts and phrases, commonly known as *Rotlichtbestrahlung* (red light radiotherapy) simply achieved the opposite effect to that desired. As one report correctly assessed: 'There is not a surfeit of politics amongst young people, but rather in the way that it is presented to them.'[220] The rigid political structures also provided little scope for imagination, and pupils viewed the annual election of their FDJ council to be a farce rather than an important experience of 'democratic centralism'; as election results could be accurately predicted in advance, many questioned the value of voting.[221] The system as a whole was in need of new blood; many long-standing FDJ members exceeded the age of 25, so-called 'Youth Brigades' at workplaces frequently consisted of middle-aged workers, and the SED's leaders were past the age of retirement. Those who attempted to rejuvenate the system, however, found their suggestions rejected by officials who feared the consequences of change; the principle of laying trust and responsibility in young people, a concept which the party so often hailed as central to its youth policy, appeared little more than a verbal promise lacking practical application, and enthusiasm quickly turned into resignation and grumbling conformity.

Many young people also found it difficult to relate to a youth organisation which posed as both the 'helper and reserve of the SED' and the 'representative of the interests of young people', for few felt that the FDJ had the right to speak on their behalf. Despite the party's tentative attempts to promote the inclusion of minority groups such as homosexuals and punks in the late 1980s, official discourse still referred to 'the youth' as one entity, not as a diversity of individuals or different interest groups. Lacking a true representative voice, many saw their actions to be futile, and increasingly questioned the validity of FDJ campaigns which rarely appeared to bring about any real change.[222] By 1988, only 18% of young people felt that their personal contribution to politics over the previous two years had aided the further development of the GDR.[223] Feeling neither that they were being taken seriously, nor that their actions were of any political influence, many simply paid their FDJ membership fees in order to placate the organisation, and 'buy' themselves personal space. Rather than rearing a generation of politically active patriots, the FDJ instead created large numbers of young people who were highly skilled at using the political system to their own personal advantage.

In the attempt to reverse this trend, the political demonstrations of the SED and FDJ became ever more elaborate in nature. Yet the effect created was often one of superficiality and pretence, and young people were reported to have dismissed the 1979 National Youth Festival as a 'propaganda show', likening it to a 'play at the theatre or a circus show', at which their responses and apparent cries of enthusiasm had been previously rehearsed.[224] In the eyes of many, the cost of such events far exceeded the bounds of the reasonable, and in light of material shortages, shabby housing and outdated technology, young people saw little justification for such unnecessary expense. The widening gap between the existing world of socialism and that which was propagated was even causing young people to question whether the SED's patriotic propaganda was, in fact, in the interests of the state: 'Do we really need to pat ourselves on the back on 1 May, and tell ourselves how good we are? . . . Would it not make more sense simply to work especially hard on this May bank holiday, or on 7 October, to produce real goods?'[225] Whilst this view, along with many others, opposed the party, it is interesting that it also showed support for one of the central principles of socialism, namely the desire to be productive for the republic, thus displaying a potential source of patriotism.

The GDR media naturally helped maintain the divide between reality and propaganda, for articles or reports which questioned any tenet of socialism or its success were likely to endanger the future of a newspaper, magazine or radio station. The ban on the Soviet news digest *Sputnik* in 1988, for example, following its publication of an article which implicated the role of German communists in Hitler's rise to power, aimed to maintain stability by preventing ideologically unsound material from entering the GDR. The result, however, was simply to highlight the growing unrest amongst the young generation, for the ban triggered an explosion of scepticism towards the party's strict control of the media, a sentiment which had been growing throughout the 1980s. Many became increasingly unwilling to support a party and state which refused to present its population with credible information on both local and national affairs, and the withdrawal of *Sputnik* provoked intense debate at many FDJ meetings. Interestingly, these discussions saw the involvement of members who had never even read the journal, as well as the broader questioning of principles such as democracy and trust in the population.[226] The fact that this publication came from the Soviet Union rather than a Western capitalist country unsettled many, for fears spread that other Soviet papers such as *Pravda* or *Neue Zeit* would also be banned and the GDR would be gradually isolated. Some individuals even left the FDJ in protest, one claiming: 'I regard this measure to be despotism committed by our state against its citizens. I don't want to be in an organisation which, in my eyes, supports this.'[227] Designed to control the population, this measure ironically pushed many into active political opposition, awakening them from their apathy.

As many of the above examples demonstrate, it was frequently the way in which the SED chose to exercise power rather than its fundamental principles which young people found unacceptable, and as a ZIJ survey from 1988 revealed, only 4% of young people were in complete agreement (22% partial agreement) with the way in which questions of societal development had been solved in the GDR.[228] One student thus typically stated that she agreed with the idea of socialism, its morals and its commitment to society, yet concluded: 'I don't like the realisation of these ideas.'[229] In this way a large proportion of the young generation held the potential for active political participation in reforming society, as the ideal of a socialist GDR frequently remained an attractive proposition: 'This degenerated, decayed, inhuman and tsarist system must be changed. But no capitalism! Instead, a socialism which follows the grand ideals!'[230] Yet the party continued to quell all enthusiasm, denying the young generation any sense of self-worth, and withholding from them the opportunity to make a difference. As one young citizen pleaded: 'I was born in this country, and I *want* to stay here. But I must also have the chance to take part in life within the community.'[231]

Identification with the material and political achievements of the GDR clearly decreased throughout the 1980s. On the one hand this was caused by the realities of life in the GDR, such as goods shortages, low living standards and a stagnant political system, all of which undermined the content of patriotic propaganda. On the other hand, it seems that the unwavering course of SED policy,

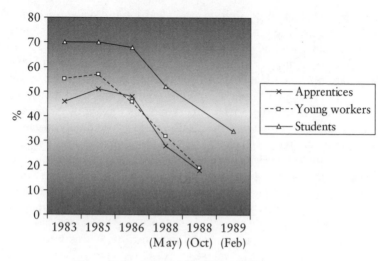

Figure 3 Identification with the GDR, 1983–89
(percentage responding 'close/very close' to the statement 'I feel very close
to the GDR')

Source: Walter Friedrich, 'Mentalitätswandlungen der Jugend in der DDR',
APuZG, B16–17 (1990), 25–37 (p. 30).

which heavily relied on censorship and costly displays of 'staged'
patriotism, pushed many young people into apathy or rebellion,
despite the fact that many actually agreed with the basic ideal of
socialism. Indeed, as one youth report observed, SED policy was
actually diminishing the accomplishments of GDR socialism which
had hitherto largely been accepted.[232] Patriotic education thus
clearly did shape the attitudes of young people – only not in the way
the SED intended. Rather than creating a vanguard of young patriots, it instead provoked many to reject socialist patriotism, and seek
ways of using the political structures of society for their own personal needs. These trends were reflected in ZIJ surveys of the time,
all of which documented a weakening GDR identity from the mid-
1980s onwards. By March 1989, only 22% of young people felt
closely attached to the GDR,[233] and as figure 3 demonstrates, this
dwindling loyalty was representative of all sectors of young people,
even students, traditionally the most loyal sector of the GDR's
young generation.[234] Moreover, the proportion of young people
attempting to flee the GDR even before the summer of 1989 was

relatively high,[235] revealing that it was not only the achievements of the present that failed to stimulate patriotic feelings through emotional attachment, but also the projected future of socialism.

Conclusion

Identity formation amongst young people in the GDR was clearly a more complex and multi-faceted phenomenon than that suggested by Eberhard Aurich and Josef Joffe at the start of this chapter. As the above analysis demonstrates, young people were subject not only to a rigorous programme of patriotic education, but also to a variety of other influences, ranging from the private to the public, and the local to the international. In many ways, it was the elements outside state control which gained most influence over young people's attitudes. Within the international sphere, the Cold War tensions of the early 1980s, followed by détente and the election of Gorbachev, all proved central in shaping attitudes towards military service, the 'imperialist' West and the concept of proletarian internationalism. In contrast, the private sphere provided individuals with their most immediate form of identity. Family and friends were thus influential in persuading or preventing young men from committing to extended military service; parents' involvement in church circles often created resistance in their offspring to the regime and national holidays, along with rituals such as the *Jugendweihe*, were welcomed not for their ideological importance but for their value in the private sphere. Regional loyalties also remained important, with local history proving popular, alongside concern for the natural environment and enthusiasm in looking after one's immediate environs. Through these elements, many young people showed attachment to the GDR as their 'Heimat', an apolitical home to familiar landscapes, childhood memories and, above all friends and family, but failed to perceive their country in political terms as the 'socialist fatherland'. Territorial and political identities thus began to develop quite separately, and the political basis of socialist patriotism, which was so crucial to its survival, ultimately found little resonance amongst young people.

Despite young people's distanced attitude towards the political world, archival files repeatedly reveal support for the fundamental principle of socialism, even amongst some groups, such as punks, who had chosen to 'opt out' of socialist society. It was rather the realisation of socialism in the GDR, and the SED's methods of rule, to which many young people objected. This was demonstrated in all areas of patriotic education, each of which revealed the ineffective and frequently counter-productive nature of the party's patriotic programme. Four main causes for this trend can be identified. Firstly, repetitive and dry teaching methods did little to inspire the active interest of pupils, and only where activities received more innovative treatment away from the classroom, such as residential camps or outdoor environmental projects, did they attract positive attention. The outdated socialist language used in textbooks, combined with old-fashioned teaching methods, merely resulted in disengaging pupils from their subject matter. Secondly, the rigid and predictable nature of the FDJ, whose leaders far exceeded the age of 25, proved increasingly unattractive to a young generation which preferred to follow the fashions and culture of the West. The few who attempted to bring about reform simply found that their suggestions fell on deaf ears, and the SED's principle of placing trust and responsibility in its youth was rarely practised. Young people's personal interests thus increasingly conflicted with those of the collective. Thirdly, the SED's censorship of ideologically dubious material proved nothing more than counter-productive. As revealed in areas of history (such as Stalin's crimes and the Third Reich), popular culture (Western pop music), the media (the withdrawal of *Sputnik*) and many other areas, the attempt to shield young people from such influences simply created in them a heightened interest and curiosity. In the case of rock music and the fashion industry, this policy backfired to such an extent that the SED was forced to adopt elements of Western culture simply to placate the young generation. Patriotic propaganda was, thus, partially shaped from below, revealing the frequently 'fuzzy' boundaries between state and society. Fourthly, the party's emphasis on large-scale events and achievements only served to highlight their neglect of the everyday and their inability to listen to the real needs of young people. Whilst the young generation frequently deplored the lack of consumer goods, the shortage of basic foodstuffs and the absence of affordable fashion items, the party continued to provide lavish displays of state power during national festivals and congratulate its engineers and cosmonauts on advances made in space travel. As a result, the gap between reality and propaganda became ever more pronounced, and young people felt increasingly isolated from the world of their political leaders.

The SED was, in many ways, fighting a losing battle from the early 1980s onwards, for despite warning signs and advice from youth workers that a more differentiated approach was needed,[236] the party did little to change its course. Although the FDJ tried to present itself as more inclusive and accepting of minority groups, the continued insistence on its status as the sole representative of young people merely proved the opposite. Rather than creating new methods with which to attract young people, the reliance on tried and tested means simply demonstrated the party's stagnant nature and inability to place trust in its youth. By the late 1980s, the various attempts to intensify patriotic sentiment had simply resulted in the opposite effect, driving the majority of young people away from the grasp of the party and into the private sphere. As seen in many areas, however, young people became adept at using the structures of patriotic education for their own interests, or in their pursuit of '*Eigen-Sinn*'. Many teenagers would, for example, join the GST in order to take their driving test, show apparent commitment to festivals of international friendship in order to gain a holiday place, or show enthusiasm for the *Jugendweihe* as a celebration of family and personal values. Few, however, embraced these structures for the purpose of displaying genuine patriotic sentiments and, as chapter 5 will reveal, it was this personal element of interaction with the regime that was central to young people's experience of the GDR, and proved most influential in shaping their loyalties in the longer term.

The SED's aim of creating a loyal youth through the imposition of patriotic norms clearly proved far from effective during the GDR. This is not to say, however, that all aspects of patriotic propaganda were rejected, or that young people chose to display their dissatisfaction in the same way. Indeed, reactions to patriotic education were varied, and contrary to the SED's concept of a single youth, young people formed far from a monolithic group. Whilst a small minority of loyal patriots did exist, who offered the regime support, the majority could be described as apathetic conformists, who co-operated with the system to the bare minimum in order to assure for themselves a relatively comfortable and hassle-free future. By outwardly conforming with the norms of patriotic behaviour and choosing not to display their discontent, this group allowed the regime to function, giving the GDR a semblance of stability. Others, however, chose to demonstrate their lack of support for the SED's version of socialist patriotism in a range of forms. On the one hand, extremists, such as skinheads and punks, neglected all social responsibility, and attempted to contravene the socialist order through their appearance and rowdy behaviour. On the other hand, some young people, perhaps best described as 'concerned critics', attempted to achieve change from within society. Often involved in church or environmental groups, these young citizens co-operated with the system to a certain extent, yet protested against specific elements of patriotic policy, such as the over-emphasis on military affairs, in the attempt to achieve moderate reforms. Displaying genuine concern for the future of the GDR state, this group was potentially the most patriotic of all, yet frequently found its activities fiercely repressed by the SED.

By the late GDR, the objections of extremists and concerned critics to patriotic propaganda found increasing influence over the young masses, the former within the sphere of fashion and the latter drawing greater numbers into active resistance. The SED and its youth organisations held decreasing influence over a young generation that was rebelling against patriotic education, and not only was the party having difficulty in maintaining a politically loyal youth but it was latterly also struggling to keep young people within its borders. As chapter 3 will reveal, the end of SED dominance brought about an unexpected turn in the loyalties of many young people, yet until this moment, the party simply succeeded in distancing the majority of young people even further from the GDR state.

Notes

1 Eberhard Aurich at the IX. Pädagogischer Kongreß: 'Patriotisch, parteilich und tatbereit – das ist unsere Jugend', *Neues Deutschland (ND)*, 15 June 1989, p. 5.

2 Josef Joffe, 'Die Beton-Blamage', *Die Zeit*, 33, 9 Aug 2001, p. 1.

3 BArch, DC4/306, 'Das staatsbürgerliche Bewußtsein der Jugendlichen', ZIJ, Mar 1989, p. 17.

4 Wilfried Schubarth, 'Geschichtskult contra Geschichtsbewußtsein: Nachholbedarf der DDR-Jugend', *Deutsche Jugend – Zeitschrift für Jugendarbeit (DJ)*, 10 (1990), 449–53 (pp. 449–50).

5 Some of this section has been previously published in ' "Wenn es so wäre wie im Geschichtsbuch": The Historical Consciousness of East Germany's Youth before and after Unification', *Field Studies: German*

Language, Media and Culture, CUTG Proceedings, vol. 5, ed. by Carol Fehringer and Holger Briel (Bern: Lang, 2005), 177–95.

6 SAPMO-BArch, DY30/IV2/2.039/237, Eberhard Aurich, 'Diskussionsbeitrag auf der 7. Tagung des ZK der SED', 1–2 Dec 1988, p. 126; SAPMO-BArch, DY24/113274, Letter from Delia Göttke (FDJ First Secretary, *Bezirk* Magdeburg) to Eberhard Aurich, 7 Dec 1988, p. 7.

7 BArch, DC4/305, 'Zum Geschichtsbewußtsein von Jugendlichen der DDR', ZIJ, Mar 1989, p. 12.

8 BArch, DR2/A.3875, 'Zur Analyse im Fach Geschichte', Jul 1987, p. 4.

9 DIPF/BBF/Archiv: Sign.: 16.137, 'Staatsbürgerkunde – Kontrollarbeiten', 1983.

10 BArch, DC4/305, 'Zum Geschichtsbewußtsein . . .', Mar 1989, p. 91.

11 DY30/IV2/2.039/234, 'Stimmen von Teilnehmern an der Premiere . . .', 1984, p. 13.

12 See Val D. Rust, 'Transformation of History Instruction in East German Schools', *Compare*, 23/3 (1993), 205–17 (p. 209).

13 BArch, DC4/305, 'Zum Geschichtsbewußtsein . . .', Mar 1989, p. 90.

14 BArch, DR2/A3875, 'Ergebnisse und Tendenzen der mündlichen Abschlußprüfung . . .', Magdeburg, 1 Jul 1985, p. 6.

15 DIPF/BBF/Archiv: Sign.: 11.106/Ia, 'Zur Herausbildung eines sozialistischen Vaterlandsbewußtseins . . .', 1988, p. 17.

16 Freya Klier, *Lüg Vaterland: Erziehung in der DDR* (Munich: Kindler, 1990), p. 193.

17 BArch, DC4/305, 'Zum Geschichtsbewußtsein . . .', Mar 1989, p. 23.

18 *Ibid.*, pp. 26, 36.

19 SAPMO-BArch, DY30/JIV2/2/2329, 'Protokoll Nr 20 der Sitzung des Politbüros des ZK der SED vom 23.5.1989. Anlage 9: Bericht des Zentralrats der FDJ . . .', May 1989, p. 49.

20 DIPF/BBF/Archiv: Sign.: 11.106/Ia, 'Herausbildung von Wertorientierungen und Verhaltensweisen . . .', Aug 1988, p. 3.

21 BArch, DY24/14090, 'Analyse der politisch-ideologischen Situation . . .', ZR der FDJ, 11 Sep 1989, p. 14.

22 BArch, DC4/305, 'Zum Geschichtsbewußtsein . . .', Mar 1989, p. 31. A considerable imbalance was also found amongst pupils.

23 SAPMO-BArch, DY30/IV2/2.039/233, 'Einschätzung der Wirksamkeit politisch-ideologischer Arbeit . . .', 9 Oct 1989, p. 109.

24 BArch, DC4/305, 'Zum Geschichtsbewußtsein . . .', Mar 1989, pp. 10, 76.

25 *Ibid.*, p. 34.

26 BArch, DC4/307, 'Zur staatsbürgerlichen Identität und ihren Merkmalen im Bewußtsein Jugendlicher', ZIJ, Apr 1989, p. 7.

27 Schubarth, 'Geschichtskult contra Geschichtsbewußtsein . . .', p. 450.
28 E.g. Antje, 29, 06/04/02; Frank, 30, 6/4/02. All interviewees have been given pseudonyms, and will be referred to in this format (name, age, date of interview).
29 BArch, DC4/306, 'Das staatsbürgerliche Bewußtsein . . .', Mar 1989, p. 70.
30 BArch, DC4/305, 'Zum Geschichtsbewußtsein . . .', Mar 1989, p. 66.
31 This sometimes gave rise to the use of 'Jew' as a term of abuse, for young people had heard it, yet did not know its full meaning. E.g. LA Magd.-LHA-, Rep.M1, vorl.16997, 'Meldung eines besonderen Vorkommnisses', Rat des Kreises Gardelegen, 22 Jan 1987.
32 Ansgar Weißer, 'Die Darstellung des Dritten Reiches und der Holocaust in Geschichtslehrbüchern und Unterrichtsmaterialien der DDR 1949 bis 1989', Schriftliche Hausarbeit, Erste Staatsprüfung, Westfälische Wilhelms-Universität Münster, 1999.
33 *Gemeinsame Geschichte – Geteilte Ansichten: Jugendliche aus der Bundesrepublik und der DDR begegnen deutscher Geschichte*, ed. by Kommunales Jugendbildungswerk der Stadt Witzenhausen (Witzenhausen: Zweckverband Evangelische Jugendarbeit Witzenhausen, 1986), p. 99.
34 BArch, DC4/305, 'Zum Geschichtsbewußtsein . . .', Mar 1989, p. 108.
35 *Ibid.*, p. 57.
36 E.g. LA Magd.-LHA-, Rep.P13, vorl.22240, 'Information über außergewöhnliche Vorkommnisse', Volksbildung Bezirksschulrat, 18 Feb 1988, p. 99.
37 A number of files reveal the reverence of Hitler amongst isolated circles throughout *Bezirke* Magdeburg and Halle, e.g. LA Magd.-LHA-, Rep.M1, vorl.16996 (1986); BStU, BV-Mdg, AKG/33 (1987).
38 BStU, HA, IX/748, 'Information', 9 Nov 1989, pp. 1–5.
39 BArch, DR2/A2677, 'Information über die Entwicklung außergewöhnlicher Vorkommnisse . . .', 7 Jun 1988, p. 5.
40 Some of this section has been previously published in 'Growing up on the Front Line: Young East Germans and the Effects of Militarism during the 1980s', *Debatte*, 13 (2005) 3, 283–97.
41 BArch, DR2/A9989, 'Orientierung zur Erhöhung des Niveaus der patriotischen Erziehung . . .', Feb 1981, p. 2.
42 *Ibid.*
43 BArch, DR2/A3340, 'Information über außergewöhnliche Vorkommnisse', 30 Mar 1988, p. 2.
44 SAPMO-BArch, DY30/IVB2/14/129, 'SED zensiert DDR-Kirchenzeitung', Jürgen Röder, DLF, 5 Feb 1983, 14.05, p. 32.
45 SAPMO-BArch, DY30/IVB2/9.05/50, 'Information zum Wehrunterricht', 10 Apr 1980, p. 2.

46 BArch, DR2/D438, 'Bericht über die Durchführung der Wehrausbildung . . .', 30 Aug 1983, p. 1.

47 BStU, BV-Mdg, 73/AKG, 'Rückinformation . . .', Magdeburg, 15 Mar 1984, p. 103.

48 E.g. LA Magd.-LHA-, Rep.P13, IV/E-2/14/538, 'Informationsbericht', Sektor Kirchenfragen Magdeburg, Sep/Oct 1982, p. 96; LA Magd.-LHA-, Rep.P13, IV/E-2/14/539, 'Informationsbericht über die kirchenpolitische Situation', 6 Oct 1983, p. 251.

49 BArch, DR2/D437, 'Bericht Magdeburg', 1982, p. 4; BArch, DR2/D471, 'Information über die Durchführung der Wehrausbildung', 1989, p. 3.

50 Christian Sachse, *Die Entwicklung der (vor)militärischen Ausbildung in der DDR und die Auswirkungen auf das Friedensbewußtsein Jugendlicher* (Kiel: Projektverbund Friedenswissenschaften Kiel, 1995), p. 19.

51 Markus G., cited in *Erziehung für das Militär? Erziehung für den Frieden! Unterrichtsmaterialien zur Auseinandersetzung mit der vormilitärischen Erziehung in der DDR* (Potsdam: Medienpädagogisches Zentrum Land Brandenburg, 1995), p. 98.

52 Jörg M., cited in *ibid.*, p. 100.

53 E.g. Barbara, 30, 09/04/02; Antje, 29, 06/04/02; Anna, 31, 10/4/02; Michaela, 29, 20/09/01.

54 Peter Förster and Mathias Daug, *Entwicklungstendenzen und -bedingungen der Verteidigungsbereitschaft und des Engagements in der vormilitärischen Ausbildung* (Leipzig: ZIJ, Jan 1989), pp. 52, 94.

55 Events at this school received specific attention, for not only were many pupils the children of high-ranking SED members, such as Egon Krenz, but one of the instigators of the demonstration, Philipp Lengsfeld, was the son of the peace activist and former SED member Vera Wollenberger (now Lengsfeld). Whilst it was, thus, an unusual case, events here triggered protests and demonstrations in other schools.

56 SAPMO-BArch, DY30/IVB2/14/43, 'Vier Schüler von Pankower Schule geschmissen', Zionskirchgemeinde, 16 Oct 1988, pp. 126–8.

57 SAPMO-BArch, DY30/IV2/2.039/201, 'Gewinnung des militärischen Berufsnachwuchses', no date [1986?], p. 6.

58 See BStU, BV-Mdg, AKG/29, 'Berichterstattung zu politisch-operativ bedeutsamen Problemen . . .', Schönebeck, 19 May 1987, p. 268; Robert, 28, 25/09/01.

59 SAPMO-BArch, DY24/14121, 'Entwurf des Standpunktes zur Verantwortung der FDJ . . .', no date [1988?], p. 6.

60 LA Magd.-LHA-, Rep.P13, vorl.28510, 'Information für die Bezirkseinsatzleitung', 25 Apr 1988.

61 SAPMO-BArch, DY24/10593, Letter from Horst Dübner to Egon Krenz, 12 Apr 1982, p. 3.

62 BStU, BV-Mdg, AKG/127, 'Lageeinschätzung zu Wehrdienstverweigerern', 24 May 1988, p. 53.

63 LA Magd.-LHA-, Rep.M1, vorl.16323, 'DFD Bericht', Bezirksvorstand Magdeburg, 18 Apr 1989, pp. 1–2; 'Einsatz in der POS "Germer"', 7 Mar 1988, p. 3.

64 LA Magd.-LHA-, Rep.P13, vorl.28510, 'Information für die Bezirkseinsatzleitung', 25 Apr 1988, p. 5.

65 SAPMO-BArch, DY59/314, cited in 'Bericht über den Inhalt und die Ergebnisse der persönlichen Gespräche . . .', 24 Feb 1987, p. 9.

66 LA Magd.-LHA-, Rep.P15, vorl.44773, 'Protokoll der Volksbildungsaktivtagung', Kreis Gardelegen, 3 Sep 1987, p. 3.

67 LA Magd.-LHA-, Rep.P13, IV/E-2/14/540, 'Information', Rat des Bezirkes Magdeburg, 17 Jan 1984, p. 4.

68 LA Magd.-LHA-, Rep.P13, IV/D-2/12/618, 'Information über die politische Grundhaltung der Wehrpflichtigen . . .', Wehrbezirkskommando Magdeburg, 10 May 1980, p. 5.

69 M-D-A, 13.1.1.18, 'Nach 18 Monaten Wehrdienst als Bausoldat', open letter written by two former *Bausoldaten* to 'Kirchengemeinden und Kirchenleitungen', Sep 1989, p. 1.

70 BStU, MfS-JHS/21496, 'Diplomarbeit', 19 Apr 1980, pp. 8–9.

71 BStU, BV-Mdg, Abt XX/2927, 'Die politisch-operative Bearbeitung von Initiatoren . . .', Magdeburg, 20 Jul 1988, p. 10.

72 BArch, DC4/267, 'Jugendliche über den Sinn ihres Lebens', ZIJ, Oct 1982, p. 38.

73 SAPMO-BArch, DY24/10596, cited in letter from Horst Glaßl (FDJ First Secretary, *Bezirk* Magdeburg) to Egon Krenz, 10 May 1982, p. 2.

74 Konrad Weiß, 'Die neue alte Gefahr: Junge Faschisten in der DDR', *Kontext*, 5 (1989), pp. 25–6.

75 BStU, MfS, BV-Halle, AKG/1920, 'Information zu aktuellen Erscheinungsformen gesellschaftswidrigen Auftretens . . .', 1986, p. 39.

76 SAPMO-BArch, DY30/vorl.SED/26118, 'Bericht des Bezirksausschusses Magdeburg . . .', 18 Mar 1981, p. 9.

77 SAPMO-BArch, DY24/11226, 'Notiz über die Verwirklichung der Anordnung . . .', 15 Apr 1982, p. 3.

78 BArch, DR2/D484, Letter from Peter L., Löbau, to Ministerium für Volksbildung, Abteilung Wehrerziehung/Wehrausbildung, 10 Jul 1985.

79 SAPMO-BArch, DY24/11246, cited in letter from Egon Krenz to Erich Honecker, 8 June 1983, p. 1.

80 SAPMO-BArch, DY24/14487, 'Zu pädagogischen Maßnahmen an der EOS "Carl von Ossietzky"', 1988, p. 8.

81 SAPMO-BArch, DY30/1352, Letter from Unteroffiziere des TT, Tautenhain, no date [1989?], p. 135.

82 BArch, DO4/85, Sender Freies Berlin, 'Das Thema – Schwerter zu Pflugscharen . . .', *Die Zeitschriftenschau*, 15 Mar 1983, p. 11.

83 BStU, BV-Mdg, Abt XX/2945, 'Information zur Forderung nach "Zivilen Wehrersatzdienst" ', 27 Jul 1988, pp. 9–12.

84 SAPMO-BArch, DY30/IV2/2.039/235, 'Information über die Führung von Gesprächen . . .', 1984, pp. 42–3.

85 *Ibid.*, p. 50.

86 M-D-A, 10.11.2, 'Interviews mit Jugendlichen aus Weimar und Apolda', in 'Bevölkerung in West und Ost: Nein zur Raketenstationierung und Militarisierung', no date [1983?].

87 LA Magd.-LHA-, Rep.P13, IV/E-2/14/538, 'Notizen zum Gespräch am 3. Juni 1982', pp. 10–11.

88 SAPMO-BArch, DY24/11803, 'Einschätzung der politischen Lage unter der Jugend', 9 Oct 1989, p. 21.

89 LA Magd.-LHA-, Rep.P16, IV/D-5/1/146, Education report, Stadtleitung Mdg, no date [1979?], p. 1.

90 Michael Rauhut, 'Rock und Politik in der DDR der achtziger Jahre', in *Jahrbuch für zeitgeschichtliche Jugendforschung 1994/5*, ed. by Jan Foitzik, Helga Gotschlich, Daniel Küchenmeister *et al.* (Berlin: Metropol, 1995), pp. 76–97.

91 Cited in *ibid.*, p. 80.

92 SAPMO-BArch, DY30/IV2/2.039/242, 'Bericht über Ereignisse am 6., 7. und 8. Juni 1987 . . .', p. 11.

93 SAPMO-BArch, DY24/11458, 'Erkenntnisse, Erfahrungen und Schlußfolgerungen . . .', 28 Jun 1988, p. 2.

94 SAPMO-BArch, DY30/IV2/2.039/242, Letter from Egon Krenz to Erich Honecker, 20 Jun 1988, p. 57.

95 BStU, MfS, BV-Halle, Sach AKG/433, 'VVS Hle 049 – 123/81', 1981, p. 16.

96 DIPF/BBF/Archiv: Sign.: 11.106/Ia, 'Zuarbeit zum Bilanzmaterial Erziehung . . .', Apr 1988, p. 27.

97 SAPMO-BArch, DY30/IV2/2.039/246, 'Zum Entwicklungsstand . . . unserer Jugend', Jul 1987, p. 68.

98 E.g. LA Magd.-LHA-, Rep.P13, vorl.22239, 'Staatsfeindliches Auftreten von Schülern in Genthin', May 1989, p. 16; LA Magd.-LHA-, Rep.M1, vorl.16996, 'Meldung eines besonderen Vorkommnisses', Wernigerode, 22 Apr 1986.

99 BArch, DR2/A.2677, 'Information über die Entwicklung außergewöhnlicher Vorkommnisse', Mar 1989, p. 3.

100 SAPMO-BArch, DY30/IV2/2.039/246, 'Zum Entwicklungsstand . . . unserer Jugend', Jul 1987, p. 68.

101 BStU, BV-Mdg, AKG/154, 'Rückinformation zu ausgewählten Problemen . . . im Jahre 1984', Magdeburg, 1 Mar 1985, p. 135; SAPMO-BArch, DY30/IV2/2.039/233, 'Zu den verschärften Angriffen des imperialistischen Gegners . . .', 17 Jul 1987, p. 21.

102 BStU, MfS, BV-Halle, Abt.XX/1925, 'Operative Information', Roßlau, 4 Oct 1989, p. 43.

103 LA Magd.-LHA-, Rep.P15, IV/D-4/07/110, 'Parteiinformation zu aktuellen Problemen . . .', no date [1980?], p. 2.

104 SAPMO-BArch, DY30/JIV2/2/2258, 'Welche hauptsächlichen aktuellen Erscheinungen . . .?', no date [1987?], p. 110.

105 'Ende makabrer Mutproben: Anklagebank', *JW*, 5 May 1988.

106 BStU, HA IX/748, 'Information', 9 Nov 1989, p. 1; BStU, BV-Halle.

107 BStU, BV-Halle, Abt. XX/774, 'Hinweis auf geplante Aktivitäten von Skinhead-Anhängern', 6 Feb 1989, p. 64; 'Auch mit türkischem Honig kann man sich eine WM-Suppe versalzen', *Magdeburger Volkstimme (MV)*, 13 Apr 1989, p. 5.

108 LA Magd.-LHA-, Rep.P16, IV/D-5/1/146, Education report, Stadtleitung Mdg, no date [1979?], p. 1.

109 BStU, MfS, BV-Hale, Abt. XX/1867, 'Unbehagen, Protest, Provokation . . .', no date [1987/8?], p. 99.

110 SAPMO-BArch, DY30/IV2/2.039/313, 'Skinheads in der DDR', ARD, 21.00, 19 Jul 1988, p. 77.

111 Klaus Michael, 'Macht aus diesem Staat Gurkensalat: Punk und die Exerzitien der Macht', in *Wir wollen immer artig sein . . .*, ed. by Ronald Galenza and Heinz Hauemeister (Berlin: Schwarzkopf und Schwarzkopf, 1999), pp. 72–93 (p. 74).

112 BStU, MfS, BV-Halle, AKG/1920, 'Information zu aktuellen Erscheinungsformen gesellschaftswidrigen Auftretens . . .', 1986, p. 39.

113 BStU, MfS, BV-Halle, Abt. XX/1535, 'Einschätzung aktueller Erscheinungsformen gesellschaftswidrigen Auftretens . . .', Halle, Jan 1989, p. 6.

114 Marlies Menge, 'Stehen Sie mal gerade!', *Die Zeit*, 3 Mar 1989, p. 4.

115 BStU, BV-Halle, AKG/442, 'BEL Jugend', June 1984, p. 14.

116 SAPMO-BArch, DY30/IV2/2.039/313, 'Skinheads in der DDR', ARD, 21.00, 19 Jul 1988, p. 77.

117 BArch, DO4/808, 'Bericht zu Problemen der "offenen Jugendarbeit" im Bezirk Magdeburg', 1984, p. 2.

118 BStU, MfS, BV-Halle, Sach AKG/433, 'VVS Hle 049 – 123/81', 1981, p. 17.

119 BStU, BV-Mdg, AKG/73, 'Rückinformation aus der Einschätzung der politisch-operativen Lage . . .', Magdeburg, 15 Mar 1984.

120 BStU, BV-Mdg, AKG/419, 'Einschätzung zu ausgewählten Problemen . . .', 11 Feb 1985, p. 5.

121 BStU, BV-Mdg, AKG/5, 'Einschätzung zu ausgewählten Problemen . . .', 10 Feb 1983, p. 6.

122 Birgit, 30, 5/4/02; Anna, 31, 10/4/02.

123 DIPF/BBF/Archiv: Sign.: 11.106/Ia, 'Herausbildung von Wertorientierungen . . .', Aug 1988, p. 17.

124 SAPMO-BArch, DY30/IV2/2.039/236, 'Analyse der politisch-ideologischen Situation . . .', ZR der FDJ, 1987, p. 117.

125 BArch, DR2/A.2576, 'Information zu ausgewählten Problemen . . .', Abteilung Volksbildung, Rat des Bezirkes Halle, 2 Oct 1989, p. 2.

126 DIPF/BBF/Archiv: Sign.: 11.106/Ia, 'Herausbildung von Wertorientierungen . . .', Aug 1988, p. 16.

127 SAPMO-BArch, DY24/113259, Letter from Delia Göttke to Eberhard Aurich, 6 Oct 1987, p. 2.

128 E.g. LA Magd.-LHA-, Rep.P15, IV/D-4/08/144, 'Einschätzung zur Auswertung der Rede des Genossen Erich Honecker in Gera', 27 Nov 1980, p. 2.

129 DIPF/BBF/Archiv: Sign.: 11.106/Ia, 'Herausbildung von Wertorientierungen . . .', Aug 1988, pp. 4–5.

130 BArch, DC4/290, 'Die Jugend und der XI. Parteitag der SED', ZIJ, Jun 1986, p. 82.

131 SAPMO-BArch, DY24/9624, Letter from Horst Dübner to Egon Krenz, 8 May 1979, p. 184.

132 SAPMO-BArch, DY30/IV2/2.039/236, 'Analyse der politisch-ideologischen Situation . . .', ZR der FDJ, 1987, p. 116.

133 SAPMO-BArch, DY24/113263, Letter from Delia Göttke to Eberhard Aurich, 7 Jan 1988, p. 2.

134 SAPMO-BArch, DY24/9624, Letter from Horst Dübner to Egon Krenz, 7 Mar 1979, p. 124.

135 SAPMO-BArch, DY24/11803, 'Einschätzung der politischen Lage unter der Jugend', 9 Oct 1989, p. 18.

136 BArch, DC4/307, 'Zur staatsbürgerlichen Identität . . .', Apr 1989, p. 4.

137 'Festivalstudien der ZIJ', Apr 1977, in *Das Zentralinstitut für Jugendforschung*, ed. by Friedrich *et al.*, p. 110.

138 SAPMO-BArch, DY24/11803, 'Einschätzung der politischen Lage unter der Jugend', 9 Oct 1989, p. 18; *Das Zentralinstitut für Jugendforschung*, ed. by Friedrich *et al.*, p. 85.

139 SAPMO-BArch, DY24/14301, Wolfgang Kirkamm, Abteilungsleiter des ZR der FDJ, 'Die Jugend der DDR . . .', Sep 1989, p. 5.

140 SAPMO-BArch, DY24/111324, Letter from Horst Glaßl to Eberhard Aurich, 6 May 1985, pp. 1–2.

141 E.g. LA Magd.-LHA-, Rep.P15, vorl.43534, 'Reisebericht', 4 Oct 1983, pp. 1–2.

142 SAPMO-BArch, DY24/10593, Letter from Horst Dübner to Egon Krenz, 24 Dec 1982, p. 2.

143 SAPMO-BArch, DY30/IV2/2.039/236, 'Analyse der politisch-ideologischen Situation . . .', ZR der FDJ, 1987, p. 125.

144 Andreas Müggenburg, *Die ausländischen Vertragsarbeitnehmer in der ehemaligen DDR* (Berlin: Die Beauftragte der Bundesregierung für die Belange der Ausländer, 1995), pp. 4–6.

145 SAPMO-BArch, DY30/IV2/2.039/246, Walter Friedrich, 'Expertise zur Lage der Jugend 1988', Jun 1988, p. 104.

146 BStU, MfS, BV-Halle, XX/1535, 'Einschätzung aktueller Erscheinungsformen gesellschaftswidrigen Auftretens . . .', 19 Jan 1989, p. 7.

147 E.g. LA Magd.-LHA-, Rep.M1, vorl.16995, 'Meldung eines besonderen Vorkommnisses', Sep 1986.

148 LA Magd.-LHA-, Rep.M1, vorl.16992, 'Meldung besonderes Vorkommnis', 6 Mar 1985.

149 SAPMO-BArch, DY21/17, 'Bericht des Sekretariats zur Tagung des Zentralen Ausschußes am 12. Mai 1982', p. 193.

150 Jan Foitzik, 'Einige Bemerkungen zum Bild DDR-Jugendlicher von "Sowjetmenschen" und "Russen" ', in *Deutsche Teilung – Deutsche Wiedervereinigung: Jugend und Jugendpolitik im Umbruch der Systeme*, ed. by Helga Gotschlich and Edeltraud Schulze (Berlin: Metropol, 1996), pp. 103–4.

151 BArch, DC4/345, 'Zum Anlauf des "FDJ-Aufgebotes DDR 40". . .', ZIJ, May 1988, p. 21.

152 BArch, DC4/469, 'Student 89', ZIJ, Aug 1989, p. 7.

153 Ilko-Sascha Kowalczuk and Stefan Wolle, *Roter Stern über Deutschland* (Berlin: Ch Links, 2001), p. 207.

154 *Ibid.*, p. 209.

155 SAPMO-BArch, DY24/9753, Letter from Horst Dübner to Egon Krenz, 13 Oct 1980, p. 66.

156 SAPMO-BArch, DY30/IV2/2.039/243, 'Auszüge zu besonderen Vorkommnissen mit polnischen Reisegruppen', 1988, pp. 245–58.

157 SAPMO-BArch, DY24/10593, Letter from Horst Dübner to Egon Krenz, 18 Nov 1981, p. 3.

158 BStU, MfS, JHS/21546, 'Möglichkeiten der Qualifizierung der IM-Arbeit . . .', Hettstedt, Jun 1989, p. 24.

159 Uta Rüchel, '. . . *auf deutsch sozialistisch zu denken* . . .' *Mosambikaner in der Schule der Freundschaft* (Magdeburg: Landesbeauftragte für die Unterlagen des Staatssicherheitsdienstes der ehemaligen DDR in Sachsen-Anhalt, 2001), p. 92.

160 *Ibid.*, p. 82.

161 Michael Feige, *Vietnamesische Studenten und Arbeiter in der DDR und ihre Beobachtung durch das MfS*, Sachbeiträge (10) (Magdeburg:

Landesbeauftragte für die Unterlagen des Staatssicherheitsdienstes der ehemaligen DDR in Sachsen-Anhalt, 1999), pp. 63–70.

162 DIPF/BBF/Archiv: Sign.: 11.106/Ia, 'Zur Herausbildung eines sozialistischen Vaterlandsbewußtseins . . .', 1988, p. 17.

163 *Ferien bei Freunden*, ed. by ZR der FDJ (Berlin: Junge Welt, 1987).

164 Feige, *Vietnamesische Studenten und Arbeiter in der DDR*, pp. 44, 60.

165 LA Magd.-LHA-, Rep.P13, IV/D-2/9.02/550, 'Eine Schule der Freundschaft entsteht in Staßfurt', no date [1981?], p. 1.

166 Müggenburg, *Die ausländischen Vertragsarbeitnehmer in der ehemaligen DDR*, p. 29.

167 SAPMO-BArch, DY21/16, 'Bericht an den Zentralen Ausschuß zur Tagung am 6.5.1980', p. 187.

168 Cited in Rüchel, '. . . *auf deutsch sozialistisch zu denken* . . .', p. 86.

169 Feige, *Vietnamesische Studenten und Arbeiter in der DDR*, p. 82.

170 LA Magd.-LHA-, Rep.P15, vorl.40622, 'Information, SED-Kreisleitung Stendal', 11 May 1983, p. 2.

171 Issue addressed by Jonathan Zatlin, 'Race and Economy in Soviet-style Regimes: The East German Case', paper delivered at the 2003 German Studies Association Conference, New Orleans, 20 Sep 2003.

172 E.g. LA Magd.-LHA-, Rep.M1, vorl.16996, 'Meldung eines besonderen Vorkommnisses', 11 Nov 1986, pp. 1–2.

173 Friedrich, 'Mentalitätswandlungen der Jugend in der DDR', *APuZG*, B16–17 (1990), 25–37.

174 SAPMO-BArch, DY30/IV2/2.039/246, 'Zum Entwicklungsstand . . . unserer Jugend', July 1987, p. 58.

175 Manfred Stock and Philipp Mühlberg, *Die Szene von Innen: Skinheads, Grufties, Heavy Metals, Punks* (Berlin: Links, 1990), pp. 15–16.

176 SAPMO-BArch, DY30/IV2/2.039/246, 'Zum Entwicklungsstand . . . unserer Jugend', 1987, p. 65.

177 See Rüchel, '. . . *auf deutsch sozialistisch zu denken*. . .', p. 90.

178 BStU, MfS HA XX, AKG/79, 'Bericht: Pfingsttreffen', May 1989, p. 55.

179 BArch, DC4/307, 'Zur staatsbürgerlichen Identität. . .', Apr 1989, pp. 4–7.

180 BArch, DC4/721, 'Expertise zur Untersuchung "Sport 87". . .', ZIJ, Mar 1988, pp. 7–9.

181 SAPMO-BArch, DY30/IV2/2.039/313, 'Skinheads in der DDR', ARD, 21.00, 19 July 1988, p. 76.

182 SAPMO-BArch, DY30/838, 'Entwicklungstendenzen der DDR-Rockmusik . . .', May 1987, p. 137.

183 LA Magd.-LHA-, Rep.P13, IV/D-2/9.02/542, Letter from Dietrich Kessler, Leiter *Magdeburg*, to Konzert- und Gastspieldirektion Magdeburg, 21 Sep 1981, pp. 162–5.

184 SAPMO-BArch, DC4/728, 'DDR-Rockmusik und DDR-Jugend: Teil I', ZIJ, Dec 1988, pp. 32–5.
185 LA Magd.-LHA- , Rep.P13, IV/E-2/16/567, 'Information: "Friedensaufgebot der FDJ" ', 1983, p. 9.
186 SAPMO-BArch, DY21/18, 'Bericht des Sekretariats des Zentralen Ausschusses', May 1983, p. 55.
187 Catarina D., cited in *Wir denken erst seit Gorbatschow: Protokolle von Jugendlichen aus der DDR*, ed. by Vera-Maria Baehr (Recklinghausen: Bitter, 1990), p. 71.
188 BArch, DC4/306, 'Das staatsbürgerliche Bewußtsein . . .', Mar 1989, pp. 8, 12.
189 SAPMO-BArch, DY24/14090, 'Analyse der politisch-ideologischen Situation . . .', 11 Sep 1989, p. 21.
190 SAPMO-BArch, DY30/IV2/2.039/233, 'Zu den verschärften Angriffen . . .', 17 Jul 1987, p. 45.
191 SAPMO-BArch, DY30/IV2/2.039/237, 'Analyse der politisch-ideologischen Situation . . .', Aug 1988, pp. 40–1.
192 E.g. SAPMO-BArch, DC4/300, 'Zur Lage unter der Jugend (1988)', ZIJ, Jun 1988, pp. 42–3.
193 BArch, DR2/A3633, Report on *Staatsbürgerkunde* lessons, Halle, 1984/5, p. 14.
194 DIPF/BBF/Archiv: Sign.: 11.106/Ia, 'Zur Herausbildung eines sozialistischen Vaterlandsbewußtseins . . .', 1988, p. 4.
195 *Ibid.*, p. 7.
196 E.g. LA Magd.-LHA-, Rep.M1, vorl.16998, 'Besonderes Vorkommnis 65/87', Nov 1987.
197 SAPMO-BArch, DY30/IV2/2.039/236, 'Information über die 29. Zentrale MMM', 1985/6, pp. 62–3.
198 SAPMO-BArch, DY30/IV2/2.039/237, 'Analyse der politisch-ideologischen Situation . . .', Aug 1988, p. 34.
199 SAPMO-BArch, DY24/11803, 'Einschätzung der politischen Lage . . .', 9 Oct 1989, p. 16.
200 SAPMO-BArch, DY24/113273, letter from Delia Göttke to Eberhard Aurich, 7 Nov 1988, p. 9.
201 LA Magd,-LHA-, Rep.M1, vorl.17018, 'Information über außergewöhnliche Vorkommnisse', May 1989, p. 99.
202 BArch, DC4/300, 'Zur Lage unter der Jugend (1988)', ZIJ, June 1988, p. 46; BArch, DC4/299, 'Beweggründe Jugendlicher zum Verlassen der DDR', ZIJ, May 1988, p. 4.
203 SAPMO-BArch, DY24/11458, 'Entwurf des Amtes für Jugendfragen . . .', 1989, p. 8.
204 SAPMO-BArch, DY30/JIV2/2/2329, 'Bericht des Zentralrats der FDJ . . .', May 1989, p. 49.

205 BStU, BV-Mdg, AKG/48, 'Bericht', Zerbst, 14 Dec 1987.
206 SAPMO-BArch, DY30/IV2/2/2.039/236, 'Analyse der politisch-ideologischen Situation . . .', 1987, p. 122.
207 DIPF/BBF/Archiv: Sign.: 11.106/Ia, 'Zur Herausbildung eines sozialistischen Vaterlandsbewußtseins . . .', 1988, p. 10.
208 SAPMO-BArch, DY24/9753, Letter from Horst Dübner to Egon Krenz, 7 Aug 1980, p. 47.
209 This was an increase from approximately 70% in 1979 (according to FDJ statistics). See Dorle Zilch, *Millionen unter der blauen Fahne* (Rostock: Jugend und Geschichte, 1994), pp. 14–15.
210 SAPMO-BArch, DY30/vorl.SED/26119, 'Abschlußstatistik des Jugendstundenjahres 1981/2', June 1982.
211 SAPMO-BArch, DY30/IV2/2.039/233, 'Zu den verschärften Angriffen . . .', Jul 1987, p. 31.
212 BArch, DC4/284, 'Die politische Organisiertheit der jungen Werktätigen', ZIJ, Jul 1985, p. 5.
213 SAPMO-BArch, DY30/IV2/2.039/233, 'Zu den verschärften Angriffen . . .', Jul 1987, p. 31.
214 SAPMO-BArch, DY24/113264, Letter from Petra Günther (FDJ First Secretary, *Bezirk* Halle) to Eberhard Aurich, 5 Jan 1988, p. 1.
215 Katharina, 31, 15/4/02.
216 BStU, Z4140, 'Information über durchgeführte Maßnahmen . . .', 6 Jun 1979, p. 13.
217 BStU, BV-Mdg, AKG/111, 'Abschlußbericht zur Aktion "Jubiliäum 30"', Magdeburg, 10 Oct 1979, p. 149.
218 LA Magd.-LHA-, Rep.M1, vorl.16996, 'Besonderes Vorkommnis', Rat des Kreises Wolmirstedt, Dec 1986.
219 Cited in SAPMO-BArch, DY21/19, 'Referat "Ergebnisse des Jugendweihejahres 1984/5 . . ."', p. 72.
220 DIPF/BBF/Archiv: Sign.: 11.106/Ia, 'Zuarbeit zum Bilanzmaterial Erziehung – Informelle Gruppen Jugendlicher', Apr 1988, p. 19.
221 E.g. Robert, 28, 25/9/02.
222 SAPMO-BArch, DY24/10375, Letter from Horst Dübner to Egon Krenz, 25 Mar 1983, p. 4.
223 BArch, DC4/303, 'Politisch-historische Einstellungen der Jugendlichen', ZIJ, Dec 1988, p. 18.
224 BStU, MfS, ZAIG, 4140, 'Erste Hinweise zur Reaktion der Bevölkerung der DDR . . .', May 1979, pp. 6–7.
225 LA Magd.-LHA-, Rep.M1, vorl.17020, 'Besonderes Vorkommnis – Abschrift', 18 Apr 1989, p. 1.
226 SAPMO-BArch, DY24/113274, Letter from Petra Günther to Eberhard Aurich, 8 Dec 1988, p. 5.

227 SAPMO-BArch, DY30/IV2/2.039/237, 'Information über erste Reaktionen von Jugendlichen . . .', 24 Nov 1988, p. 125.

228 BArch, DC4/303, 'Politisch-historische Einstellungen der Jugendlichen 1988', ZIJ, Dec 1988, p. 25.

229 BArch, DC4/469, cited in 'Student 89', ZIJ, Aug 1989, p. 23.

230 *Ibid.*

231 SAPMO-BArch, DY24/14286, Letter from theology student to Eberhard Aurich, 12 June 1988, p. 38. Emphasis in original.

232 SAPMO-BArch, DY24/14090, 'Analyse der politisch-ideologischen Situation . . .', 11 Sep 1989, p. 10.

233 BArch DC4/306, 'Das Staatsbürgerliche Bewußtsein . . .', Mar 1989, p. 8.

234 BArch, DC4/300, 'Zur Lage unter der Jugend (1988)', ZIJ, Jun 1988, p. 3.

235 BStU, BV-Mdg, AKG/41 9, 'Einschätzung zu ausgewählten Problemen . . .', Magdeburg, Feb 1985, p. 27.

236 E.g. SAPMO-BArch, DY30/JIV2/2/2258, 'Welche hauptsächlichen aktuellen Erscheinungen . . .?', no date [1987?], p. 113.

3

October 1989–October 1990: the rise and fall of a GDR identity

Someone suddenly uncovered an FRG flag . . . and faster than we could see, a car stopped. Someone, someone else came from behind . . . and they, they took the flag down, got into the car, and were gone. It all happened in a minute and a half. . . And I said to myself, ooh, what's going on here . . . (Jens' recollection of Aschersleben on 7 Oct 1989)[1]

The fortieth anniversary celebrations of the GDR on 7 October 1989 marked not only the last major demonstration of SED power, but also the realisation amongst many young citizens that the party was losing control over the East German people. Rioting was evident on this day not only in Berlin and larger regional centres, but also in smaller towns such as Aschersleben. Even the most politically loyal of citizens began to realise the gravity of the situation, as they were called upon to help keep some semblance of order.[2] Yet the discontent of many citizens had been spreading during the summer and early autumn; thousands of East Germans were fleeing their homeland, some via the West German embassies in Prague and Warsaw and others through Hungary and Austria. Once Hungary officially opened its border in September, the stream of refugees became a veritable flood and, as was frequently joked at the time, reunification of the Germans was taking place, but on West German soil only. Only two days after the fortieth anniversary, citizens witnessed demonstrations of another kind: those organised by members of newly formed opposition groups, such as *Neues Forum*, who called for reform of the socialist system. Although Leipzig was at the centre of these demonstrations, other major towns throughout the GDR witnessed similar events, and the evening service in Magdeburg cathedral, for example, attracted 4,000–5,000 people.[3] Following the peaceful conclusion to demonstrations on 9 October throughout the republic, Monday night demonstrations around the country swelled in number, with as many as 150,000 people congregating in Leipzig on 16 October.[4] The pressure finally proved to be too great for the leadership, and on 18 October an ill and aged Honecker was dismissed by the Politbüro and replaced by Egon Krenz, who famously promised the coming of a *Wende*. Despite a number of changes, such as the commencement of discussions with the Church, the legalisation of *Neues Forum* and the lifting of the ban on visa-free travel to Czechoslovakia, the SED maintained its constitutional claim to sole leadership. Discontent thus increased, and on 4 November more than half a million people congregated at Alexanderplatz in East Berlin in demonstration against the SED regime.

Change came sooner than expected, for two days after the resignation of the entire East German government on 7 November, events took an unexpected turn. On the evening of 9 November, government spokesman Günter Schabowski announced at a press conference that travel to the West would be allowed 'immediately, without delay . . . at all border crossing points',[5] triggering one of the most memorable events in twentieth-century history: the opening of the Berlin Wall. Over the following days and weeks, millions of East Germans took part in the pilgrimage to West Berlin and West Germany, many gaining their first taste of capitalism. Whilst the majority returned to their Eastern homeland, as many as 2,000 per day continued to leave permanently; along with calls of 'We are one people' and 'Germany, united fatherland', it became clear that the future of the GDR was far from stable.

Events continued at a rapid pace: on 14 November Hans Modrow was appointed Prime Minister of the GDR to replace Willi Stoph; on 1 December the GDR parliament withdrew the SED's constitutional right to political leadership, and two days later Krenz and the entire Politbüro resigned. Whilst the SED remodelled itself as the SED–PDS (later simply PDS: Party of Democratic Socialism) under Gregor Gysi, power shifted away from the party towards the government. Round Table talks also began on 7 December between opposition groups on the one hand and delegates from the government, the former bloc parties and mass organisations on the other, acting as a consultative body and watchdog for the process of reform.

Despite such progress, the severity of the country's economic and environmental problems rapidly became evident, and it was clear that the state would need more than a simple overhaul of the system in order to survive in the long term. Although many still hoped at this early stage for a type of democratic socialism somewhere between capitalism and communism, this seemed increasingly unfeasible and, following the agreement of the '2+4' formula (the meeting of the two German governments with the four former wartime Allies) in Ottawa in mid-February, the process of unification slowly took shape. The sweeping victory of the CDU-led 'Alliance for Germany' in the GDR elections of 18 March 1990, which saw Lothar de Maizière become the first (and last) freely elected Prime Minister of the GDR, marked a clear turning point, highlighting the population's desire for unification and, above all, the Deutschmark (DM). This was followed by currency union on 1 July, setting the seal for political unity. With increasing economic difficulties in the GDR, the need for rapid unification became all the more pressing, and on 23 August the GDR parliament voted in favour of unification on the basis of art. 23 of the FRG's Basic Law. This provided for the simple accession of 'other parts' of Germany to the FRG, rather than requiring the adoption of a new constitution, the more lengthy procedure presented in art. 146. Speed and simplicity thus won over, a move which would, in future, provide fuel for the claims of annexation and colonisation of the East. Five new *Länder* based largely on historic territories were created out of the old GDR *Bezirke*, and official unification took place on 3 October 1990, thus concluding the final chapter of GDR history.

Whilst the period between the first major demonstrations and official unification barely constituted a year, it was an intense, emotional time during which the sentiments of GDR citizens towards both German states were brought to the fore. The concept of patriotism radically changed during these months, for once the power of the SED was broken, loyalty to the GDR no longer also entailed loyalty to the party. For the first time in their lives, young people were able to express patriotic commitment, or lack of it, without having to consider the political consequences. This chapter will explore the ways in which young people revised their loyalties towards the GDR and the FRG during this year, and ask how loyalty to each state developed in the absence of any officially sponsored patriotic programme. The discussion will fall into three main time periods, each of which represents a separate stage of the unification process. The first begins with the demonstrations of 9 October, and ends one month later with the fall of the Wall. Whilst the structures of GDR society remained in place during this month and the question of unification remained largely taboo, this period witnessed the beginning of major changes, and above all the emergence of a new mass politics. The second period, from 9 November to the GDR elections on 18 March 1990, was marked by the undecided nature of the state's future, whereas transition during the third phase from mid-March to official unification on 3 October was clearly channelled towards unification. In order to underpin attitudes during these three phases, however, an initial section will outline the central reform processes within the youth sphere.

Reform and renewal: education and youth work during the *Wende*

9 October 1989 witnessed two events in the field of youth work which represented the beginnings of reform. Firstly, *Junge Welt* published images and articles relating to the fortieth anniversary celebrations of two days earlier. Whilst, like the majority of other GDR newspapers, it declared the victorious atmosphere of this day, the FDJ newspaper also dedicated sizeable column space to the street battles which had taken place in Berlin and Dresden, even publishing photos of these incidents. In this unprecedented move, a first step was taken towards a more realistic media representation of events. Amongst its pages was also a lengthy letter from the author and president of the Writers' Association of the GDR, Hermann Kant, who highlighted the biased nature of newspaper reporting in the GDR, and directed gentle criticism at the SED regime. He ended by stating the best and worst things about the GDR: 'That it exists', and 'That it exists in its present state', once again an unexpected sign of change from a writer known for his loyal stance.[6] Secondly, the highest-ranking youth leaders of the GDR sent a report to Honecker presenting in no uncertain terms the position of young people towards their state: 'There is a rapid loss of trust in the party and state leaders, in their decisions and in the mass media, because they [the youth] do not find that their questions are adequately considered.'[7] Certain passages also revealed the ineffective nature of socialist patriotic education, claiming that a significant number of young people identified themselves primarily as Germans rather

than specifically GDR citizens. Despite the accuracy of this report, Honecker did his utmost to prevent it from being presented at the following Politbüro meeting, declaring: 'this is the first time in the history of the GDR that the FDJ leadership has attacked the politics of the party and its Central Committee in a united fashion.'[8] This reaction simply underlined the significance of the report, for not only did it highlight the leadership's disregard for the truth, but it marked the emergence of severe disagreement within the political elite, and an important move towards reform for the youth organisation.

Serious discussions concerning the reform of the FDJ began at the twelfth conference of the FDJ Central Council from 26 to 27 October, yet despite the popular desire for reform, the FDJ leadership resisted all concepts of radical change, continuing to promote the leading role of the SED.[9] Subsequent articles in *Junge Welt*, such as the front page on 8 November, entitled 'For a new FDJ!', called for the reform of all tiers of the FDJ, as well as the economy, the education system, travel restrictions and many other areas; it even called for a new 'singable' national anthem. However, it still portrayed the 'new' FDJ very much in the mould of a national youth organisation which represented the interests of the GDR. Even after the change of leadership from Eberhard Aurich to Frank Türkowsky in November, alongside more radical demands for the abolition of the blue shirt, independence from all political parties and voluntary membership, its political outlook remained steadfast. Not until two months later, when Türkowsky was replaced by Birgit Schröder, did a greater break with the past emerge, although even this was far from radical, symbolised by the organisation's name 'change' to the lower-case 'fdj'. Indeed, its ideology remained largely unchanged, for alongside claims of independence, the organisation's aims closely resembled those of the SED–PDS and never strayed from the ideal of a reformed socialist GDR. As a result, the majority of young people continued to view the fdj as a representative of the party rather than an advocate of their own interests, and membership levels fell dramatically. Between the summer of 1989 and early December alone, 750,000 young people left the organisation, whilst many others simply became inactive without formally leaving.[10] The number who declared allegiance to the new fdj in January reached only 20,000, less than 1% of the former membership.[11] The final indication of its decline came on 18 March, when the fdj, together with a number of new youth organisations, won only 0.13% in the GDR elections.[12] From this point onwards, it slipped further into insignificance, and whilst it still exists in isolated areas today, it carries no notable influence.

The demise of the FDJ was counterbalanced by the rapid formation of a number of other youth organisations, all of which were keen to break the FDJ's dominance. Whilst many young people enjoyed the freedom not to take part in any organised group, 26% were members of at least one youth organisation by February 1990, and forty-two new groups had been registered in this short amount of time, alongside numerous others which did not seek official recognition.[13] Attempts to unite these organisations at the Youth Round Table, at which twenty-five groups were represented, and in the formation of the Democratic Youth Confederation in March 1990, largely failed because of a prevailing aversion to central authority and a preference for individualism and smaller interest groups. The enthusiasm for plurality following forty years of FDJ hegemony, however, created an over-abundance of emergent groups which endangered the survival of many. Indeed, those which maintained long-term stability were invariably affiliated to the main political parties, such as Young Liberal Action (JuliA), the Young Social Democrats (JuSos) and the Christian Democratic Youth (CDJ), or other existing organisations that could offer support, such as the churches and Western youth groups.

Reform of the education system was a much longer and slower process, yet moderate change had also been on the agenda before the fall of the Wall. By the time of the ninth Education Congress of the GDR in June 1989, for example, over 400 petitions had been submitted to the Ministry for Education by individuals and opposition groups, all making demands for reform.[14] Although discussions at the congress touched on the rigidity of the system and the need to introduce a less blinkered approach, little attempt was made to address true reform, and Margot Honecker's keynote speech simply reinforced the Marxist–Leninist basis of the education system.[15] It was only with the onset of mass demonstrations that schools were forced to recognise the need for change, and a number of subjects fell away from the curriculum, particularly those which were central to patriotic education. *Wehrunterricht* was the first to go, followed by *Staatsbürgerkunde*, which became a general discussion class concerning current affairs, before being completely abolished. The content of other ideologically weighted subjects, such as history, was left up to the discretion of teachers, and official syllabi were largely abandoned. The most significant date concerning the future of the GDR education system, however, was the news of Margot Honecker's resignation on 2 November for, since she had been Minister for Education since 1963, her departure symbolised the beginning of a new era.

These changes did not, however, stop petitions from flooding into the Ministry, numbering 8,000 by the end of December 1989.[16] Written by pupils, teachers, parents and institutions alike, the majority objected to the highly political nature of GDR education, particularly elements of the patriotic programme. Changes to the curriculum thus continued throughout the academic year, seeing a shifting focus away from the notion of service to the state towards the individual development of pupils, and by early 1990 many schools had begun to use textbooks donated by West German schools. The ideal of the 'socialist personality' and the emphasis on collective education were quick to disappear in all subjects, yet because of the restricted availability of teachers and resources, certain subjects, such as foreign languages, could not be transformed so rapidly, and Russian remained compulsory for the school year 1989–90. The basic school structure was also difficult to reform in the middle of the academic year, although the second half of the year saw the formal separation of the state and party in all school affairs, and the introduction of purely academic criteria for pupils wishing to take the *Abitur*. Major change then took place at the end of the school year, when all deputy and head teachers were required to reapply for their positions if they wished to remain in post.[17] East German schools were consequently to develop in accordance with the Western model and, following the regional elections of 14 October 1990, responsibility for their further development was transferred to the government of each *Land*, which secured its own school laws and structures.

Decentralisation was a major feature of the unification process for East Germany, and can be seen in institutions outside the education system, such as the *Jugendweihe*. Discussions concerning the possible reform of this ritual began in the summer of 1989, yet as in other areas it underwent considerable change only after the demonstrations of October, with the introduction of a new programme of classes and the replacement of the oath with a '*Jugendweihe* message'.[18] Whilst the revised ceremony remained true to the humanist and anti-fascist traditions, socialism and loyalty to the communist party no longer featured, and the ritual became officially separated from school life (a move which, in practice, proved more difficult). A new umbrella organisation, the '*Interessenvereinigung Jugendweihe*' was thus founded in June 1990, under which regional *Jugendweihe* groups were established in each of the new *Länder*. Decentralisation was also evident in the rapid growth of independent youth organisations, many of which were regional in character, as well as the Youth Round Table discussions, which addressed issues such as childcare and the provision of youth facilities specific to each region. In Magdeburg, for example, the Youth Round Table met between December 1989 and May 1990, and led to the development of an active regional network, now known as the Magdeburg Children's and Youth Circle (KIJUMA).[19] The ongoing establishment of regional structures such as this has become increasingly important in the long-term shaping of local communities, and one which continues to influence many areas of youth work today.

Whilst the new structures of East German society evolved under the supervision of a select group of reformers, they were largely steered by the behaviour and loyalties of the wider population between October 1989 and October 1990. To what extent did popular attitudes thus change during this period of rapid change? Did young people's attraction to the West remain constant in the build-up to unification, and how far did their support for the ideal of socialism shape any desire to retain the GDR state? Most importantly, however, to what extent did the concept of socialist patriotism prove influential in the absence of the SED's patriotic propaganda?

Hope of a reformed socialism: 9 October–9 November 1989

In the month prior to the fall of the Berlin Wall, two clear trends emerged amongst the young population. The first had begun weeks before the onset of mass demonstrations, increasing in intensity towards 9 November: flight from the GDR. The second developed during this month: the desire to stay and work for an improved, reformed GDR. Both represented hope of better things to come, and above all, escape from an ever-more depressing reality.

Those who fled the GDR sought a better standard of life and improved future prospects in West Germany, where, as 'German' citizens, they automatically received FRG passports. The proportion of young people amongst those who left was particularly high, with estimates that as many as 80% of those leaving the GDR in 1989 were under 30,[20] many of whom were skilled workers with a good chance of finding employment in the West and few binding commitments in the GDR.[21] Alongside the usual complaints concerning inadequate accommodation, unattractive youth activities and goods shortages, the SED's continuing refusal to undertake reform pushed increasing numbers of young people into the arms of the West. Eberhard Aurich's statement in *Junge Welt*, for example, that the Rock Musicians' Resolution of 18 September (which called for clear reform) should not be discussed at FDJ events, provoked a flood of angry letters to the newspaper.[22] Many also complained that, having written an 'honest expression of opinion' in *Staatsbürgerkunde* as requested, they were graded with a 5 (fail).[23] Fearful that real reform would never take place in the GDR, many fled, leaving behind friends and relatives, and renouncing all loyalty to the concept of socialist patriotism.

The flight of growing numbers of East Germans provoked an increasingly resolute reform movement amongst the large number that remained, with ever-more young people becoming proactive in the battle to create a truly democratic socialism. As the ZIJ found in November 1989, 88% of young people desired a reformed, socialist GDR, but only 5% opted for a capitalist solution.[24] Socialism clearly offered young people some benefits which could not be secured under capitalism, such as full employment and comprehensive social security. This is not to say that those who stayed were unaware of the problems in the East, and many wanted these to be openly discussed: 'I think we should first deal with the problems in the GDR, and not unemployment in the FRG. We should be able to say honestly and concretely what is wrong.'[25] Many letters sent to the FDJ were, indeed, directed against the glossy images of SED propaganda, and indicated a strong desire to clean the slate and establish a true basis on which reform could take place, thereby creating a country in which one could take real pride, rather than a fictional world created by SED functionaries. The question of unification not only remained taboo during this month, but was largely considered impossible, and the GDR of the future thus remained a state worth working for in the minds of many who stayed.

Evidence suggests that a genuine East German identity emerged amongst young people during this month, and perhaps for the first time a real sense of patriotism for the GDR state was felt amongst those who remained, for the mass demonstrations and the rapid formation of interest groups gave participants a sense of purpose and involvement which had previously been lacking. A number of interviewees claimed that this period transformed their political behaviour: 'I got to know about politics during the *Wende*. Since then I have been politically engaged.'[26] For the first time in their lives, many felt a sense of empowerment: 'You sort of had the feeling that without any direct confrontation, you were still able to do something . . .'[27] Rather than carrying out orders from above, they were acting upon their own initiative in pursuit of a common goal, sensing a 'feeling of togetherness' and collective identity.[28] The demonstration at Alexanderplatz on 4 November represented the high watermark of this identity, and in contrast to the forced jubilation of the SED's official parades, the atmosphere was one of genuine passion and excitement, even infecting those who had previously felt no allegiance to the state. As 18 year old Christian L. claimed: 'I hated this state, I hated the flag. But now this has all changed, in October, November, December '89. One of the best days of my life was 4 November, with this overwhelming demonstration on *Alexanderplatz*.'[29] Adjectives used by interviewees to describe this period similarly all evoked a sense of excitement and disbelief ('speechless', 'mad', 'mind-blowing', 'crazy', 'moving'), indicating the emotional intensity of this time.

This elated atmosphere extended far beyond the political sphere. The field of rock music, for example, experienced a sudden turnaround during this period, with new sources of inspiration producing what one commentator described as a 'minefield of creativity'.[30] In sport, GDR football fans showed unusually passionate support for the national team, and as two young fans exclaimed before the World Cup qualifier against Austria: 'Our team can rely on us. We are true fans. We will wave flags, because now we can hold the GDR flag high again with pride.'[31] The symbolism of flags during this period could hardly have been greater, and although the West German flag was evident at demonstrations, it was that of the GDR which gained increasing public prominence. Previously the object of much vandalism, it suddenly became an idolised symbol, adopted by the people as their own, and thus severed from its long-standing association with the SED. Some young people, who only weeks previously had been ashamed of the GDR flag, even hung it on their bedroom walls,[32] and having been transformed from a symbol of SED power to a symbol of the people, it regained popular acceptance as a marker of patriotic pride for the GDR state.

This new patriotism for the GDR was also evident in attitudes towards the West, and for the first time there was evident resistance amongst the young community towards the influence of the FRG. For Stefan, for example, the presence of Western media at demonstrations was unsettling, for their cameras intruded on an event which was ultimately an East German affair.[33] Others felt angry that some West Germans thought themselves qualified to comment on the situation and offer advice, although they had no experience of life in the GDR. In response to a *Junge Welt* article on West German intellectuals' remarks, for example, one reader wrote: 'Least of all can artists from the FRG pass judgement on this. I don't have anything against them, but I don't think it is appropriate that they are "suddenly" taking part in these debates so loudly. I believe we can, and must, learn to overcome *our* problems alone. Only then will we be credible and capable of acting.'[34] Few were willing to concede their newly discovered sense of autonomy and purpose to outsiders, particularly those from neighbouring Germany, who posed a threat to the rapidly developing sense of community within the GDR.

This period doubtless marked a time of heightened identification with the GDR amongst those who stayed, and surveys carried out by the ZIJ amongst school pupils revealed that although the number who felt a strong identity as Germans in November 1989 was lower than in the previous March or the following February, it was during this month that their identity as GDR citizens peaked (see figure 4). Hopes of a reformed socialism, and the potential of the GDR breaking free from its SED stranglehold created probably the most genuine expression of popular patriotism known in the state's forty-year history. Whilst a 'free' GDR failed to survive, it was the overwhelming desire and determination to create such a state that marked the collective consciousness of those who remained in the GDR in the autumn of 1989.

From socialism to scepticism: 9 November 1989–18 March 1990

Whilst attitudes towards the FRG had already begun to change with the development of a more self-confident GDR identity, it was the

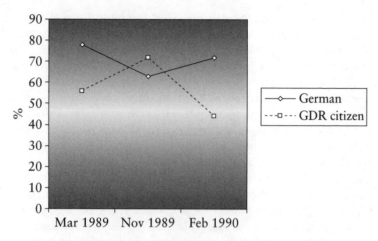

Figure 4 Pupils' identity as 'Germans'/'GDR citizens', 1989–90
(percentage agreeing with the statement 'I feel myself to be a
German/GDR citizen')

Source: Walter Friedrich, 'Mentalitätswandlungen der Jugend in der DDR',
APuZG, B16–17 (1990) p. 33.

fall of the Berlin Wall on 9 November which brought about a full-
scale revision of the German–German relationship. Personal experience of life on the other side of the Wall not only changed young
Easterners' perceptions of their West German neighbours, but also
of themselves, and over the ensuing months this event irrevocably
altered the newly founded GDR identity. How did young people's
perceptions of the West thus alter, and to what extent did this impact
on their own state loyalties and expression of GDR patriotism?
Furthermore, how far was the movement for a reformed GDR compromised by the fall of the Wall, and how did this event influence
young people's attitudes towards possible unification? As the following pages reveal, the future of the GDR was still open to discussion during this period, and unification was far from a forgone
conclusion, providing for unexpected and varied responses.

Perceptions of the West and perceptions of the self
During the weeks that followed the dramatic events of 9 November,
hordes of East Germans crossed the border in order to experience
life in the West. The FRG, which for young people had previously

been a world of colourful television images on the one hand, and a bastion of imperialism on the other, now became a tangible place. Whilst some young visitors to the West expressed surprise at what they found, large numbers claimed that it met with their expectations: 'I didn't need to change my mental picture of the FRG/West Berlin, because what we were told in school about evil capitalism and the poor unemployed people was all rubbish.'[35] In many ways, the opening of the border thus revealed the ineffective nature of the SED's patriotic propaganda concerning West Germany. Easterners' impressions of West German citizens, however, were more varied. Whilst the majority of East German visitors were touched by the generosity and welcoming nature of their Western neighbours, a number also commented on the short-lived nature of this behaviour, perceiving a fear amongst West Germans that the influx of GDR citizens might deprive them of jobs and accommodation.[36] Many who visited the West some weeks or months after the fall of the Wall failed to rediscover the initial euphoria of their neighbours, and noted instead the after-shock of events; one young apprentice even witnessed signs reading 'Easterners get out!', and 'Look after your own mess'.[37] Closer contact also alerted some to the often stereotyped images of the GDR held by many West Germans, few of which were complimentary: 'What I find worst is that they generally speak about the GDR as if we only exist as a caricature.'[38] First encounters with West Germans in the FRG were clearly mixed, yet often did little to help forge understanding between the two populations, frequently adding to the wariness that some East Germans had begun to develop during earlier demonstrations.

Experience of the West, however, also changed many young people's self-awareness as GDR citizens, and as Barbara claimed: 'I felt as if you could tell I came from the East just from looking at me. And I think it was true, because the life that we led here was completely different.'[39] Whilst a collective identity had already formed prior to the fall of the Wall, it was only in comparison with the West that this gained full definition, and for the first time many realised the personal implications involved: 'I can identify better with the people here. They're just the same as me. They work and live like our family.'[40] The anonymity and sterility felt by many visiting the West created a greater appreciation of the close-knit family atmosphere of private niches within the GDR. Even those on the outside

of mainstream society commented on this phenomenon, such as
Inga, an Eastern goth:

> When the borders were opened, we too trundled over to the West.
> We'd heard where they [Western goths] lived over there, and we were
> completely flabbergasted to start with, it really shocked us . . . because
> there were masses of people living there, but they were all like
> strangers to each other, nobody had got to know each other, like here.
> You can go there as often as you like, but you simply won't get to
> know anyone . . . Here it's like a small family . . .[41]

Differences with the West clearly highlighted the fact that socialisation in the GDR had had a notable effect on young East Germans.
However, it was not so much the formal influence of patriotic education during the GDR which shaped consequent identities, but
rather young people's personal experiences of the SED's system, and
their own individual experiences (or *eigen-sinnige Erfahrungen*) of
life in the GDR.

Comparison of the two regimes not only highlighted the positive
elements of the GDR, but also its shortcomings. Most notably, the
material wealth of the FRG underlined the relative poverty of the
East, triggering two distinct reactions amongst Eastern visitors to
the West. The first was embarrassment and shame, not so much for
the GDR but rather for one's compatriots, whose behaviour on
arrival in the West was sometimes considered unacceptable, especially whilst queuing for the 'welcome money' of 100 DM from the
FRG government: 'I found it awful at the post office in Hanover,
where we went to pick up our "welcome money", because the
people were like vultures . . . Everyone was pushing and shoving in
the queue.'[42] Those who expressed such views generally did so out
of concern for the reputation of the GDR, keen not to leave a bad
impression or to stick out. The desire to appear similar to West
Germans was thus widespread, and if successful, a boost to one's
self-confidence; as Jens said proudly of his experience of one
day spent at a West German school shortly after 9 November:
'They didn't recognise me [as an East German], and that was really
important.'[43]

On the other hand, material differences triggered a second reaction: a defensive pride, and the desire to protect Eastern values. Not
only did encounters with West Germans and their higher living standards make young East Germans feel inferior and inexperienced,

but the act of queuing in front of West Germans to receive a gift of 100 DM symbolised a clear power relationship between East and West: 'I first thought it was stupid, this "welcome money" . . . because I was too proud to accept it . . . because it was like alms for the poor, along the lines of "oh, you poor people, you've never had anything", and it wasn't like that at all.'[44] Many thus felt the need to fight the dominance of the West, and restate their identification with the GDR: 'I don't intend to lose my identity; I do come from the GDR, but I'm not stupid or have no rights. Although it seems as though that's how the other side sometimes sees us.'[45] Few were willing to accept the image of the 'poor' Eastern relative, and aspects of life which were previously cause for complaint were now defended in the face of Western criticism. As one *Junge Welt* reader commented with reference to an article in the Western newspaper *Bild* on the poor quality of GDR cosmetics: 'Reading this article is enough to make your hair stand on end, even un-styled. We find it outrageous that a young woman has made such derisive comments about our cosmetics.'[46] This newfound defensive pride was most evident, however, in resentment towards citizens who had fled the GDR prior to the fall of the Wall, but who were now returning and able to receive accommodation immediately, when thousands of citizens had been waiting for years. Large numbers of letters swamped the *Junge Welt* headquarters, proclaiming the injustice of this situation, and viewing those who had abandoned the GDR as traitors to the socialist cause.[47] Once again, a strong sense of solidarity and patriotism towards the GDR state was felt amongst those who fought to reform socialism, and a defensive pride emerged in the face of those who threatened to disrupt this new-found political community.

For a reformed GDR?

The fall of the Berlin Wall was a triumph for all GDR citizens who had taken to the streets during the previous month, for not only did it represent freedom and a sign of real change to come, but it showed that the demonstrations had not been futile and that popular demands were being taken seriously. In this way, it gave further impetus to the reform movement, and the energies of many young people remained channelled towards the renewal of the GDR during the final two months of 1989. Pupils' suggestions for the reform of subjects such as *Staatsbürgerkunde*, for example, were indicative of this new sense of patriotism, with many showing a thirst for knowledge concerning recent political events – an atmosphere far from that of the general apathy and indifference which had reigned only months earlier. Many letters from pupils to the Education Ministry thus mentioned the desire to learn about the rights and duties of GDR citizens, and yet very few spoke of unification.[48] Despite the popular slogan 'We are one people', the majority still assumed during this initial phase that the GDR would continue as an independent state, and the question of unification remained unrealistic: 'I really didn't believe it would be possible. I really didn't. I think I grew up in my own little protected world, without ever thinking that it could be different.'[49] A survey carried out amongst pupils in grade 9 at the end of November confirmed this trend, finding 69% in support of the continuance of two sovereign German states. The remaining 31% claimed to be in favour of a unified Germany, but not necessarily as a capitalist country. Indeed, 51% supported socialism as a future system, 29% advocated a 'third way', a combination of the positive aspects of both socialism and capitalism, but only 19% favoured capitalism.[50] Whilst few had believed SED propaganda concerning the evils of Western imperialism, the FRG was still seen as a separate country, in many ways still an unknown quantity to be regarded with suspicion.[51] Consequently, loyalty to the concept of socialism, and indeed to the ideal of socialist patriotism, remained prominent.

The persisting desire in late 1989 to reform the GDR lay not only in the expectation of continuing division and muted scepticism towards the West, but was also a response to the SED and the mass organisations which, despite mild reform, continued attempting to control the masses. As demonstrated by an angry letter from a group of history teachers from Magdeburg in December 1989, for example, teachers found it difficult to lay their hands on unbiased teaching materials. They expressed disbelief at the publication of the November edition of the teachers' magazine *Geschichtsunterricht und Staatsbürgerkunde*, which provided outdated information on historical and educational congresses that had taken place months earlier in 1989, and could be little more than ridiculed in the present climate.[52] The FDJ was also criticised for attempting to exert control over other youth organisations as late as March 1990, causing the JuSos to leave the Round Table discussions in Magdeburg, claiming: 'The JuSos do not want to work in a hierarchical committee which is controlled by the FDJ and its associated organisations, and which requires us to be subordinate to them.'[53] Scepticism towards the authorities was clearly still great, and was only further intensified by press reports in late November revealing the relative luxury of life in Wandlitz, home to the SED's leaders.[54] *Junge Welt* was inundated with angry letters, few of which were published, proclaiming disdain for the former party leadership. Indeed, these revelations pushed many formerly loyal supporters into opposition circles, demanding full reform of the system. As one such young man wrote, who had been a candidate member of the SED: 'I appeal to everyone: let us fight together, so that there will never again be a Wandlitz for some, but rather a Wandlitz for ALL!!!'[55] Once again, the desire to 'free' the GDR from SED control proved a major motivation within the reform movement.

By late 1989, there was still an active core of young reformers, as illustrated by a demonstration in Berlin on 20 December for an independent and sovereign GDR. Here the slogans 'Three Reichs suffice' and 'Rather Dr. Modrow than Dr. Oetker' were chanted in clear opposition to the increasingly realistic possibility of unification.[56] Attitudes, however, were beginning to change, and those who actively demonstrated for independence were dwindling in number, leaving a core of former loyal supporters and a number of concerned critics, whose ideal remained a reformed socialism. In contrast, however, the masses who had been drawn out of their apathy to fight for reform, now began to turn their sights Westwards, willing to give unification a chance.

A growing desire for unification

Support for unification strengthened as the GDR's financial and material difficulties became ever more apparent, and large numbers continued to leave for the West, amongst them a high proportion of young people.[57] Additionally, first-hand experience of the luxuries and ease of life in the Western world highlighted the inefficiencies of the socialist system, and undermined the efforts of many to improve their standard of life by pursuing a reformed socialism. By early 1990, only a minority of young people continued to cling stoically to the ideal of a reformed GDR, and the possibility of unification gained increasing acceptance. Initially, however, this was typically marked by caution and the desire for a slow integration of the two states, for there was concern that the GDR would be engulfed by the

FRG. Yet as the reform of former SED institutions and socialist organisations took place, the reliance on Western structures became ever more apparent, and a unified Germany modelled on the West seemed increasingly inevitable. The Youth Round Table in Magdeburg, for example, invited youth workers from the Braunschweig Youth Circle to their meetings in order to help them reshape their own organisations, as this was a ready source of information on democratic working structures. Consequently, the future Magdeburg Children's and Youth Circle was largely modelled on the structure of the Braunschweig organisation. Whilst this proved successful, the increasing reliance on Western structures created despondency amongst many young people, for they saw fewer opportunities to bring about change themselves.[58] Indeed, decreasing numbers of young people took part in these discussions, and the Youth Round Table became dominated by adults, a development which was typical of many other areas of life.[59]

This retreat from the public sphere, along with tacit acceptance of unification, resulted not only from a growing feeling of inevitability, but also increasing difficulties within the private sphere. A survey carried out in early 1990 amongst graduates in their first year of work revealed the immediate nature of their worries, with accommodation problems and financial issues proving to be the two most common causes for concern. Whilst 76% of respondents saw at least one of these areas to be a problem, a mere 4% named the development of socialist democracy as a concern, and only 8% of problems touched on the ideological situation.[60] Gradually the more pressing issues of everyday life began to take precedence over broader political ideals, and German unity increasingly represented an end to such troubles, promising new-found wealth and, in Helmut Kohl's words, 'blossoming landscapes'. In contrast to the ideal of socialism, which many young people had actively fought for, unification was gradually becoming accepted as a necessary measure for everyday survival, regardless of previous ideological or patriotic values.

The increasing acceptance of unification was not only a result of material difficulties, but also of emerging social insecurities. Many found their family situations suddenly unstable, either due to the absence of relatives who had left for the West, or the mounting threat of unemployment, which caused many children to fear for their parents' livelihood.[61] Others felt abandoned by friends who had already departed, and some even mourned the loss of FDJ activities. Although the youth organisation had been widely resented, many had become accustomed to its fully structured programme of activities, without which their lives felt strangely empty. The shift in emphasis from the collective to the individual, particularly within the education system, also demanded readjustment, for young people were faced with increased responsibility and required to make decisions about their futures which had previously been made for them. Some also had problems facing up to their past involvement with the regime, and Beate L. admitted to an unusual identity problem, 'fear of myself'.[62] Afraid of her previous readiness to believe in the ideals of the FDJ, and shocked at the implicit possibilities and dangers involved here, she was fearful of where her future actions might lead her. Those who had not displayed outright loyalty during GDR times clearly did not suffer this kind of problem, yet encountered a different kind of disorientation. Many members of minority groups, such as punks and goths, found that following the fall of the Wall their scene began to fall apart. The close-knit groups which they had created for themselves during the GDR had been places of refuge in which they could largely escape the hold of the state, and were thus sustained by common opposition towards the SED. Once the Wall had fallen and the power of the SED had disintegrated, many such circles found that they had lost their purpose and began to lose impetus. For these young people it was the loss of the private niche, not the official community, which created disorientation and loss of identity, highlighting once again the greater importance of individual experience of life in the GDR, rather than the effects of official socialisation.

Generational differences also proved important, and the expectations of older Germans only furthered the strain on young people, for it was commonly believed that the young would readily adapt to the new situation. As Hermann Gröhe, chairman of the CDU's youth wing, Young Union, claimed in November 1989: 'Reconciliation is easier for young people than for those – on both sides – who have experienced and witnessed violence.'[63] This only led some young people to further despair, finding themselves out of their depth: 'We are repeatedly told that we are the ones who can, and must, change the world. But how are we, as young people, supposed to do that? What means do we have?'[64] Ironically, young people were finally entrusted with the responsibility of which they had felt so deprived during the 1980s, yet at this time of turmoil in both public and private life few felt able to bear this burden. Consequently, many turned even further away from the public sphere and political involvement, and quietly accepted the advent of unification.

By the end of this phase of the *Wende*, young citizens' material and social instabilities had reached a head. In March 1990, Walter Friedrich announced that the youth of the GDR were in 'psychological chaos', and warned that only 12% wanted to maintain a lifestyle of active social commitment, whilst a considerable number were drawn towards right-wing xenophobic attitudes.[65] On the one hand, many were too preoccupied with their own affairs to be concerned with those of the GDR's future, and the few who had remained loyal to the GDR's principles found themselves denounced and ridiculed in society, causing them to flee the public sphere: 'I used to feel national pride for the GDR, but this has now vanished. I . . . was named a "red swine", a "Wandlitz bitch" and a "Stasi official" . . . What a shame for my GDR. For me, personally, it means that I will definitely leave the GDR or Germany.'[66] On the other hand, a small minority sought orientation in an extreme right-wing identity, and neonazi graffiti and attacks on foreigners increased dramatically during this period.[67] The superiority that was felt over foreigners often compensated for protagonists' own insecurities, and the notion of a united, powerful Germany provided a strong reference point amidst a world of shifting realities. Although these two trends were contradictory, one drawing back from involvement with the nation, the other adopting an overly nationalistic attitude, they were both a reaction to the loss of orientation and the influx of overwhelming new experiences.

The increasing lack of support for a reformed GDR was also closely linked to growing interest in the international sphere. As the border opened, and young people's horizons expanded beyond the socialist bloc, their visions understandably shifted away from the familiar territory of the GDR towards the unknown. Fears concerning the rebirth of nationalist thinking also pushed many groups and organisations to highlight the importance of the international community. The FDJ, however, persisted with the ideal of proletarian internationalism and special friendship with the Soviet Union, joining the SED–PDS on 3 January 1990 in a demonstration against neonazism at the recently vandalised Soviet War Memorial in Treptower Park in East Berlin. Whilst many young people supported the fight against neonazism, they also found slogans such as 'Against neofascism, for antifascism and for friendship with Gorbi's country!'[68] too similar to those of former times, and with few feelings of affinity with the countries of the former Soviet bloc many resented the compulsory status of Russian at school. In contrast, however, the desire to learn about Western nations was dominant, as was the call for a more honest appraisal of such cultures.[69] Consequently, the majority of new youth organisations turned their focus away from the restrictive world of the Soviet bloc towards Western alliances. *JuliA*, for example, emphasised the importance of a European identity: 'We want to help ensure that we, as Germans, become an equal and competent part of the community of European nations. Aware of our own, positive, national values and traditions, we oppose isolation as a result of nationalism.'[70] The adoption of a European identity was typically presented as the prerequisite of an acceptable German identity, thereby guarding against nationalism, yet still allowing for the expression of national worth. Indeed, the ready-made international community provided hope for many young GDR citizens who had lost faith in a GDR identity through the increasing difficulties of life there, but also in an all-German identity through negative experiences of the West.

The period between the fall of the Wall and mid-March 1990 was one which mirrored the month that preceded it. Whilst GDR patriotism and active participation in the pursuit of a reformed GDR spiralled to a pinnacle on 9 November, it was from this point onwards that they slowly receded. Although commitment to reform continued after the fall of the Wall, this gradually changed as practical considerations and psychological insecurities began to dominate, as well as a new relationship towards West Germany. Increasing numbers thus adopted a passive acceptance of unification, an easy option which promised to offer a solution to many emerging problems. Rather than representing a new kind of patriotism for a united German state, which might replace the values of socialist patriotism, this emerging atmosphere was instead one of resignation and recognition that GDR independence was unlikely to improve the growing difficulties experienced in everyday private life. Any hopes for independence that might have survived came to a conclusive end on 18 March with the results of the GDR elections, ushering in the final phase of this tumultuous year.

The GDR becomes history: 18 March–3 October 1990

The landslide victory of the CDU-led 'Alliance for Germany', which gained 48.1% of the vote in the East German parliamentary elections on 18 March 1990, effectively endorsed the rapid reunification process. The failure of either the PDS (16.1%) or the SPD (21.9%) to gain even half the number of votes cast for the Alliance demonstrated the clear lack of support for either independence or a longer, slower reunification process. For the few young people who had continued to pursue the ideal values of socialist patriotism, 18 March came as a huge disappointment, representing the betrayal of a utopian Round Table democracy. For some it brought with it the end of a positive identity: 'For me, our peaceful revolution has failed. In the months from September '89 to March '90, great hope grew in me. Before this, I had no relationship to the GDR, it emerged during these months.'[71] Furthermore, the local and regional elections of 6 May marked the end of provisionary decision-making bodies such as the regional Round Tables, thus ending a phase of popular politics. Whilst a minority mourned the loss of a dream, the majority looked towards the West and the international community, whilst remaining preoccupied with the practicalities of everyday life.

Once unification seemed certain, few young citizens saw any gain from looking back, and attitudes towards the GDR altered once again. A survey of 12–18 year olds during the final days of the GDR revealed the extent to which the GDR had slipped into the realm of the past; when asked what spontaneously came to mind in connection with the GDR, replies typically stated: 'subject over', 'forty years prison', 'existed from 9 October to 18 March', 'finally over', 'I'm turning the light off', 'socialism which we never had'.[72] The overwhelming impression was one of finality, conclusion and negativity, and a desire not to dwell on the past. In many ways the tendency to see the GDR in an unfavourable light was an easy way of parting with it, as this reduced any sense of loss, thus creating a clean break with the past in order to enter a new era. This was undoubtedly easier for young people than for older generations, not only because they had less cultural baggage and memories to part with, but because this change also coincided with the end of the youth phase, and entry into the FRG conveniently corresponded with entry into the adult world. The GDR could thus be effectively confined to the realm of childhood memories.

As the GDR moved from the sphere of the present to the past, young people increasingly adapted to a Western lifestyle in anticipation of unification. Consumerism rapidly became a way of life, and the confirmed popularity of Western brand names caused the death of numerous East German firms which could no longer survive the competition of the free market. A survey carried out amongst students in both the GDR and the FRG revealed that young people's values also became more materially oriented during this time. Indeed, East German students appeared to have overcompensated for their unfamiliarity with the capitalist system by adopting a more materialistic outlook than that of West German students: 77% of GDR students declared that a highly paid job was important to their future, compared to 50% of Western students.[73] Another study noted 'startling similarities' in the orientation of school pupils' values in East and West during the summer of 1990, showing that young Easterners were clearly keen to adapt.[74] This acceptance and approval of life in the West was reflected in a widespread desire for unification, which rose dramatically from 45% in November 1989 to 91% in August 1990 amongst the whole Eastern population. Surprisingly, this was lowest amongst the younger generations, with 82% of 15–24 year olds giving their general approval, but only 42% claiming to be strongly in favour of unification in August (compared to 63% of 45–65 year olds).[75] Whilst a united Germany was alive in the memories of many older Germans, this was an unknown quantity for young people who had been brought up amidst the extreme divisions of the Cold War. Although they had fewer ties to the GDR, it was also the only world they knew. Scepticism towards unity thus lay less in attachment to the past, but rather in apprehension of the future, particularly within the personal sphere. Indeed, by the late summer of 1990 as many as 90% of GDR youth viewed the future with 'mixed feelings'; the fact that this was true of only 37% of West German youth indicates the specifically Eastern nature of this insecurity.[76]

With fewer ties to the GDR than their parents, yet less affinity with a united Germany than their grandparents, it is little surprise that many young people lacked orientation. This was clearly a time of extreme uncertainty and young people's personal futures remained largely unknown, as one teenager's fears highlighted: 'At the moment I don't really have any concrete idea of where my life is going, least of all in a "unified Germany" . . . I see my future to be stressful, running from one local department to another, sometimes hopeful, sometimes beyond hope, sometimes completely distraught, always struggling against the masses.'[77] As the future of the East German economy became increasingly bleak, fear of mass unemployment, a phenomenon unknown to those raised in the East, reached unprecedented levels, worrying as many as 80% of 18–24 year olds.[78] At this point in the unification process, there appeared to be little solace, for stuck between past and present there was no existing positive identity which young people could adopt. Whilst the majority simply retreated further into the private sphere, withdrawing from political activity, a minority further explored the path of radicalism, and the number of violent attacks continued to grow.[79] As Hendrik W., an Angolan living in Staßfurt, stated: 'The provocations of young Germans have increased. We can no longer go onto the streets alone.'[80] Although foreigners were the main target of such violence, youth rioting between different factions also increased in some towns, and battles between skinheads and punks became a daily occurrence in Magdeburg over Whitsun.[81] Not only an indication of growing insecurities, these battles also demonstrated the need of young people to identify with groups which offered a strong form of identity, something which the future of unified Germany clearly failed to do.

One development did, however, offer a potential identity to young people: the formation of the five new *Länder*, which were formally constituted on 14 October 1990, the day of the regional elections. Public discussions concerning the re-establishment of the *Länder* during previous months saw the emergence of a new regional identity in many areas, and young people became increasingly aware of their more immediate roots and traditions. Newly formed regions with strong traditions, such as Thuringia and Saxony, frequently offered a positive and accessible identity to those who felt little attachment to a united Germany, for they represented the old and familiar, yet also stood for the future.[82] In Sachsen-Anhalt, however, the area claimed no single historical tradition, other than between 1945 and 1952, and consequently very few citizens, especially young people, felt immediate attachment to this area or recognised regional symbols, such as its coat of arms.[83] Arguments over the exact boundaries of the region, as well as its future capital (Magdeburg), further enhanced feelings of ambiguity towards the area as a whole.[84] This was reflected by a notable absence of letters sent by young people to local or youth newspapers concerning the formation of Sachsen-Anhalt. In many ways it was simply accepted as a further inevitable step towards unification, for it represented the breakdown of GDR centrality and the adoption of Western structures.[85] The conflicting nature of regional structures and identities in this area did, however, highlight the immediate identity of smaller local communities, which became increasingly associated with notions and feelings of Heimat.[86] As in the GDR, this local attachment was emotional and largely apolitical, for small communities provided a feeling of safety and familiarity, far from the more distant political identity of larger regions. For many, this emotional identity was confined to the smallest of areas, and as one 18 year old claimed: 'I feel calm about reunification; I've said goodbye to this country, I don't feel it's my Heimat, admittedly I've never put it to the test. My Heimat is my family, my friends, my flat.'[87] In this way, many found their immediate personal circles to be the most prominent factor in defining their identities during the final stages of the unification process, a far cry from the overt expression of GDR patriotism less than a year earlier. As the only spheres of influence to remain relatively unchanged, these circles offered emotional stability and continuity amidst the turmoil of the previous year.

Conclusion

The relationship of young people towards the GDR and the future of Germany over this single year was far from constant, reflecting the social and political turbulence of the time. Whilst the attitudes of the young generation frequently corresponded to those of older GDR citizens, the difficulties which they encountered as young people, such as pending unemployment and housing difficulties, caused greater sensitivity to the situation, rendering the personal sphere more influential in the development of any patriotic sentiment. This could be seen amongst all sectors of young people. Extremists, for example, either adopted a more radical attitude in order to provide some orientation amidst the insecurities of their immediate lives, or found their groups disintegrating in the absence of the need for private 'niches'. Former loyal supporters frequently found themselves denounced in the new society, along with their efforts to maintain only a mildly reformed GDR. As a result, many retreated into the private sphere for fear of further accusations. Concerned critics, who were among the first to demonstrate for a renewed GDR, often continued their efforts into the early 1990s for, having originally demonstrated against the SED, they held more credibility amongst the population than loyal supporters. Many, however, began to support the prospect of inevitable unification with decreasing levels of political involvement, and the majority of young people found themselves in a similar position in October 1990 as in October 1989, for the collective identity of the masses during this year turned full circle. Prior to the beginning of the *Wende*, apathetic conformists showed little political identification with the state, withdrawing into the private sphere and displaying minimal patriotic commitment. During the autumn of 1989, however, identity with the GDR rapidly increased, and alongside the hope of a reformed and democratic socialism young people became both socially and politically active. Yet as hope began to fade, and the difficulties of life in East Germany became ever more apparent, this political identity rapidly began to wither, and the majority of young people once again withdrew into the private sphere, in quiet acceptance of unification. Many thus entered unified Germany in much the same way that they had lived in the GDR, demonstrating an apolitical distance from the state, yet an emotional attachment to their immediate surroundings, finding solace rather within the private sphere. Ironically, young East Germans' patriotic attachments and sense of national identity during this period appeared at their weakest at the very moment when the official German nation was supposedly celebrating its greatest triumph.

Notes

1 Jens, 27, 25/9/01.
2 E.g. Eva, 31, 12/4/02.
3 *Magdeburg: Stadt im Aufbruch und Umbruch: Fünf Jahre deutsche Einheit* (Magdeburg: Amt für Öffentlichkeitsarbeit und Protokoll, 1995), p. 12.
4 Ehrhart Neubert, *Geschichte der Opposition in der DDR 1949–1989*, 2nd edn (Bonn: Bundeszentrale für politische Bildung, 2000), p. 855.
5 *Ibid.*, p. 876.
6 Hermann Kant, 'Ein offener Brief an die Junge Welt', *JW*, 9 Oct 1989, p. 11.

7 SAPMO-BArch, DY 24/11803, 'Einschätzung der politischen Lage . . .', 9 Oct 1989, pp. 4–5.

8 Egon Krenz, *Wenn Mauern fallen: Die friedliche Revolution: Vorgeschichte – Ablauf – Auswirkungen* (Wien: Neff, 1990), p. 37.

9 Gerd-Rüdiger Stephan, 'Die Bewertung der politischen Situation in der DDR im Sommer und Frühherbst 1989 durch die Führung der FDJ', *Jahresbericht 1992* (Berlin: Institut für zeitgeschichtliche Jugendforschung, 1992), 151–65 (p. 164).

10 'FDJ-Schwund: 750.000 gingen', *JW*, 7 Dec 1989, p. 3.

11 Andrea Grimm, Martina Holzinger and Mathias Rudolph, 'Unser Zeichen ist die aufgehende Sonne', in *Unser Zeichen war die Sonne*, ed. by Hans Modrow (Berlin: Neues Leben, 1996), pp. 155–71 (155).

12 Julian Rhys, ' "Was denn, es gibt euch noch?" The *Freie Deutsche Jugend* in the 1990s', in *East German Continuity and Change*, German Monitor 46, ed. by Paul Cooke and Jonathan Grix (Amsterdam, Atlanta: Rodopi, 2000), pp. 133–40 (136).

13 BArch, DA3/96, 'Ausgewählte Zahlen und Fakten zur Lage der Kinder und Jugendlichen in der DDR', paper given by Wilfried Poßner to the Round Table, 5 March 1990, p. 63.

14 Rosalind M.O. Pritchard, 'Education Transformed? The East German School System since the *Wende*', *GP* 7/3 (1998), 126–46 (p. 127).

15 *Deutsche Lehrerzeitung (DLZ)*, 25 (1989), Beilage.

16 Rosalind M.O. Pritchard, *Reconstructing Education: East German Schools and Universities after Unification* (New York, Oxford: Berghahn, 1999), p. 32.

17 *Bildungspolitik seit der Wende*, ed. by Hans-Werner Fuchs and Lutz R. Reuter (Opladen: Leske & Budrich, 1993), pp. 18–19.

18 See *Jugendweihe*, 6 (1989), inside of front cover.

19 Information provided during discussion with Thomas Lösche, representative of the *Evangelisches Jungmännerwerk* on the *Runder Tisch der Jugend Magdeburg* (24 Mar 2003).

20 Helga Gotschlich, *Ausstieg aus der DDR: Junge Leute im Konflikt* (Berlin: Verlag der Nation, 1990), p. 5.

21 Nikolaus Werz, 'Abwanderung aus den neuen Bundesländern von 1989 bis 2000', *APuZG*, B39–40 (2001), 23–31 (p. 24).

22 'Im Dialog', *JW*, 11 Oct 1989, p. 1. Many unpublished letters to *Junge Welt* referred to this article, in DIPF/BBF/Archiv: Sign.: JW/199.

23 BStU, BV-Mdg, Abt. XX/4362, 'Information über die Reaktion und Stimmung der Bevölkerung – Stand 31.10.1989', p. 6.

24 *Schüler an der Schwelle zur deutschen Einheit*, ed. by Deutsches Jugendinstitut (Opladen: Leske & Budrich, 1992), p. 76.

25 BArch, DR3/A.3635, Letters from pupils Anne-Kathrin Z., and Danny R., 5 Nov 1989.

26 Stefan, 29, 12/4/02.
27 Johannes, 31, 15/4/02.
28 Michaela, 29, 20/9/01.
29 Christian L., cited in Helga Moericke, *Wir sind verschieden: Lebensentwürfe von Schülern aus Ost und West* (Frankfurt am Main: Luchterhand, 1991), p. 62.
30 Wolf Kampmann, 'Ich such die DDR: Ost-Rock zwischen Wende und Anschluß', in *Wir wollen immer artig sein* . . ., ed. by Galenza and Hauemeister, pp. 368–76 (370).
31 Manfred Hönel, 'Stolz unsere Flagge zeigen', *JW*, 14. Nov 1989, p. 8.
32 Moericke, *Wir sind verschieden*, p. 63.
33 Stefan, 29, 12/4/02.
34 DIPF/BBF/Archiv: Sign.: JW/265, Sabine G., unpublished letter, early Nov 1989. Emphasis in original.
35 Apprentice, cited in Gotschlich, *Ausstieg aus der DDR* . . ., p. 63. This attitude appears as a recurrent theme throughout the comments of respondents to Gotschlich's questionnaire, completed by 6,400 young people in Feb–Mar 1990.
36 *Ibid.*, p. 46.
37 Apprentice, in *ibid.*, p. 57.
38 Kerstin N., 19, cited in Moericke, *Wir sind verschieden*, p. 69.
39 Barbara, 30, 9/4/02.
40 Pupil, 17, cited in Gotschlich, *Ausstieg aus der DDR* . . ., p. 89.
41 Inga, cited in Manfred Stock, *Jugendliche Subkulturen im gesellschaftlichen Transformationsprozeß* (Halle: Kommission für die Erforschung des sozialen und politischen Wandels in den neuen Bundesländern e.V., 1995), p. 7.
42 Anna, 31, 10/4/02.
43 Jens, 27, 25/9/01.
44 Katharina, 31, 15/4/02.
45 Apprentice, 18, cited in Gotschlich, *Ausstieg aus der DDR* . . ., p. 138.
46 DIPF/BBF/Archiv: Sign.: JW/252, unpublished letter sent to *Junge Welt*, with reference to 'Make-up im Sozialismus – So schwer haben es Frauen in der DDR', *Bild*, 25 Nov 1989.
47 E.g. DIPF/BBF/Archiv: Sign.: JW/258; JW/254; JW/265.
48 Of a collection of letters sent from pupils of two POS to the Education Ministry in December 1989, for example, none spoke of possible unification, despite the critical tone of many. See BArch, DR2/A.3635.
49 Simone, 26, 13/4/02.
50 'Zwei souveräne deutsche Staaten?', *DLZ*, Nr 51 (1989), 5.
51 E.g. Birgit, 30, 5/4/02.

52 DIPF/BBF/Archiv: Sign.: 11.351, 'Welche Perspektiven hat der Geschichtsunterricht?', letter from PH 'Erich Weinert' Magdeburg, to APW/IG Forschungsgruppe Geschichte, 7 Dec 1989, pp. 1–2.

53 'Jusos erklären Rücktritt vom Runden Tisch', *MV*, 21 Mar 1990, p. 6.

54 E.g. 'Wandlitz: Wir waren drin!', *JW*, 23 Nov 1989, p. 2; 'Türen öffnen sich . . .', *JW*, 24 Nov 1989, pp. 1–2.

55 DIPF/BBF/Archiv: Sign.: JW/257, René B., unpublished letter to *Junge Welt*, 29 Nov 1989, pp. 37–9.

56 'Wider Vereinigung!', *JW*, 21 Dec 1989, p. 7.

57 BArch, DA3/96, 'Ausgewählte Zahlen und Fakten zur Lage der Kinder und Jugendlichen . . .', pp. 49, 60.

58 Information provided during discussion with Thomas Lösche (24 Mar 2003).

59 As testified in protocols from the Round Table discussions in Magdeburg, held by Fr. Dr. Kornemann-Weber.

60 BArch, DA3/96, 'Ausgewählte Zahlen und Fakten zur Lage der Kinder und Jugendlichen . . .', p. 59.

61 See Gotschlich, *Ausstieg aus der DDR . . .*, pp. 172–214.

62 Hans-Jürgen von Wensierski, *Mit uns zieht die alte Zeit* (Opladen, Leske & Budrich, 1994), p. 161.

63 Rudolf Bauer, 'Warum sollen wir über Deutschland nicht reden?', *Rheinische Post*, 10 Nov 1989.

64 SAPMO-BArch, DY24/14285, letter from Birgit B. to FDJ, 7 Dec 1989, p. 1.

65 'Und jetzt etwas Verrücktes', *Abendzeitung*, 14 Mar 1990.

66 Pupil, 17, cited in Gotschlich, *Ausstieg aus der DDR . . .*', p. 147.

67 'Ein Amt muß sofort her!', *JW*, 4 Jan 1990, p. 3.

68 'An alle FDJler, an alle jungen Leute!', *JW*, 2 Jan 1990, p. 1; also *JW*, 4 Jan 1990.

69 BArch, DR2/A.3635, letters sent from pupils to the Education Ministry, Dec 1989.

70 'DDR-Jungliberale berichten über Schauprozesse und Mord', *Die Welt*, 15 Dec 1989.

71 Kerstin N., 19, cited in Moericke, *Wir sind verschieden*, p. 69.

72 'Vom raschen Wandel der Werte', *JW*, 25 Oct 1990.

73 Rainer Brämer and Ulrich Heublein, 'Studenten in der Wende? Versuch einer deutsch-deutschen Typologie vor der Vereinigung', *APuZG*, B44 (1990), 3–16 (p. 4).

74 *Schüler an der Schwelle zur deutschen Einheit*, p. 15.

75 Sarina Keiser and Bernd Lindner, 'Jugend im Prozeß der Vereinigung: Erfahrungen, Empfindungen und Erwartungen der Neubundesbürger aus der Sicht der Jugendforschung', in *Deutsche Vereinigung: Probleme*

der Integration und der Identifikation, ed. by Bernhard Muszynski (Opladen: Leske & Budrich, 1991), pp. 27–43 (28). Similar figures in *Schüler an der Schwelle zur deutschen Einheit*, p. 76.

76 'Aufbau in DDR läßt West-Jugend kalt', *Frankfurter Rundschau*, 12 Sep 1990.

77 Keiser and Lindner, 'Jugend im Prozeß der Vereinigung . . .', p. 29.

78 *Ibid.*, p. 32.

79 'Als die Skinheads die Straßenbahn stürmten . . .', *MV*, 28 May 1990.

80 'Die neuen Leiden des Hendrik W.', *MV*, 15 Jun 1990, Beilage, p. 3.

81 Benno Hafeneger, 'Nationalismus, Rassismus und Rechtsextremismus bei Jugendlichen in der DDR', *DJ*, 7–8 (1990), 319–24 (p. 320).

82 'Im Galopp durch die Gründerzeit', *Süddeutsche Zeitung*, 27 Jul 1990; 'Eine Lanze für die Länder', *Die Zeit*, 12 Oct 1990.

83 Mathias Tullner, *Geschichte des Landes Sachsen-Anhalt* (Magdeburg: Landeszentrale für politische Bildung Sachsen-Anhalt, 2001), p. 174.

84 'Bald wieder auf der Landkarte: Sachsen-Anhalt', *Hannoversche Allgemeine Zeitung*, 26 Mar 1990; 'Die Mehrheit unseres Landes will es', *MV*, 1 Sep 1990, p. 1.

85 Everhardt Holtmann and Bernhard Boll, *Sachsen-Anhalt: Eine politische Landeskunde* (Magdeburg: Landeszentrale für politische Bildung Sachsen-Anhalt, 1997), pp. 27–8.

86 'Vom raschen Wandel der Werte', *JW*, 25 Oct 1990.

87 Thorsten W., 18, cited in Moericke, *Wir sind verschieden*, p. 12.

4

Civic loyalties in the wake of unification

The aim of the education and training of young people . . . is to nurture free personalities who, in the spirit of tolerance, are prepared to bear responsibility for coexistence with other peoples, as well as for future generations. (Constitution of Sachsen-Anhalt)[1]

After a tumultuous year, five new *Länder* entered the Federal Republic on 3 October 1990. Eleven days later, regional elections took place in the east, ushering in a new phase of regional autonomy. As in the March elections earlier that year, the CDU emerged as the strongest party, once again demonstrating the popular desire to embrace the values of a new unified Germany. The formal conclusion of the GDR and the adoption of more apparently universal values did not, however, bring an end to division, and surveys from the 1990s revealed a growing divide between the populations of east and west.[2] It is no surprise that this coincided with a growing number of problems in eastern Germany, such as high unemployment, economic inertia, environmental pollution and right-wing extremism; unification was far from the ready-made solution many had hoped for and, whilst it satisfied many immediate material desires, it became increasingly evident that this alone could not meet the longer-term needs of the east German community.

Not only did unification bring widespread social, economic and political transformation to eastern Germany, but it also radically changed the agenda for notions of patriotism within education and youth work. All traces of socialist patriotism and the socialist personality disappeared from public discourse and, as the constitution of Sachsen-Anhalt demonstrates, calls were made instead for tolerance and the development of the 'free personality'. This chapter explores the extent to which young people have adapted to these new structures and values, examining the five thematic areas of

GDR patriotic education discussed in chapter 3 (subsuming western influence and proletarian internationalism into one section on foreign influence). In doing so, it poses two sets of questions: firstly, to what extent have the emphasis and importance of these themes in united Germany changed, and how do this society's different methods of transmitting patriotic values today change the way in which they are received? Secondly, how have young people's experiences of GDR socialisation influenced their subsequent loyalties? Did this generation's ultimate rejection of patriotic values in the GDR allow them to adapt more easily to a united Germany, or has their socialist upbringing rather left them sceptical of contemporary society? By examining such questions, this chapter assesses the longer-term effects of GDR patriotic education and its influence in united Germany, thereby helping us to further understand the nature of both the GDR state and the concept of patriotism. The analysis pays particular attention to the differences in attitude between the two groups of interviewees in 2001 and 2002: 'teenagers' (aged 17–21), who experienced little formal education in the GDR, and 'young adults' (aged 27–31), who spent their most formative years there. First, however, a brief introductory section will outline the major structural changes that have taken place in the east, especially within the field of education and youth work.

Societal change and education in the absence of the blue shirt

Following the *Wende* it rapidly became clear that the east would be unable to sustain its manual-intensive workforce and large number of outdated and inefficient industrial works, which were not only economically unviable but also seriously damaging to the environment. As plants were closed or downsized, unemployment inevitably mounted, reaching an average of 18.8% in March 2002 in the east, and as much as 20.3% in Sachsen-Anhalt, compared to an average of 8% in the western *Länder* (see figure 5). Not only did unemployment hamper optimism in the area, but crime levels and incidents of right-wing extremism also increased after 1990, and the German People's Union (DVU) election success of 12.9% in the Sachsen-Anhalt regional elections of 1998 rang alarm bells throughout Germany. At the opposite end of the political spectrum, the relative popularity of the PDS, attaining around 20% in all eastern *Länder* at the 1998 *Bundestag* elections,[3] caused many

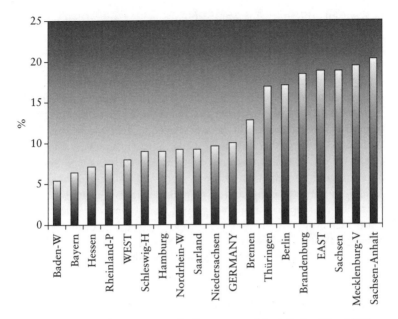

Figure 5 Unemployment rates in Germany and its *Länder*, Mar 2002

Source: Bundesanstalt für Arbeit, cited in 'Sachsen-Anhalt bildet weiterhin das Schlusslicht', *MV*, 10 Apr 2002.

to question eastern support for the values of a federal democracy. Despite such concerns, the political sphere has above all been dogged by apathy, for not only did membership of all political parties fall dramatically between 1990 and 1997,[4] but so too did participation rates at elections, showing the lowest levels in the east.[5]

Unification has brought with it a plethora of problems, but clearly also greater freedoms, decentralisation and plurality, all of which are reflected in the field of education and youth work. Major structural change occurred here only after October 1990, when schools became the responsibility of each individual *Land*. Although decentralisation has given rise to some variation within the education system, such as in the precise structures of secondary schools, all eastern *Länder* have aligned themselves to the western system, thus replacing the ten-year POS with a multi-layered system in which pupils are segregated according to their ability. Following primary school, children may thus attend a *Hauptschule* or *Realschule* (or, in Sachsen-Anhalt, a *Sekundarschule*), leaving school either after year 9 or year 10. Alternatively, those who wish to attain the *Abitur* will complete twelve or thirteen years of education at a *Gymnasium* (or, occasionally, a *Gesamtschule*). Such changes have not, however, always proved popular, for many parents complained that the new system stigmatised those who failed to gain entry to the *Gymnasium*. Indeed, by 1995, as many as 58% of east German parents claimed they would have preferred to keep the former GDR structures and simply change the pedagogical content of classes; in contrast only one-fifth said they were happy with the new system.[6] Similarly, the introduction of the thirteen-year *Abitur* in the eastern *Länder* (except Saxony and Thuringia, where it remains twelve years) caused uproar amongst pupils, parents and teachers alike, many of whom saw the extra year to be unnecessary, and simply an attempt to conform with the west. Consequently, this decision has been reversed in both Sachsen-Anhalt and Mecklenburg-Vorpommern, demonstrating a strong desire to maintain an element of autonomy in the east.[7]

Other structural changes have included a high turnover and reduction of teaching personnel, as many teachers were forced to leave because of their prior involvement with the SED regime. By 1992 4,500 teachers had lost their jobs in Sachsen-Anhalt alone, and a further 1,400 were forced to take early retirement.[8] This was also a reflection of the dramatic fall in the birth rate, which had more than halved in all eastern *Länder* between 1988 and 1992,[9] necessitating the closure of a number of schools by the late 1990s and early 2000s. A lack of funds led to the closure of facilities such as crèches, kindergartens and after-school clubs, all of which had been taken for granted during GDR times, yet were vociferously fought for once threatened with closure. Whilst ideological and political changes were thus welcomed by the majority, it seems that structural changes were not always unproblematic.

Youth work outside the formal education system has also seen major changes since unification and has been affected by similar problems. Most notably, the lack of funding has brought about large-scale closure of state-run youth clubs and in contrast to western *Länder*, whose youth departments dedicated 9% of their budget to such needs, this amounted to only 2.7% of those in the east, whose priorities lay elsewhere.[10] Furthermore, the historical absence of independent youth groups meant that those outside the influence of the state, or those not affiliated to a pre-existing organisation, were slow to become established. Of the youth groups that did emerge, however, the majority fell into four broad categories. Firstly, the Catholic and Protestant churches continued to attract a sizeable number of young citizens, albeit in much smaller numbers than during the *Wende*, providing mainly cultural and musical activities. On the political front, the second category consisted of youth groups connected to the established political parties, which also lost considerable influence following the political enthusiasm of the *Wende*. Thirdly, the youth wings of (mainly western) trade unions were active in preparing young people for the working world, offering courses and seminars, as well as organising excursions and holidays, and establishing advice centres and youth cafés. Finally, a number of other youth organisations established themselves following western models, such as the *Bund der Pfadfinderinnen und Pfadfinder* (scouting movement), the CVJM (Christian Union for Young People, YMCA), or the *Internationaler Bund* (international association). With no foundations in the east, these organisations initially relied on western structures, often learning from visiting youth workers, or attending courses in the west, and many now receive support from their regional Youth Circles.[11] Whilst the diversity of groups and activities is far greater than during the GDR, the number of young people belonging to such a youth organisation was estimated to be 25–31% of 14–17 year olds and 19–25% of 18–22 year olds in 1993,[12] thus demonstrating their relatively minor hold over the young generation, especially in comparison with the role of the FDJ in the GDR.

The new structural plurality of youth work in east Germany is clearly also reflected in the aims of formal education. References to identity in educational documents are consequently marked by a policy of inclusion and tolerance, highlighting values such as freedom and individuality. The Schools Law of Sachsen-Anhalt thus typically states:

[S]chools are particularly required to:

1. educate pupils to respect the dignity of human beings, show self-determined responsibility towards those with different opinions, accept and commit to ethical values, respect religious beliefs, exercise responsible use of freedom and a fundamental commitment to peace,

2. prepare pupils to take on political and social responsibility according to the free-democratic basic order,
3. impart knowledge, aptitude and skills to pupils, with the aim of
   promoting the free development of the personality and talent,
   autonomous behaviour, and a readiness to work,
   . . .
8. educate pupils in tolerance towards cultural diversity and international understanding, as well as enable them to recognise the
   meaning of Heimat in a united Germany and a common Europe.[13]

The emphasis here is clearly very different to that found in education documents from the GDR, for the black and white images of
love and hate are replaced by values such as tolerance and diversity,
the notion of the 'socialist personality' gives way to the 'free development' of the personality, and the values of socialist patriotism
prove redundant in a society which highlights the importance of
'Heimat' both at home and in Europe. Although the term 'patriotism' is absent from the above passage, and is rarely used in post-
Wende educational documents, it does, however, remain present as
a concept, for loyalty to the state's social and political structures is
still called upon, whether explicitly or implicitly, through the promotion of its wider system of values. The terms and emphasis
of patriotic education have clearly changed, yet the central aim
remains constant: to rear a young generation which will support and
uphold the basic values of the state in which they live. Patriotism,
the expression of loyalty to the civic institutions of the state, clearly
remains an important potential force in post-*Wende* Germany.

The double burden of overcoming the past: historical consciousness in united Germany

During and after the *Wende*, GDR historical propaganda rapidly
became history itself: textbooks were consigned to the rubbish bin,
teachers were forced to alter their approach and the all-pervading
environment of socialist tradition gradually disappeared as streets,
schools and factories were renamed, memorial days became forgotten and the familiar flags and uniforms disappeared from sight.
Young people were faced with questions concerning not only the
nature and morality of the GDR state, but also the role played
within the regime by teachers, parents, friends and, ultimately,
themselves. Not only was their immediate GDR history under

radical revision, but also that of the Third Reich, which suddenly became part of their official heritage. Rather than fading into the past with the challenge of creating a new Germany, these periods of history instead gained prominence during the 1990s, dominating a number of public debates, particularly those concerning the *Wehrmacht* exhibition, Daniel Goldhagen's book *Hitler's Willing Executioners*, the Holocaust memorial in Berlin and the Walser–Bubis controversy.[14] Furthermore, discussions concerning the nature of the GDR as an *Unrechtsstaat* (a state not governed by the rule of law), the influence of authoritarian styles of socialist education and the responsibility of the PDS for the SED legacy also filled acres of newspaper print.

Against this background of public debate, history teaching, which had previously been employed to legitimise German division and the GDR state, was suddenly charged with a radically different task: to promote and strengthen the unity of Germany. In order to do so, calls were made for a common view of history. Reinhard Höppner, prime minister of Sachsen-Anhalt, for example, advocated a 'mutually accepted image of the GDR', without which he claimed that celebrations of the Federal Republic's fiftieth anniversary could not be truly inclusive.[15] To what extent, however, can a united historical consciousness be achieved, and how obstructive really are different visions of German history to a collective identity and expression of patriotism? This section examines how young easterners have adapted to changes in historical propaganda and teaching, and asks how far their experiences of the GDR still prove influential.

History teaching in united Germany: theory and practice
In contrast to the 'progressive' socialist view of history disseminated in GDR schools, pupils in unified Germany are encouraged to develop independent thinking and explore varying angles on even the most difficult historical periods. Yet despite the evident structural and ideological differences, many of the broader aims of history teaching remain similar to those of the GDR, promoting pupils' sense of national and regional identity as well as their political, social and moral consciousness. History teaching thus remains linked to the present and future, and is frequently used to advocate the prevailing ideology of the state. The 'overcoming' of the two dictatorships and the victory of democracy, human rights and basic freedoms is consequently a theme that has marked much political

rhetoric in post-*Wende* Germany. As in the GDR, history clearly cannot be separated from questions of identity and whilst there are few direct references to patriotism in official documents or teaching materials today the aim is to encourage young people to support the democratic order, and to identify with a larger civic community in Germany.

The practical application of these theoretical aims, however, has often proved problematic in eastern Germany, particularly concerning the teaching of GDR history. Difficulties emerged shortly after the *Wende*, when western schoolbooks were donated to eastern schools, for they depicted the GDR in a completely different way to that which pupils were accustomed. Written for a western audience, the angle of historical events such as the Berlin blockade, the division of Germany and the uprising of 17 June 1953 was frequently turned 180 degrees, and whilst some drew direct comparison between the GDR and the Third Reich, others applauded the economic superiority of the West over the East.[16] With 75% of their content concerning West Germany, and designed for a young audience on the Western side of the Cold War, these books clearly did not take into account the needs of a young eastern readership.[17] What little pupils did learn about their immediate heritage was marked by a clear West German bias, thus failing to promote a sense of self-confidence or openness towards the west. Textbooks written since 1990 are less polemic in their outlook and attempt to portray the GDR from a greater variety of perspectives.[18] However, a clear western bias can still be detected, and critics claim that some books provide only a superficial examination of the GDR whilst others make assumptions about the nature of its regime.[19] One question directed at pupils in a 1996 textbook, for example, asks: 'Give reasons for the fact that a national [i.e. GDR] consciousness could not be achieved in the GDR',[20] allowing no consideration of the notion that a type of GDR identity may have developed which still influences collective consciousness. Similarly, a number of textbooks and curricula use the concept of totalitarianism with reference to the GDR without allowing any further discussion of the issue; some also use it to draw parallels between the GDR and the Third Reich and, in doing so, show little progress from older western materials.[21] More than a decade after unification, problems of interpretation continued to discolour history teaching in the east, and as a representative of one teachers' union claimed in 2001:

'Schoolbooks are often out of date and always written by western authors. GDR history is portrayed from a western viewpoint – but the teachers are mainly from the east. Some teachers change their position by 180 degrees, others say "that's not how it was", and withdraw.'[22] In recognition of such problems, a proposal for a 'uniformly prescribed historical image' of Germany in schoolbooks was rejected by Sachsen-Anhalt, Brandenburg and Niedersachsen at the 1996 Conference of Ministers for Education. As Reinhard Höppner claimed at the conference: 'Those who write interpretations of GDR history often do not have the faintest idea how wrong the interpretations are.'[23]

Not only are historical portrayals biased, but critics such as Marianne Birthler, head of the Stasi archives, claim that GDR history features too little on curricula, where it figures considerably less than the history of National Socialism, and is viewed only in comparison to the FRG, thus undermining its independent value.[24] The neglect of GDR history is also noticeable in areas of youth activity outside state control, such as in the post-socialist *Jugendweihe*, where accompanying guides and brochures frequently contain brief *Jugendweihe* histories yet dedicate minimal space to the development of the ceremony during the GDR.[25] Similarly, voluntary events that take place prior to the *Jugendweihe* ceremony rarely, if ever, include sessions on GDR history. For a ritual which gained widespread popularity in the GDR this absence is notable, and not only implies to young people the irrelevance of their immediate historical roots but also suggests that pride in the GDR past is incompatible with the values of present-day society.

Historians and professionals in education who advocate the accurate dissemination of GDR history also criticise the tendency of educative materials to avoid emotional issues concerning the GDR legacy.[26] The structures of the Stasi, for example, feature in many textbooks, yet few provide an in-depth examination of its function, or portray its influence on everyday life.[27] As a result, the onus is on the teacher to promote more detailed discussions, and innovative activities and controversial issues are thus frequently kept at a safe distance, preventing the true understanding and emotional involvement of pupils. In contrast, the portrayal of the *Wende* period and the role of the GDR masses in 1989 forms an important emotional part of the history syllabus, particularly where local history is concerned, and pupils are encouraged to interview citizens who took part in protests, discuss placards from this period and collect relevant materials.[28] Yet this emotional involvement is rarely carried through to the study of united Germany, for the process of unification is invariably treated in a dry and calculated fashion, with the details of treaties, agreements and institutional reform providing little inspiration for young people.[29] As in the GDR, pupils' emotional involvement with historical material is essential in contributing to its effective transmission, and highly influential in forming young people's loyalties. The variable nature of teaching materials since 1990 and the difficulties concerning recent periods of history, however, fail to provide a consistent basis for the development of patriotic sentiment.

National Socialism: the past that remains present?

The National Socialist past, which has consistently undermined the expression of patriotism in the FRG since 1945, yet never received in-depth treatment during GDR times, became a major focus of public consciousness in eastern Germany following unification. Interest has been great, as many still feel the need to confront this period following its neglect during the GDR, and the 'educational overkill' that is frequently witnessed in west Germany appears not yet to have affected the east.[30] As an Allensbach survey found in 1995, 42% of west Germans, and only 13% of east Germans, believed that the German media dedicated too much space to the Holocaust. In contrast, 10% in the west and 23% in the east believed it received too little attention.[31] Interestingly, the survey also revealed that younger age groups were least eager to see an end to discussions on this subject,[32] a finding confirmed by a group of Magdeburg school pupils in 2000 who advocated earlier and more detailed examination of this period.[33] In contrast to the west, interest clearly remains high in the east, yet how do perceptions of this period impact on the expression of patriotism?

Despite experiencing very different systems of education, the two age groups interviewed for this project revealed surprisingly similar attitudes to National Socialism, visible in three clear trends. First, and in contrast to attitudes in the GDR, a strong sense of emotional involvement with this period was notable, particularly amongst older interviewees aged 27–31, who saw the National Socialist past to bear great relevance to present-day German life.[34] Not only did both groups of interviewees rank the Second World War above all other events, including the *Wende* and unification, as the most important event of the twentieth century for the future of Germany, but many expressed feelings of shame and responsibility for crimes committed during the Third Reich: 'I think sometimes you really have to be a bit ashamed of the past'; 'I see us as part of the tradition, . . . I wouldn't go so far as to say that I share the blame . . . but I definitely feel some responsibility.'[35] This period thus often marked the whole of German history in a negative way, highlighting the dangers of a nation based on ethnicity and often preventing the expression of patriotism in the traditional sense: 'I also have real difficulties with our national anthem, because it is a song that was also sung in, sung during the Nazi period, and now two verses have just been left out . . . and to just, just carry on singing it, as if nothing happened . . . I can't do that.'[36] This historical period has clearly conditioned the way many young people now express their national loyalties, and responses to the question 'Would you say you are proud to be German?' were invariably sceptical, many claiming that 'it has negative connotations' or it is 'something that you simply don't dare say'.[37] A small number of interviewees also noted the need to remain vigilant, believing that such atrocities could be repeated in Germany. Matthias even displayed an essentialist belief in the destructive nature of Germans as a race: 'Germany has this latent problem of a mob mentality, I believe . . . when Germans are together, . . . it can become quite dangerous, especially if they are not particularly educated and don't think.'[38] In view of such comments, which are far removed from the images portrayed in GDR propaganda, the influence of GDR education appears to have had little long-lasting effect. This is further strengthened by the fact that older interviewees, who experienced GDR education to the full, revealed the most emotional involvement with this period, and showed greater wariness towards the overt expression of patriotism.

The second trend relates to young people's experiences abroad, for many interviewees felt that the National Socialist past unfairly reflected on their present identity, especially when travelling outside Germany. Antje, for example, complained that, as a German, she was always associated with the Nazi past when abroad, and whilst rarely asked about contemporary events such as unification, the Third Reich frequently came up in conversation with foreigners.[39] Similar situations were experienced by others, sometimes forcing young people to think consciously about their identity, and provoking Simone to comment that at times 'it's really not so nice being German'.[40] Young people clearly do not want to forget the events of the past, yet they feel that these should now be seen as history, rather than directly shaping the present and future, and whilst many still feel shame and even responsibility towards Nazi crimes few believe they should be personally associated with events that took place long before they were born. Instead, the majority would rather be asked about their experiences and memories of the *Wende* period – or, indeed the GDR itself – both of which they feel are of more direct influence on their futures.

The interplay of memories of the GDR and perceptions of life in the Third Reich forms the third trend, for interviewees commonly judged Germans who lived during the Third Reich harshly as immoral conformists, yet GDR citizens emerged as freer and morally stronger. Katharina's comment was typical of both age groups: 'I think that during Nazi times people were convinced, they simply went along with things without thinking, and I think it was different then [in the GDR], you thought about things, and you talked about them, and you didn't tolerate things so silently, although many *Wessis* say, yeah, how could you put up with everything.'[41] This trend was, however, strongest amongst young adults, who often felt the need to justify their own experiences of life in the 1980s in the face of critical west Germans. Furthermore, their knowledge that it was possible to lead a private life in the GDR which was, in essence, far removed from party politics, contrasted with perceptions of political loyalty and discipline during the Third Reich: 'I believe the flags that were waved there were done so with conviction, yes. But that wasn't always the case in the GDR'; 'Hitler Youth in the Third Reich, FDJ in the GDR . . . but back then you had to join, you were forced into it . . . and it wasn't like that in the GDR.'[42] Such comparisons not only led to a harsh judgement of Germans' complicity in the National Socialist regime, but also to a romanticisation of life in the GDR, for in order to mark out the differences between the two regimes the interpretation of each frequently became more extreme. As Simone fondly claimed: 'I think the majority of GDR citizens were here of their own free will.'[43] However, these findings are in stark contrast to those of a research group at the University of Hanover, which claims that a 'cumulative heroisation' of former Nazis is evident, particularly in east Germany.[44] According to this study, experience of the GDR has led east Germans to a more sympathetic portrayal of former National Socialists, for they understand what it is like to live under a dictatorship. Such findings may be explained by two aspects of the Hanover study: firstly, the average age of its sample was much older than the interviewees for this study and, secondly, its focus on individual histories of family members enhanced the likelihood of favourable portrayals, particularly for older Germans whose personal histories are closer in time to the period of National Socialism and its protagonists. In contrast, the findings of this present study are specific to the youngest GDR generation, who are several generations removed from the period of National Socialism and unlikely to have such a close relationship with family members who once supported the regime. Moreover, having only experienced the GDR in the 1980s from a youthful perspective, when the regime was largely at its most lenient with respect to youth culture, this generation's comparison of the two regimes is more likely to fall in the GDR's favour. As a result, young people are unwilling to lay the two regimes side by side or accept the image of the GDR as totalitarian, as portrayed in some post-*Wende* educational materials.

All three of the above trends show how young people's exposure to previously neglected elements of the National Socialist past has undermined any potential sense of patriotism towards the Federal Republic. As has long been the case in western Germany, young easterners' newfound emotional proximity to this period perpetuates shame rather than pride in the history of their country, not only at home but also abroad. Additionally, the prominence of this period within the public sphere has produced inevitable comparisons between the two dictatorships, leading the young generation to a largely positive appraisal of the GDR, and even to a defence of life under socialism. Whilst attitudes have clearly changed towards the National Socialist past, this period simply appears to have deflected potential loyalties away from the Federal Republic.

The GDR: a world of childhood

In contrast to the history of the Third Reich, it is commonly believed that the legacy of the GDR will gradually fade with time and, as one kindergarten teacher claimed of her class in 1995, 'They will no longer ask about the GDR'.[45] Interviewees from both age groups, however, revealed an interest in GDR history and, whilst those who experienced their teenage years there showed a particularly high emotional attachment to this period, younger interviewees were still keen to find out about their immediate heritage, often with the view to passing down an oral tradition to their children in the future. Yet how do experiences and memories of this past influence the way in which it is perceived, and how do they affect the expression of loyalty towards united Germany?

Teenagers and young adults regarded the GDR in a number of similar ways. Most prominently, they were united in the face of western attitudes, and studies have revealed that young easterners typically regard the GDR more favourably than western youth.[46] Furthermore, they view the GDR past in a more positive light than the way in which their western contemporaries regard their own history. To quote Bodo von Borries' 1995 study:

> Each side appraises achievements in its own state between 1949–1989 considerably more favourably than in the other state . . . the *east German youth emphasise the superiority of their Heimat much more blatantly* than the west Germans . . . The correlation between 'GDR acceptance' and 'eastern origins' is one of the very strongest to be found in our study.[47]

Other opinion polls and surveys have also found that this trend is particularly concentrated amongst today's young generation,[48] and evidence suggests that this results from two phenomena.

Firstly, having experienced the GDR only as young children and teenagers, this generation's memories are often far removed from the realities of the political state and typically presented as: 'a great childhood and youth, which didn't have so much to do with the system itself, but simply with normal growing up.'[49] The common tendency is thus to remember only the positive sides, and as Katya admitted, 'my memories do, of course, glorify childhood'.[50] Secondly, however, the portrayal of eastern history since 1989 enhances young people's bias towards the GDR, and many object to the western domination of history books and GDR research. According to one *Spiegel* survey, for example, 97% of easterners in 1995 believed that only those who had lived in the GDR were qualified to pass an opinion on it.[51] Indeed, young people have sometimes found themselves learning that they suffered under the GDR regime, whereas personal experiences tell them that life there was much more differentiated, experiencing a situation which Detlef Oesterreich compares to schizophrenia.[52] In reaction to the common western desire to condemn every aspect of GDR history, a phenomenon which was often perceived as arrogance, many eastern Germans thus began to assess the GDR in a new, positive light, identified by Borries as 'posthumous identification' with the GDR.[53] Yet interviewees' comments that the GDR 'wasn't so awful' or 'not that bad' demonstrate that this identity can hardly be seen as retrospective patriotism for the GDR; their defence of the GDR was designed to counter common western images rather than display their genuine enthusiasm for the former state. In a similar way, the desire to retain a number of former GDR institutions, such as outpatients' clinics, the 'baby year' (a year's maternity leave), subsidised transport and after-school clubs, is all the stronger in the east, as their value is rarely recognised in the west. As Henryk Broder commented in the *Spiegel*, 'Nobody wants to have the GDR back again. But no-one wants to have it taken away from them',[54] and the western tendency to overplay the negative sides of life in the GDR yet ignore the positive aspects, creates a defiant identity with the GDR. These trends illustrate the problematic nature of patriotism in eastern Germany today, for easterners are unwilling to fully commit to a united Germany which continues the traditions of the former West German state and neglects those of the GDR.

Whilst teenagers and young adults both resisted the western dominance of GDR history, each group also revealed a number of cohort-specific trends. Above all, young adults emphasised their personal experiences of the GDR, which were often considered to be enriching and something to be proud of. Amidst the many positive elements named by this group, one was mentioned with greater frequency than all others: the feeling of solidarity in the GDR. Indeed, concepts such as 'cohesion', 'communal spirit', 'feeling of togetherness' and 'community feeling' were brought up nineteen times in twenty interviews. In addition, aspects of the socialist state such as full employment, social security and subsidised rents were named eleven times, and perceptions that life in the GDR was 'easier' for young people, and that it was a safe, protected place, were also popular.[55] In the face of western standards, however, this age group was keen to highlight the 'normality' of the GDR state: 'I mean it was, above all in my time, it was simply a country like any other . . . without any kind of political presence.'[56] Having represented the norm for the first part of their lives, some were even reluctant to label the GDR as a dictatorship: 'Of course force prevailed to a certain extent, but everything was somehow arranged in such a way that the majority of people could live in some kind of peace and freedom there . . . Of course it was more dictatorial than, let's say, today . . . it wasn't a democracy, but God knows, it wasn't a dictatorship, definitely not.'[57] As this comment demonstrates, young adults sometimes overplayed the sense of community, yet they were not oblivious to the negative sides of life in the GDR; whilst Paul rejected the term 'dictatorship', for example, he did recognise that the GDR was not a democracy, and that methods of force were used. Indeed, none would have wanted to return to the GDR and its drawbacks were clear, with lack of freedom being mentioned most frequently (sixteen times), followed by economic problems or goods shortages (nine times) and 'pressure' or 'coercion' exercised by those in power (eight times). The last of these was frequently mentioned in connection with the strong sense of solidarity that was felt, and as Anna said: 'The things that are now perceived to be good, or which I myself perceive as good, resulted partly from pressure.'[58] Despite having experienced only their youth in the GDR, the majority of interviewees in this group thus portrayed the GDR in largely realistic terms, wary of overemphasising its positive or negative sides. Of the 114 'key words' named by this cohort to describe the GDR, for example, twenty-two were negative and fifteen positive, the vast majority simply being descriptive, or 'neutral' in meaning (such as 'POS', 'neckerchief', 'cinema evenings', 'planned economy', 'holiday camp').

Of all their memories, those of the *Wende* proved most poignant amongst young adults. Coinciding with the coming of adulthood, this period was frequently experienced as an emotionally intensive time, and those who took part in the demonstrations still felt pride in their actions over a decade later. Indeed, in contrast to widespread inhibitions concerning the expression of pride in relation to the German nation, this was abundant in references to the *Wende*: 'Yeah, I was there at the first demonstration in Magdeburg, I'm kind of proud of that'; 'I'm proud that I come from East Germany . . . to have been there on the streets'; 'despite everything it ended without bloodshed . . . I think we can be proud of that.'[59] National surveys have also revealed that the *Wende* occupies a special place within east German memory,[60] revealing that identification with East German history is not merely a reaction to western portrayals of the GDR or contemporary circumstances, but also a response to the collective sense of achievement resulting from the peaceful events of 1989: 'what I'm proud of is that we, that reunification took place in Germany . . . And I'm really more proud of the east Germans, because the initiatives came from here in the region, from East Germany, and less from West Germany.'[61] The tendency to heroise the role of the GDR citizen during the *Wende* undoubtedly also relates to this generation's condemnation of the masses during the Third Reich, for having experienced an atmosphere of revolt in the GDR, they denounced those who made no such visible efforts under National Socialist rule. Personal experience of the GDR and the *Wende* have thus clearly been influential in shaping attitudes towards both the German past and present.

In contrast, teenagers' perceptions of the GDR were influenced to a greater extent by older relatives and family histories, media images and contemporary circumstances, for their memories of GDR times extended little beyond sketchy images of kindergarten, GDR coins and notes, or the wearing of the Pioneers' blue neckerchief. Kassandra's recollection of the *Wende* demonstrates the extent to which their perceptions of the GDR never left the realm of childhood: 'my first thought after the Wall had fallen, so to speak, was that in future we would be able to buy our own jelly babies, and wouldn't have to wait for jelly babies from the West any more.'[62] Whilst many recognised that their memories bore little relevance to the real state of affairs in the late 1980s, a number still valued these experiences, finding it 'cool' that the GDR had been part of their lives.[63] However, many over-estimated this experience. Thorsten, for example, was only four in the autumn of 1989, yet still claimed to find the 'basic principle of the GDR' agreeable;[64] the very existence of personal memories, however negligible, often created amongst teenagers a sense that they 'knew' what the GDR was like. This generation's impressions of the GDR were thus largely based on 'second-hand' information, predominantly passed down by parents. However, the heavy reliance on a single source of information often resulted in biased views. Annette, whose mother worked at a museum and documentation centre on the site of a former Stasi prison, for example, readily admitted that her mother's research into Stasi crimes and activities had created in her a low estimation of the GDR regime.[65] Whilst a similar stance was evident amongst interviewees whose parents had been active in the church, the majority of views adopted from parents and older relatives were more positive, particularly where families had experienced financial difficulties since unification, and the security of employment, sub-sidised rents and transport costs in the GDR gained heightened emphasis. As a number of comments highlighted, relatives' views were commonly accepted as realistic, whereas those portrayed in the media, particularly the western media, were rather treated with sus-picion,[66] and teenagers once again veered towards defence of the GDR in sweeping statements such as 'it was really quite okay'.[67]

Largely reliant on second-hand images of the GDR, teenagers were more likely to pigeonhole aspects of GDR life rather crudely into 'good' and 'bad' categories than older interviewees. This polemic view of the GDR is demonstrated by the 'key words' named by this age group to describe the GDR, for although they amounted to little more than half those given by the older group, the number with positive or negative connotations remained roughly the same, and thus proportionally much higher. Furthermore, many of the purely descriptive words were repeated numerous times – Erich Honecker, the Wall and the Stasi, for example – were named three times more frequently by younger interviewees, demonstrating their less differentiated view of the GDR. In contrast to young adults, however, who all showed some awareness of the drawbacks of the GDR, many teenagers appeared surprisingly uncritical: 'The bad sides . . . were there any bad sides? . . . as a child you didn't really have any problems'; 'In the GDR there weren't really any [bad sides]. There must have been some, but . . .'[68] Having never con-sciously experienced goods shortages, censorship or travel restric-tions, these were easier to ignore, and some interviewees even convinced themselves that they would have liked the situation as it was: 'well, I didn't realise there were any shortages . . . and I somehow quite liked it . . . I didn't have a problem with it'; 'if the *Wende* hadn't come, then I wouldn't really have had a problem with it.'[69] As a number of commentators have suggested, it seems that the collective memory of this age group has gained some mythical and legendary qualities.[70]

Teenagers' over-emphasis on the positive qualities of the GDR has also resulted from their own negative experiences in post-*Wende* Germany, particularly youth unemployment. Many younger inter-viewees thus drew direct comparison between the two regimes: 'I found the GDR much better, because . . . everyone had a job, an apprenticeship etc.',[71] and this age group named the GDR's social policies such as full employment, social security and subsidised prices twice as often as young adults. Young people's concerns about their future careers and education were also emphasised in their portrayal of the GDR as a place where life was 'easy' for young people, and 'you didn't have to worry so much about what the future would bring' in contrast to the 'achievement-orientated' approach of the present day.[72] Interviewees who had experienced most difficulties over the past decade consequently presented the GDR in a more positive light, thus highlighting the importance of their contemporary circumstances, and whilst their attitudes towards the GDR were more distanced than those of older generations they were also more polarised and judgmental. Despite the efforts of present-day education to present this history 'in its universality, including its contradictions',[73] it seems that personal experiences, both in direct and 'second-hand' forms, have dictated the attitudes of this youngest generation. Only one teenager referred to history teaching in schools, thus emphasising the fact that formal education appears, once again, to have adopted a secondary role in the formation of young people's historical consciousness.

The GDR past evidently continues to influence teenagers' and young adults' loyalties towards the modern German state. Whilst their frequently favourable assessment of the GDR, especially amongst the younger age group, suggests nostalgia for the past, a closer analysis in fact reveals that this is primarily caused by dissatisfaction with the present, whether caused by the biased treatment of history or contemporary social and economic circumstances. Where the defence of GDR history is particularly strong, a lack of patriotic commitment towards the present-day German state is thus often in evidence.

A fractured history: a fractured identity?

Much twentieth-century history is clearly problematic for the expression of patriotic sentiment in Germany, yet older regional history is less contentious, and provides a potential source of positive identity. As a result, numerous efforts have been made in recent years to foreground local history in the eastern *Länder*. Whilst this has been easier in regions such as Thuringia and Brandenburg, which have been geographical units for considerably longer, newer regions such as Sachsen-Anhalt have also drawn on older historical traditions, as demonstrated by the '2002 Guericke Year' and the exhibition 'Otto the Great, Magdeburg and Europe' in 2001. Not only are older historical periods and figures untainted by the controversies of twentieth-century history, but many also offer an element of continuity from GDR history teaching through to the post-*Wende* period, for they have been less marked by the sudden revision of history. Although figures such as Luther and Otto the Great, for example, were portrayed in a different light in the GDR, their presence as historical figures grew throughout the 1980s following the broadening of historical propaganda. By the end of the decade they were considered important local figures, often symbolised by specific buildings and towns which continue to provide a focal point of interest today. The legacies of other less political local figures, such as the scientist Otto von Guericke and the composer Georg Philipp Telemann in Sachsen-Anhalt have remained largely unaffected by post-*Wende* changes, thus further offering strong regional continuity.

Interviewees expressed a general interest in local history, a number showing particular interest in the Middle Ages or in regional features such as the cathedral in Magdeburg, and reports of local projects have been favourable.[74] However, areas of prime interest lie elsewhere, most notably in the twentieth century. Of all sixty-four areas of historical interest that were named by interviewees, for example, 44% lay in the twentieth century, whereas only 3% concerned local history, results which were similar in both age groups. Despite the fact that local history has been promoted in the school curriculum and in local government projects, it seems that this cannot compete with periods such as the Third Reich and the GDR, which consistently form the foci of public debate and appear more directly influential on young people's personal lives. Whilst older periods of regional history offer a respectable source of pride, far removed from the dictatorships of the twentieth century, it is ironically this distance from the present which gives rise to their secondary importance and, as in the GDR, the historical interests of young people lie rather in the controversial events of recent history.

The fractured German past has, in many ways, led to a fractured historical consciousness, for not only do young people's perceptions in east and west differ, but also within the east itself. There is little doubt that this has influenced civic loyalties in the present, as well as identification with the German nation. Where young easterners' attitudes prove largely united, namely towards the National

Socialist past, they find no source of positive identity, but rather grounds for shame and reticence in expressing pride in national history and with it their contemporary German state. Similarly, unity in the face of the west only provides a source of negative identity in the rejection of 'the other', a phenomenon which prevents young people from embracing commitment to a unified Germany. In contrast, the GDR past offers some source of positive identity to young easterners, particularly young adults who participated in the demonstrations of the *Wende*. Attitudes towards the GDR, however, depend on the extent to which young people experienced it first hand, as well as the role that they and their families played within the regime, and the economic situation in which they have found themselves since. A 'common image' of the past, as called for by Höppner, is clearly still a long way off. Indeed, this may be an unattainable, and even undesirable goal, for individuals' personal experiences of their own past and present are of primary importance in shaping their perception of history. As the dominance of western interpretations of history has demonstrated, the attempt to present one 'correct' view of history ultimately proves counterproductive to the patriotic cause. Instead, it seems that a state which accepts and respects the validity of individual experience within its collective history is more likely to gain the respect and loyalty of its population in return.

Military loyalties in the absence of the enemy

The end of the Cold War not only brought about the radical revision of history but also the dramatic restructuring and downsizing of the armed forces in Germany, sealing the fate of the NVA. On 3 October 1990, the Federal Ministry for Defence thus took charge of approximately 90,000 soldiers from the East, creating a *Bundeswehr* of 585,000 soldiers, which was to be reduced to no more than 370,000 by the end of 1994.[75] As a result, former NVA soldiers were either faced with unemployment (58% had lost their jobs by January 1991[76]), or with working for the army of the former 'enemy', an act which only a year earlier would have represented the greatest betrayal of patriotic values. Alongside these structural changes, the highly militaristic and authoritarian nature of the NVA gave way to the more democratic image of the *Bundeswehr*, which portrays soldiers as 'citizens in uniform' and foregrounds the concept of 'inner leadership'.[77] In its new role, the *Bundeswehr* is also presented as an institution which supports and actively promotes German unity: 'Especially in the new *Länder*, military service helps to anchor the *Bundeswehr* in the consciousness of the population. It promotes the exchange of young people from the eastern and western federal regions. In this way, the *Bundeswehr* also contributes to the inner unity of Germany.'[78] Furthermore, the new political climate has resulted in increased *Bundeswehr* participation in UN and NATO peace-keeping missions, an important step for an army which was founded only a decade after the end of the Second World War and whose activities were previously strictly confined to defence. The most significant decision of the 1990s was taken on 12 July 1994, when the Federal Constitutional Court ruled that German soldiers should be allowed to participate in missions outside the NATO area, provided that each case is approved by a simple majority in the *Bundestag*. As a result, the *Bundeswehr* took part in military operations in former Yugoslavia and for the first time in its history adopted an attacking position in the NATO air strikes of 1999 in Kosovo.

Despite the army's growing international role, young people in post-*Wende* Germany are considerably less exposed to military influence today than during the GDR, for the paramilitary GST was disbanded and military classes were abolished from the school curriculum. Whilst military service was retained, the introduction of *Zivildienst* in the east, a civilian alternative involving service to the community, meant that young men could avoid all contact with military life if they so wished. Furthermore, by 2002 the length of military service had been reduced from twelve months to nine months, and *Zivildienst* from fifteen to twelve months, with continuing discussions concerning the further shortening of both. School has thus remained the only forum where young people are confronted with compulsory education featuring military issues. Although this takes place in a variety of subjects, such as history, geography, politics and *Sozialkunde*, it occupies minimal space on the curriculum,[79] and with much emphasis on the importance of international alliances and peace-keeping missions, the role of the army within Germany is largely neglected. Contrary to the promotion of the NVA in the GDR, school materials today clearly do not present the army of united Germany as an institution which is symbolic of the German state or nation. How influential have such changes thus been to young people's military loyalties and sense of patriotism since 1990, particularly in view of prior experience of GDR military education? Has the *Bundeswehr* proved to be a unifying force in post-*Wende* Germany or have military influences instead provided a source of tension for young east Germans?

Military service and the Bundeswehr after the Cold War: symbols of German pride?

The portrayal of the *Bundeswehr* as a guardian of peace is reminiscent of NVA propaganda, yet in the post-Cold War era the relevance of the army proves radically different. Indeed, in the absence of an apparent enemy, the immediate significance of the army was lost on many interviewees, even a matter of months after the terrorist attacks of 11 September 2001. Similarly, a number of surveys carried out by the *Bundeswehr*'s Social Science Institute (SOWI) in the early-to-mid-1990s found that young people's sense of security in post-*Wende* Germany was rarely influenced by the army. The *Bundeswehr* was thus considered irrelevant by over 50% of 16–25 year olds in 1991 in both east and west, and although approximately 25% associated the army with feelings of safety in the west, this was true of only 20% in the east.[80] Instead, perceptions of security were more commonly associated with health, living standards, crime, environmental conditions and social and political relations. The level of living standards was particularly important to young people in eastern Germany, where rapid change had not only caused widespread material and social insecurities, but fear of violence and crime also proved considerably more prevalent than in the west.[81] Consequently, many young easterners placed civilian organisations above the armed forces for their importance in maintaining security, and as Birgit typically claimed, 'I don't feel safer, or safe, because of the *Bundeswehr*.'[82]

Despite the new international conditions, the existence of military service ensures that the army still retains immediate relevance for young men. It also remains central to the concept of patriotism, as those who opt for military service must swear to 'loyally serve the Federal Republic of Germany'.[83] Many young men, however, consider this to be an unwelcome obligation rather than an honourable patriotic duty, and enthusiasm for military service has been low since the *Wende*, with only 22.6% of young men surveyed in the east, and 17.4% in the west, regarding it positively in 1993.[84]

Slightly higher levels of acceptance persisted in the east until the end of the decade,[85] partly, it seems, because of the heightened influence of militarism in the GDR, where military service was considered a standard and central part of a young man's biography. As seen in chapter 2, *Bausoldaten* suffered severe discrimination and, despite their increasing acceptance in society towards the later 1980s, such behaviour was considered highly deviant from the norm. In this way, military service was frequently seen as a rite of passage into masculinity, a phenomenon which remained strong in the immediate post-*Wende* years in the east. As one male interviewee stated: 'I'd say it's life experience, becoming familiar with guns and things',[86] and many simply followed the well-trodden path, not even considering the alternative: 'I just did what the call-up papers said . . . I really didn't think hard about it.'[87] As in GDR times, however, enthusiasm was minimal and often aroused only by the promise of good sporting facilities, flying lessons, or financial reward: 'I want to sign up for four years . . . Why? Don't know. . . it's an experience, and the money's good of course . . . I'd also go abroad for that reason, because you earn 70,000 Marks a year.'[88] Once again, reasons for serving in the army rarely displayed inner conviction for either the military or the patriotic cause.

This lack of enthusiasm has seen a rise in the popularity of *Zivildienst*, particularly amongst those with higher levels of education.[89] Surveys have also revealed that around two-thirds of young people in both east and west view *Zivildienst* to be more important for society than *Wehrdienst*.[90] Valued above all for its support of the social state, *Zivildienst* is thus often considered to be of greater patriotic worth than *Wehrdienst*, a trend which correlates closely with young people's tendency to dismiss the role of the military in maintaining inner security. This enthusiasm is, however, only relative, for an atmosphere of apathy reigns with respect to both types of service, the chosen one often being simply the lesser of two evils. With reference to *Zivildienst*, for example, one interviewee typically stated, 'It's better than crawling through mud'; whereas of *Wehrdienst* another claimed that 'cleaning out bed pans isn't really my thing'.[91] Few see either to be an expression of responsible citizenship or service to the state, often begrudging the time which is lost. To quote Thorsten: 'It's just a year of hanging around for me . . . What's the state done for me? . . . I have to find my own apprenticeship . . . training . . . I have to do everything for myself. And all of a sudden I have to do something in return. I don't see why. I think it's stupid, totally stupid.'[92] Here, expectations are still based on the GDR principle that vocational training and apprenticeships were found for young people by the state and, having to fend for themselves to a greater extent than their parents or even older siblings, it is not surprising that many young people are unwilling to dedicate a year of their lives to the state. Indeed, 63% of interviewees wanted to see an end to compulsory military service through the creation of a professional army, a trend confirmed in other surveys.[93] Far from representing a patriotic duty, military service requirements have instead created resentment towards those in power, once again demonstrating how the enforcement of norms to protect the state rarely produces enthusiasm for the patriotic cause.

Interestingly, young people's attitudes towards military service do not correlate with their views of the *Bundeswehr* as an institution, which enjoys relatively high acceptance. In 1997, for example, 79% of young east Germans saw the federal army in a positive light, compared to 60% in the west, levelling out to approximately 70% in both areas by the turn of the decade.[94] Furthermore, a study carried out in Sachsen-Anhalt in 2000 found that the *Bundeswehr* came top of the list of institutions trusted by young people, above the law courts, the police, school, political parties and the government.[95] This positive assessment of the *Bundeswehr*, coupled with scepticism towards military service, reflects the widespread existence of apathy, for on the one hand young people are willing to lay their trust in the army – and, indeed, see it as a self-evident institution – but on the other hand they are unwilling to support it with their own actions. As Benjamin typically claimed: 'Germany needs, well it's a country that needs an army . . . but it doesn't inspire me.'[96] Similar attitudes can be witnessed regarding international military involvement, for studies have revealed highly favourable attitudes towards international organisations such as NATO, and the *Bundeswehr*'s provision of humanitarian aid within the international sphere was positively noted by numerous interviewees, even justifying its very existence.[97] Yet in 1999, 59% of eastern youth opposed *Bundeswehr* participation in NATO military actions, compared to only 36% of western youth,[98] a trend which was also evident concerning German involvement in both Kosovo and Bosnia. Although young eastern citizens (aged 16–25) were found to be more supportive of an active foreign policy than their elders, they were clearly more content to see Germany take a back-seat role than their western peers.

Whilst these trends suggest that GDR socialisation may have caused some scepticism towards *Bundeswehr* deployment, reticence towards military action can be found amongst young easterners of all ages, including those who are too young to have experienced GDR education. Instead, attitudes towards the military find their roots in two principal causes. Firstly, the fact that many in the east have had to adapt their lives, retrain, move to find employment, or cope with increasing social unrest has meant that few can muster enthusiastic support for large-scale military action abroad when they see the need for more resources at home. Similarly, many interviewees advocated a smaller and more technical army which would not only see the abolition of military service but also save money. As in the GDR, the army was often seen to be superfluous to the needs of the population, and many regarded it to be a drain on finances which could be better used to improve their immediate situation through investment in job creation schemes or youth work. Secondly, young people's attitudes have been influenced by their heightened historical awareness of the National Socialist legacy following the *Wende*. One young man completing his military service in the east in 1992, for example, explained that he felt uncomfortable about military intervention because 'We Germans have twice started a war . . . I think it's better if we hold ourselves back a bit.'[99] Interviewees' concern for their image abroad was of most influence here, for many still felt they were associated with the overbearing militarism of their past: 'What's negative is that the medium of Germany – Hitler and all that is still there – and also the *Bundeswehr*, are still connected to war and things, and then other countries naturally think it's still a danger.'[100] As a result, many interviewees stated that they would like to see greater emphasis on crisis management and humanitarian aid, rather than defence,[101] and soldiers' work following serious flooding, most notably in the early autumn of 2002, only heightened this image, winning respect for the army. Young people's reticence towards military action is thus clearly shaped by their concern for both the present and the past; lack of support for the military does not thus necessarily imply a lack of patriotic commitment, but rather the desire to tend to the immediate problems of life in eastern Germany, and to remain responsible in the face of history.

Although it may be accepted as an institution, the *Bundeswehr* clearly benefits from little active support from the young population, and in 1992 only approximately 30% of young people interviewed by SOWI in both east and west regarded it to be a symbol of united Germany.[102] It seems that concepts such as the 'citizen in uniform' and 'inner leadership' have been lost on many, who still associate the armed forces with aggressive policies dominated by conflict and war. Many interviewees, for example, saw the *Bundeswehr*'s duties primarily to involve war preparations, one typically claiming: 'For me the army always means a willingness to go to war.'[103] The government's attempts to present the *Bundeswehr* as a champion of 'democratic consciousness, tolerance and civil courage'[104] appear to have largely failed, even amongst younger interviewees who have attended *Sozialkunde* lessons on the *Bundeswehr*, rather than *Staatsbürgerkunde* lessons on the NVA. Whilst associations of aggression and military conflict have caused scepticism and reticence amongst the majority, they have also provoked a number of small-scale demonstrations, particularly in 1995, the year of the *Bundeswehr*'s fortieth anniversary. On 26 October, for example, a public swearing-in ceremony for new army recruits in Dessau's town square was countered by a group of 160–200 young protesters, who shouted anti-military slogans and carried banners, one of which read '*Bundeswehr* – murderous fascination'.[105] Although these demonstrators were denounced by a CDU politician as 'riot tourists',[106] a number of other incidents indicate a small core of active resistance amongst young people towards demonstrations of military power. In 1995, for example, objections were raised concerning organised school visits to the *Bundeswehr* show 'Our Air Force',[107] and since 1992 regular demonstrations have taken place against the military manoeuvres on the Colbitz-Letzlinger Heide in protest at the environmental damage caused by the *Bundeswehr*'s military training operations.[108] It is significant that all these demonstrations have been dominated by supporters of the far left, especially PDS sympathisers who were dissatisfied with the contemporary political status quo. As a result, protests have not only targeted the militaristic nature of the *Bundeswehr* but also aimed to demonstrate its allegedly undemocratic nature. Whilst this tactic proves similar to anti-military protests in the GDR, there remains one important difference: the effect of such protests since 1990 has been minimal, and cannot be seen as a potential threat to

the existing political order, as was evident in the GDR. The majority of young people are instead marked by a feeling of apathy
towards the *Bundeswehr* and although they disagree with elements
of military policy they recognise the army's necessity and adhere to
the credo: '*Bundeswehr* yes, but without me.'[109]

'*Army of unity*': soldiers united for a new Germany?

The *Bundeswehr* was one of the few places where intensive contact
between eastern and western citizens took place from an early stage,
as many young men from the east travelled west to complete their
military service due to poor facilities in the former GDR. For many
young east Germans, this was their first taste of life in the west,
which was often an eye-opening and unsettling experience. Indeed,
insecurity amongst eastern soldiers was not uncommon, with
reports of eastern officers being intimidated by new western recruits,
and western superiors acting in an insensitive and arrogant
manner.[110] This was not helped by the fact that western soldiers
earned considerably more than eastern colleagues, despite the fact
that they frequently worked side by side; consequently resentment
was felt more strongly here than in the population at large, where
comparisons could not be drawn so directly. The *Bundeswehr*, presented as a leading force in the unification process, was clearly far
from united. Comparisons between the *Bundeswehr* and the former
NVA were also inevitable, often providing further cause for a mental
divide amongst troops. Those who had experienced GST training,
or heard about NVA training through older siblings and friends, for
instance, commonly regarded service in the *Bundeswehr* to be too
easy and lacking in necessary discipline, and in 1992 over 90% of
east German soldiers believed the NVA to have been tougher than
the *Bundeswehr*,[111] an attitude which often gave eastern soldiers
some validity and sense of self-worth in the face of their perceived
inadequacy. East Germans completing military service thus frequently complained of boredom, frustration and disappointment
that they were being treated as cheap labour. Even after twelve years
of unity, this view was still evident in the comments of young people
concerning friends or relatives who had served in the *Bundeswehr*.
Julia said of her cousin, for example, 'he was at home more than he
was there', whilst Nadia claimed: 'My God, it's really not bad, they
could even do it for a bit longer!'[112] Others found that friends' experiences in the army only strengthened their negative perceptions of

the *Bundeswehr*, and soldiers' personal experiences, often fuelled by conflict between east and west, have clearly infiltrated the wider population, rather than promoted a unified atmosphere as the basis for a new patriotism.

The image of the *Bundeswehr* as a unifying force has also been marred in recent years by the presence of right-wing extremism amongst troops. As in the GDR, a clear correlation exists between the extreme right-wing and support of militarism,[113] and with many left-wing supporters opting for *Zivildienst*, military service has attracted a greater concentration of right-wing youth.[114] This has given rise to a number of right-wing incidents in the *Bundeswehr* such as vandalism, verbal abuse and physical violence, triggering legal proceedings which reached their height in Sachsen-Anhalt in 1996 (eighteen cases), 1997 (fourteen cases) and 1998 (twenty-one cases).[115] Whilst this was clearly a minority trend, and was far from characterising the *Bundeswehr* as a whole, it received considerable publicity and provided fuel for anti-military campaigners. In August 1997, for example, the press spokesman of the Green party sent a letter to the *Magdeburger Volksstimme* newspaper, claiming: 'The *Bundeswehr* is clearly the crowd that magically attracts brown-minded shithouse flies. German conceptions of order, fanaticism for weapons, esprit de corps and strict heirarchical structures, where could fascist sympathisers be better placed than in the *Bundeswehr*?'[116] This letter naturally caused uproar within the army and amongst the general public, as well as triggering a heated debate in the regional parliament. Although many strongly disagreed with this claim, the incident left its mark in two ways: firstly, it did little to improve the democratic image of the army, only strengthening the scepticism of many, and secondly it further widened the political divide between the left-wing and centre-right parties concerning the role of the *Bundeswehr* in Germany, as demonstrated by the subsequent and unusually heated parliamentary debate.[117]

In many ways the *Bundeswehr* thus appears to have been a divisive, rather than a uniting force, far from representing a platform for patriotic behaviour in united Germany. Whilst young people view it generally to be a necessary institution of the state, they resent many aspects of its presence in German society, and view it rather with apathy and complacency. A number of these resentments, such as the perception that the army spends too much public money, or that military service represents a waste of time, resemble sentiments during the GDR. However, the absence of GDR-style militarism, the introduction of *Zivildienst* and the *Bundeswehr*'s integration into international democratic bodies, have diluted the strength of opposition, which is unlikely ever to endanger the state's stability, as the SED feared it would in the GDR. Whilst the army has not become a platform for patriotic behaviour, the new conditions have ensured that it has not become the opposite.

International allegiances in a new world order

Along with the NVA, the bi-polar concepts of proletarian internationalism and western enmity also became redundant, replaced by western integration and the promotion of international understanding. The broad aims of these new values, however, remain surprisingly similar to those they replaced: to strengthen inclusive patriotic values and to guard against ethnic nationalist beliefs by encouraging support for international alliances and promoting cultural diversity. Curriculum aims today thus fall into two principal categories. Firstly, pupils are encouraged to identify with Europe through a process of familiarisation and critical appraisal,[118] and educational activities are required to 'help stimulate pupils to want Europe'.[119] The second aim is to promote acceptance of cultural difference and to guard against nationalist trends. Activities that encourage pupils to find out about different nationalities living in their neighbourhood, or to research a variety of cultural traditions, thus aim to bring about an understanding of cultural diversity which, in accordance with the democratic order, enriches German culture.[120] Outside the formal education system, a number of other organisations promote these principles, specifically in the battle to curb xenophobic attitudes. The association *Miteinander*, for example, works towards interracial understanding through exhibitions, workshops and political debates, whilst other independent organisations have joined together to develop initiatives for young people, such as the 'Project for tolerance and democracy' in Sachsen-Anhalt, supported by government funding.[121] International youth projects in the east have also increased dramatically since unification, with exchanges to western countries as well as former socialist countries proving highly successful.[122]

Clearly the political climate of post-*Wende* Germany has supported greater cultural diversity and acceptance in the east, and the move away from the restrictive values of proletarian internationalism towards western integration has, in many ways, mirrored the young generation's loyalties of the 1980s. Can lines of continuity thus be drawn from the 1980s through to the 1990s in terms of international attitudes? Do young people continue to show avid interest in the western world on the one hand, yet express superiority over foreigners from non-western cultures on the other, or has this changed in the absence of the SED's overbearing programme of proletarian internationalism?

The realities of western democracy

American culture and lifestyles, highly symbolic of western democracy and consumer culture, have continued to prove influential in the lives of young people today. This can be witnessed in the German language, which has imported numerous phrases such as 'cool', 'Fast-food' and 'fun', as well as in the spheres of music, film and fashion, which are dominated by American products. However, this influence has lost the political importance it used to hold in the GDR, for the readily available nature of American goods has diminished their value as status symbols. Although surveys show that attitudes have generally remained positive towards America since unification, they also reveal dwindling enthusiasm, especially since the events of 11 September 2001.[123] Perhaps unsurprisingly, attitudes also appear to correlate with age, for empirical data show that younger east Germans are more accepting of American culture than their parents,[124] and younger interviewees proved more enthusiastic than their elders, with 74% claiming they were interested in American society, compared to only 35% of the older group (with 9% and 35%, respectively, answering negatively).

Growing scepticism appears to be founded in negative stereotypes of American mass culture, which created amongst many the impression that they knew what America was like without having been there: 'but America just, like, gets on my nerves . . . everything's very sweet and plastic'; 'America is a kind of over-determined subculture, where you quickly believe that everything's good if it's American or similar.'[125] Ironically, many such stereotypes, often relating to consumerism, decadent lifestyles or perceived arrogance, prove similar to images propagated in the GDR, which were so vehemently rejected by young people. This dramatic change in young attitudes has most notably been caused by the influx of American goods and cultural products following the *Wende*, which saturated the east German market. Whilst they were initially welcomed with open arms, young people gradually became increasingly sceptical of the overbearing dominance of American mass culture. Closer insight into the political sphere of the USA, alongside reports of party scandals and affairs, has also produced further resistance, and as Paul claimed: 'That country isn't any freer than we are. I believe it is more capitalistic, more Tayloristic.'[126] This image was particularly prominent in the wake of 11 September, for the heightened patriotism of many Americans only made the country appear more aggressive and bellicose in the minds of many. Young people's attitudes towards American culture are, thus, not entirely dissimilar to the way in which Soviet culture was viewed during the GDR, for an atmosphere of over-saturation and dominance has triggered resistance and scepticism. The fact that American influence is not championed by the present German government, however, and that young east Germans do not feel materially superior to their American counterparts, means that their resistance remains less vocal, and clearly has less bearing on their civic loyalties.

In contrast, the European Union is a force which has been actively promoted by the government since 1990, and which provides a potentially important marker of identity. Despite increasing European co-operation, however, and efforts in education to enhance the profile of Europe, there was little genuine enthusiasm for a European community amongst interviewees. Although they all accepted the need for European co-operation, some voiced concern that this should remain limited, fearful that Germany would lose its distinctiveness. More commonly, however, a general indifference and apathy reigned, particularly amongst teenagers, many of whom considered European issues to be too closely linked to the political world: 'I don't have a clue about that [Europe] . . . that's politics isn't it? . . . well, I'm not bothered about that.'[127] This correlates closely with the results of *Jugend 2000*, which found that interest in Europe increased with age and education, and was higher amongst males: aspects which also influenced young people's interest in politics (see the later section in this chapter on political loyalties). Furthermore, the study found that interest in Europe was lower amongst young people in the east, where political apathy was higher, concluding that 'Europe leaves the youth cold'.[128] This is not helped by the frequent emphasis on European political structures in educational materials, which fail to engage young people emotionally or inspire active involvement.[129] It seems that Europe as a political entity is unlikely to provide a ready form of identity for this generation.

Since the introduction of the Euro in January 2002, however, young people have been forced to confront the issue of European integration, and opinions on the new currency reflected an increasing willingness to accept a European identity amongst older interviewees, 70% of whom welcomed the Euro. However, only 35% of the younger age group welcomed this change, once again revealing a strong scepticism towards European structures. Whilst their reticence was partly a result of the lower political interest of teenagers, it is notable that their attachment to the DM was also greater than that of their elders, with twice as many teenagers as young adults stating that they missed (or would miss, depending on the interview date) the DM. As the only currency they could remember (or remember using), it held more emotional value, and as Dirk lamented: 'For me, money was always the western Mark, . . . and when you're supposed to call that [the Euro] money, then I do sometimes have a problem.'[130] Another young interviewee had attached the full set of old DM coins on his keyring out of nostalgia for the old currency and in symbolic resistance to the Euro.[131] In contrast, the large majority of older interviewees claimed that they had not had time to develop a strong emotional attachment to this currency. The fact that they had already undergone one change of currency in 1990 meant that the conversion to Euros was not so traumatic, and any notable resistance was instead caused by the visible increase in prices, as elsewhere in Europe, rather than an overt emotional attachment.

Attitudes towards America and Europe have revealed a grudging acceptance of the western world and Germany's position within it, yet at the same time an ambivalence and, especially amongst younger interviewees, an apathetic stance towards the international political sphere. Western cultures have clearly lost the symbolic status they once held in the GDR, and their omnipresence today has caused a reversal of attitudes amongst many young people, revealing once again how individuals' personal experiences of their immediate surroundings often prove more central in shaping their loyalties than the influence of either past or present education.

From socialist patriotism to xenophobia?

Whilst young people show scepticism towards elements of western culture and politics, surveys reveal that American and western European citizens are consistently viewed more favourably by young people than citizens from the former Soviet bloc, Africa, or other less privileged countries.[132] This trend has caused considerable concern since unification, for the number of cases of xenophobia and right-wing extremism rose dramatically during the 1990s amongst young people in eastern Germany, with 71% of protagonists in Sachsen-Anhalt being under the age of 21 in 1999.[133] The apparent concentration of xenophobic violence in the east has given rise to a number of theories concerning the roots of right-wing extremism in eastern Germany, the majority of which focus either on the socialisation of young people in the GDR, or on situational factors in the present day (see introduction, p. 6). As a result, the ongoing debate has frequently been popularised by the media into an east–west dual, in which the GDR past is effectively defended or demonised. Attention has, however, hitherto centred on the worrying but sensational trend of extremism, which is carried out by only a very small number of protagonists; wider xenophobic tendencies have largely been neglected and, although the two are closely linked, xenophobia need not be extremist in nature.

Studies have shown that xenophobia is not only more evident amongst eastern youth than western youth,[134] but that it has also increased with time. As figure 6 demonstrates, the number of pupils rejecting violence against foreigners in Sachsen-Anhalt rose between 1993 and 2000, yet those who believed the number of foreigners in Germany to be too high also dramatically increased during the same time period, indicating the possible existence of 'latent xenophobia'.[135] Furthermore, in contrast to the west, young eastern citizens, whose socialisation in the GDR was minimal, have revealed higher levels of xenophobia than their elders.[136] Interviewees' comments confirmed this trend, for young adults generally recognised Germany's need for foreigners, yet those ten years younger proved considerably more critical, a number making remarks such as: 'they don't behave properly' or 'they live off the state'.[137] Although xenophobic attitudes existed before the *Wende*, rising levels since 1990, above all amongst young citizens, indicate the presence of influences other than GDR socialisation.

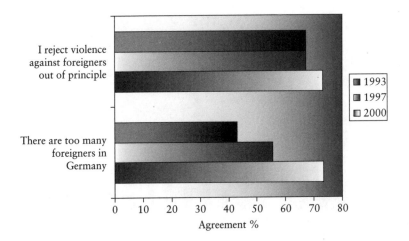

Figure 6 Attitudes towards foreigners amongst 14–15 year olds in Sachsen-Anhalt, 1993–2000

Source: Heinz Hermann Krüger et al., 'Projekt "Jugend und Demokratie in Sachsen-Anhalt" Zwischenbericht' (Martin-Luther-Universität Halle-Wittenberg, 2001), p. 132.

One evident cause of lacking cultural tolerance can be found in the small number of foreigners living in the five new *Länder*, as demonstrated in figure 7. This is clearly a remnant of GDR policy, and although numbers are now higher than they were during the GDR, young people in the east still have considerably less frequent contact with foreigners than their western counterparts.[138] A number of interviewees remarked that they had little or no contact with foreigners, and those who did have foreign friends or colleagues noted the general lack of foreigners in the east to be a hindrance to their integration in society. As one young adult claimed: 'Magdeburg citizens need more [foreigners], in order to think beyond the confines of the border.'[139] This is evidently an important point, yet it is not a new situation, and provides little reason for a worsening of xenophobic attitudes since the *Wende*, thus indicating the significance of other causes.

The single most influential factor to emerge since 1989 is that of education, for xenophobia is noticeably higher amongst young people with lower levels of education.[140] School types such as the *Hauptschule* or *Realschule* thus typically produce greater proportions of pupils with negative attitudes towards foreigners

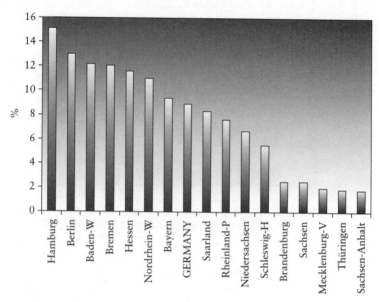

Figure 7 Percentage of foreigners living in Germany and its *Länder*,
31 Dec 2001

Source: Statistisches Bundesamt Deutschland,
http//www.destatis.de/jahrbuch/jahrtab2.htm, accessed on 23 Aug 2003.

than the *Gymnasium*.[141] It seems that this is less a reflection of the education itself but rather of the career prospects and expectations of pupils. Those with lower educational qualifications, for example, frequently experience greater insecurities and lack of orientation than those with a clear path of further education ahead of them. These insecurities are inevitably linked to unemployment, and whilst studies have revealed that unemployed young people do not actually reveal higher levels of xenophobia than those in work or education,[142] it is the fear of unemployment, and thus the perceived threat of losing one's status, or never even attaining one's desired status, which creates insecurity. The majority of interviewees thus recognised Germany's need for foreign workers and their crucial role in carrying out jobs which Germans themselves are unwilling to do. Many instead objected to foreigners who appeared to live off the state, and as Johannes typically stated: 'whoever really lives here and has a normal job is okay.'[143] Such comments were often further qualified: 'as long as they work for their money, and don't live off the "daddy-state" . . . The foreigners, Russians, live in renovated blocks of flats, paid for by the father-state. The Germans live in old buildings. I think that's crap.'[144] Foreigners who appear to gain more privileges than Germans themselves are thus often resented, for the feeling that one is ranked second to foreigners results in a perceived loss of status, especially where insecurity is already high in the east: 'Well, I think the *Ossis* are considered third-rate; first comes the *Wessi*, then the foreigner, and then the *Ossi*.'[145] Resentment towards foreigners thus has as much to do with one's own perceived status within the state as with foreigners themselves.

With the fall of the Wall, young people were clearly confronted with a string of changes, all of which added to personal insecurities. Unlike in the GDR, decisions concerning further education and future careers lay in young people's hands, competition for jobs and places in higher education required a new independence and resilience to which many were unaccustomed, and the arrival of full-blown westernisation overwhelmed many who lay in its path. As Wilhelm Heitmeyer claims in his 'instrumentalisation theory', modern society and individualisation have created a certain 'pressure of self-achievement', resulting in increasingly violent social relations.[146] In this way, other people, often those considered inferior, become 'instrumentalised' or mentally depersonalised into objects for one's own needs and security, a process which ceases only when one feels satisfied with one's own life. Whilst Heitmeyer's study took place in Bielefeld, west Germany, where changing social, industrial and economic structures was a gradual process, eastern Germany experienced such change almost overnight, thus producing heightened reactions. The lack of orientation that some experienced before the *Wende* rapidly multiplied, especially in the personal sphere, where parents' sudden unemployment shook family units, the previous authority of teachers became undermined and local personalities or sometimes even close friends were revealed as informants. It is perhaps no surprise that regions such as Sachsen-Anhalt, which suffered large-scale economic problems and consequent social unrest, have seen election successes for minority parties which promote xenophobic ideals.

Finally, the status of east Germans as a collective group has also radically changed, as eastern Germany, previously seen to be the richest and most successful country in the eastern bloc, suddenly became a poor and needy area, no longer even a country in its own right. Lack of a stable collective identity clearly only compounded personal instabilities, and it is no surprise that comparative east–west studies have noted identity problems in the east, but not in the west.[147] Ulrike was one of several interviewees to recognise this problem: 'I think we are really the problem. We ourselves. As long as we're not completely happy with ourselves . . . then anyone else is, in this sense, disruptive.'[148] Similar comments revealed the direct relationship to foreigners: 'Well, I would slowly close the borders . . . And when we are able to cope here, then we can see.'[149] In the face of personal and collective insecurities, foreigners thus appeared to be threatening and disruptive to the status quo, and the need for a stable individual and collective identity thus often temporarily resulted in the 'instrumentalisation' of foreigners. Whilst xenophobia clearly also exists in the west, and amongst all sectors of society, its high levels in the east since unification point towards the social, financial and psychological effects of the *Wende*.

The rise in xenophobia since unification does not, thus, appear to be a statement of nationalist pride but rather an expression of insecurity and lack of confidence. As in the GDR, it could be argued that it is the very lack of patriotic sentiment in eastern Germany that has prevented the acceptance of cultural difference. Although unification added depth to the problems of xenophobia, it was clearly not the sole cause of the problem, for racial tensions existed prior to the *Wende*. Instead, it acted as a catalyst for a number of processes that had already begun under socialism, exacerbating previous feelings of disorientation and further threatening young people's individual and collective identities. Ironically, it appears that for the majority, personal and localised identities prove more influential in shaping negative attitudes towards foreigners than any national or civic loyalties. Indeed, European surveys have confirmed that, together with the arrival of modern westernised culture and increasing individual insecurities, xenophobia has become a Europe-wide phenomenon.[150] The situation in eastern Germany is clearly neither exceptional, nor primarily a result of socialisation in the GDR, but is simply heightened by the events of recent history.

United yet divided? Social, economic and political trends since the *Wende*

Throughout this chapter, a number of themes have proved recurrent, most notably unemployment, political apathy, shifting personal identities and, above all, east–west tensions. Whilst it was to be expected that unification would arouse greater questions of identity in the east than the west, it is surprising that some elements of a divided mentality appear to have grown. Brunner and Walz, for example, found that east Germans' perceived status as second-class citizens actually increased after 1995.[151] Clearly the optimism which reigned immediately after the fall of the Wall has gradually been dampened by the social and economic conditions in eastern Germany, and whereas 56% of east Germans in 1992 expected that it would take between six and ten years to reach the living standards of west Germany, this was true of only 34% in 1997, by which time 50% believed that it would take more than ten years.[152] Even by 2002, the promises of blossoming landscapes were still to be ful-filled, and many in the east continued to feel neglected and subject to inferior treatment. To what extent, however, is eastern identity based on difference in the present, rather than experiences and memories of the past, and how does it relate to the expression of regional and national identities? This section addresses these ques-tions through the examination of young people's attitudes towards firstly social and economic conditions, secondly cultural develop-ments and thirdly political interest and engagement in contempo-rary society.

Young Ossis: *defined by contemporary social and economic conditions?*

Of all sectors of the population, it was commonly assumed that the young generation would overcome the tensions between east and west most rapidly. Yet in 1998, 56% of young respondents in one survey believed that more separated east and west Germans than united them,[153] and four out of five interviewees in 2001 and 2002 still claimed that Germany was divided along the former border, many typically referring to the west as 'drüben' (over there) – a term used in the GDR. Perceptions of continuing division were also com-monly expressed in stereotyped images. *Wessis* were thus typically described as 'show-offs', and considered to be arrogant and super-ficial, with teenagers' terms of expression being more openly clichéd than those of young adults. Older interviewees thus used expressions such as 'more anonymous', 'act very self-confidently', 'lack warmth', whereas the younger age group described west Germans as 'arro-gant', 'know-it-alls' and 'insincere'. There was little discrepancy, however, in the way that east Germans were viewed, for both cohorts considered them to be genuine, reliable, modest, to value true friendship and to make the best of any situation. It is no surprise that comparisons between east and west thus typically favoured the former.

Young people were clearly aware of the stereotyped nature of these terms, causing many such as Anna to qualify their remarks: 'We also have west German lecturers here, and for me they're not really *Wessis* . . . Anyone who's genuinely open and asks questions and can listen is neither an *Ossi* nor a *Wessi*.'[154] However, interviewees continued to perpetuate common stereotypes, often countering western stereotypes of easterners, such as that of the whinging *Ossi*. The conflicting nature of Benjamin's account proves typical, particularly of the younger age group:

> I still find that east and west are compared quite strongly . . . and in my opinion Germany is one unit, and . . . I'd say that there's no need to draw grand comparisons any more.

> BUT:

> the *Ossis* . . . they will somehow approach you in a much more relaxed fashion, that's what I find, but the *Wessis*, they are so inhibited.[155]

Writing in the *Spiegel*, Stefan Berg suggests that such clichés may simply be self-perpetuating, triggering counter-clichés, and producing little more than a 'contest of phantoms'.[156] On the one hand, the media draws attention to such stereotypes, for differences between east and west have continued to make front-page news in the new millennium, and are successfully marketed by publishing houses such as 'Eulenspiegel'.[157] These inevitably infiltrate popular attitudes, and become perpetuated in the perceptions of the population at large. On the other hand, however, a number of prejudices are founded in real economic and social difference.

The economy, and above all the job market, is a prime cause of tension between east and west, for not only is unemployment higher in the east, but this area has been subject to lower rates of pay in many professions. Furthermore, as a result of the strong GDR emphasis on work as a focal point for identity creation, it has been found that more people in the east look for identity and security in their work, only heightening the effects of unemployment.[158] As shown in table 2, almost one in five young people feared a

Table 2 Young people's concerns in east and west, spring 1991 (selected answers to the question: 'With key words, please say what most depresses you', ages 16–21, in %)

	East	West
Future career	18.1	6.3
Parents' future	15.7	0.3
Unemployment	23.7	4.7
General deterioration of living conditions	17.6	1.7
Problems with national identity	5.9	–
Problems with the society of the Federal Republic	13.9	1.7
Number of respondents	*461*	*364*

Source: Detlef Oesterreich, 'Jugend in der Krise', *APuZG*, B19 (1993), 21–31 (p. 26).

worsening of their living conditions in the east compared to under one in fifty in the west, thus decreasing the likelihood of young easterners displaying attachment or loyalty to their new state. As interviewees revealed, such fears were still strong ten years later, with unemployment continuing to stigmatise eastern Germany as a whole: 'Unemployment is the first thing that comes to mind . . . we're still at the bottom of the heap, like.'[159] As a result, many young easterners have moved to the west, and in 2001 over 18% of school leavers from Sachsen-Anhalt moved to a western *Land* for professional training;[160] by 2001, the area had lost a total of 300,000 people, giving rise to sensationalist headlines such as 'Dramatic migration of young people threatens east Germany' and 'Is Sachsen-Anhalt bleeding to death?'.[161] Whilst those in work experienced more stability, many earned considerably less than their western counterparts, and even in 2001 an employee in the manufacturing industry earned on average one-third less in Sachsen-Anhalt than in neighbouring Niedersachsen.[162] As figure 8 demonstrates, this was true for many professions, particularly for manual workers. Such discrepancies have given rise to widespread discontent, provoking demonstrations in the east,[163] as well as widespread feelings of despondency. As Michael highlighted, this is more than an economic issue, for it reflects on the collective image of east Germans: 'Somehow you have the feeling that if we earn less money in the east for the same work, we're being told we're lazy, unproductive.'[164] The inequality of wages has thus perpetuated

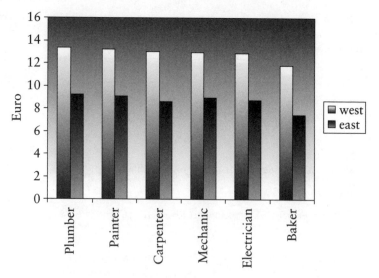

Figure 8 Gross hourly wages for manual workers in east and west
Germany, 2002

Source: Statistisches Bundesamt Deutschland,
www.destatis.de/basis/d/logh/loghtab15.htm, accessed on 31 Aug 2003.

stereotyped images of east and west in much the same way as sensationalist headlines, neither of which help to promote confidence
in a floundering regional economy.

Despite such problems, wealth and economic success remain
markers of pride for many young easterners, accounting for 41% of
all items providing a sense of positive identity for younger interviewees (and 16% for older interviewees). Traditionally a source of
West German pride, however, economic success bears little relevance
to an eastern Germany hampered by unemployment and factory clo-
sures, thus with west German economic standards commonly acting
as a yardstick, it is hardly surprising that this age group finds the
present economic situation in the east to be a major handicap to their
confidence in united Germany. Older interviewees did not place so
much pride in capitalist success, a fact which results partly from their
GDR socialisation. As Anna claimed, for example: 'I didn't see
socialism to be ideal . . . but I also learned enough of socialism not
to find, say, capitalism in the west to be ideal.'[165] Experience of consumer society has also made some older interviewees place greater

retrospective value on certain aspects of GDR society, and as Robert remembered: 'Somehow you had to really save for a tape player, and . . . you were happy about just a little thing back then, you know . . . and today there aren't any little things any more.'[166] Although older interviewees' characterisation of west Germans was less stereotyped than that of teenagers, we see here that their former experiences of life in the GDR did fashion a critical stance towards western culture. Their position is, however, marked by an appreciation of the qualities of eastern society rather than the feeling of neglect which more commonly characterises younger interviewees.

Perceptions of inferiority in the east stemming from economic problems have extended into the social sphere, where the dominance of western culture has caused the marginalisation of eastern interests. This was experienced even by very young citizens, for Katya demonstrated the emergence of a clear *Trotzidentität* at the age of only 12: 'in year 7 we had a teacher who always said "we in the West", and "my pupils over there" could always do things better than us, and we got so completely annoyed . . . that we founded a kind of club for repressed *Ossis*.'[167] The feeling that east German interests were ignored in the unification process was symbolised for many by the decision to unite according to art. 23 of the Basic Law, rather than allowing for a new constitution. Furthermore, political discourse has frequently – if only tacitly – promoted western standards as the norm. As the (east German) *Bundestag* President Wolfgang Thierse said in 2001, for example, when speaking of eastern integration: 'Only the upper third is successfully integrated, and corresponds to the western model of the middle classes.'[168] As a result, some young people felt as if they had been conquered in war, and robbed of their identity, one claiming: 'It would perhaps be good if the east Germans could preserve something like an east German culture, or an east German temperament, but I don't think we can afford to do so, because we're not the ones who can do what we want, we're rather the ones who have to adapt.'[169] A number of older interviewees thus expressed regret that some positive aspects of east German society have become negated, particularly its warmth and friendliness. Paul, for example, made his point using the symbolism of the bread roll:

Well, it's kind of . . . a typical example of the puffed-up self-importance that we have today, in general terms . . . I can still remember well how our relatives from near Dortmund visited us back then, and brought food from their journey with them. . . they had bread rolls, they were really big . . . yeah, enormous bread rolls, and you bit into them, and there was basically nothing. More or less puffed-up, like this showy puffed-up self-importance, that's very, very prevalent today.[170]

In contrast, younger interviewees felt less discrimination based on the qualities of a past community, but rather experienced neglect in the present, some even claiming to feel like foreigners in their own country. Others said they felt exploited and abused by westerners: 'They came over here to get their money, and then went back to the west again, and live there and have good lives.'[171] For both age groups, however, westerners' lack of interest in eastern affairs provided a notable cause of irritation, and many felt that this led to an unjust portrayal of eastern Germany: 'only the negative things in the east are talked about . . . there's hardly a positive piece of news about the east. It's always just rising unemployment, and everyone complains.'[172]

In view of the apparent neglect of eastern German qualities and interests, and the pressure to conform, it is hardly surprising that a large number of young people in the east claim to feel as though they are being treated as 'second-class' citizens (see figure 9). As Brunner and Walz have found, this perceived 'second-class' status has changed in meaning between the early and late 1990s; whereas it was initially a feeling of inadequacy based on historical difference, it has evolved into a sentiment founded on perceived discrimination.[173] Although this was true of both age groups, it was most evident amongst younger interviewees, whose opinions were fashioned to a greater extent by difference in present-day society. As a result, they found it hard to pledge loyalty to a state which they believed primarily represented western interests. Older interviewees, however, who compared old and new regimes more directly, often lamented the way in which the positive aspects of the former were negated by the influence of the latter, yet they were likely to assign their loyalties in a more rational way.

Ostalgie *and cultural expressions of 'easternness'*
Alongside continuing perceptions of division, the expression of *Ostalgie* has motivated a number of cultural phenomena since the early 1990s, from GDR parties to films such as *Sonnenallee* (1999) and *Good Bye Lenin!* (2003), as well as *Ostalgie* websites and TV shows. To what extent, however, is nostalgia for the past expressed

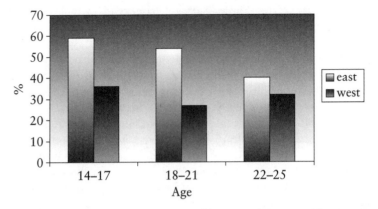

Figure 9 East Germans as 'second-class citizens', Jan–Feb 2001
(agreement with the statement: 'East Germans are treated as "second class
citizens" in Germany')

Source: Forsa, in 'Ost-Jugendliche: DDR war nicht schlecht', *MV*, 8 Feb 2001.

in the everyday lives of teenagers and young adults through cultural
phenomena such as consumer products, pop music and the
Jugendweihe? Does nostalgia manifest itself as a longing for
selected aspects of GDR society that have now disappeared, or
should young people's behaviour be characterised rather as
'pseudo-nostalgia': a response to, or criticism of, an unsatisfactory
present?[174]

Commercial *Ostalgie* has largely been driven by the desire to
recreate former GDR products, many of which were considered
outdated and unattractive in 1990, and were rapidly replaced by
western products. By December 1990, however, 50% of surveyed
households claimed to prefer eastern over western products, a figure
which rose to nearly three-quarters only one year later, and to 82%
by the end of 1993;[175] by 1999, the annual trade fair for eastern
products, 'Ostpro', attracted as many as 63,712 visitors over three
days.[176] The marketing of eastern products suggests that this
growing interest is more than simply an expression of nostalgia, for
although many former GDR products have retained the same name
and a similar form of packaging, few draw directly on their GDR
roots for advertising purposes. Instead, one of two concepts is
usually employed: the (apolitical) sense of 'Heimat', or the (politicised) concept of a 'feeling of easternness'. The former can be seen

with products such as 'Burger Knäcke' crispbreads, which success-fully adopted the slogan 'A crispy piece of Heimat' in 1991, occu-pying 65% of the crispbread market in the east by 1993, yet only 15% in the west.[177] A number of regional products also carry logos marking their origin, and promote themselves with images of green countryside, rolling hills and local landmarks, thus encouraging consumers to identify with their local area.[178] Other brands, however, exploit the emergent sense of easternness in reaction to the dominance of western culture and perceived discrimination. 'Karo' cigarettes, for example, renowned for their strength, were adver-tised in late 1991 under the provocative slogan 'Attacking the taste of unity'; similarly the 'Cabinet' brand was marketed as 'unscented and unadulterated', thus as reliable, down-to-earth cigarettes with none of the show of the west.[179] 'Rondo' coffee also found immedi-ate success after its relaunch in Magdeburg in 1997, bearing a slogan which spoke to the emotions of east Germans: 'Yes, that's exactly how the *Ossi*-heart wants it!'[180] Whilst East German coffee was distinctly inferior to West German brands during GDR times, the success of 'Rondo' today reveals the effective nature of targeted advertising, and the emergence of a contemporary eastern identity in the face of western dominance.

Interviewees revealed considerable support for local products, with 65% of young adults and as many as 83% of teenagers showing some level of loyalty to eastern products. Whilst many recognised this was simply a matter of habit, often influenced by the consumer patterns of their parents, others claimed not to pay attention to the geographical origin of products, yet still smoked 'f6' cigarettes, used 'fit' washing-up liquid and washed their clothes with 'Spee', all produced in the east. In this way, consumer behaviour had become self-perpetuating, based on consumer tra-ditions rather than a political agenda or nostalgia. The majority who claimed to shop consciously for eastern products did so to support the local economy, thereby strengthening its economic position in unified Germany, rather than as a moral stand against the west. The purchase of eastern products is thus less an expres-sion of retrospective nostalgia and instead a way of supporting the interests of one's immediate community. In contrast to claims that this trend proves an obstacle to German unity,[181] it is rather a form of regional identity that can exist alongside loyalty to a united state.

Similar to consumer products, GDR rock music was a poor second to its western equivalent prior to the *Wende*. Although western bands have maintained their popularity in the east since 1990, the fortunes of some eastern bands have changed, a number gaining considerable support in the east. On the one hand, a number of groups such as *Die Puhdys* attract fans who remember its founding years, and whilst the group has written many new songs since 1989, a certain sense of nostalgia is hard to avoid.[182] On the other hand, the music tastes of the young generation are based less on nostalgic instincts, but rather on regional loyalties. The popularity of many eastern groups and singers is thus rooted in post-GDR society, with some having successfully played on the problems experienced by young people in post-*Wende* east Germany. The single 'Deutschland' (2001), by *Die Prinzen*, for example, produced an uproar in the media because of its criticism of German society as arrogant, intolerant and violent.[183] Although the group claimed that their portrayal was ironic, it spoke to a young eastern public whose experiences in unified Germany had often left them feeling despondent. Similarly, Kai Niemann's 2001 single 'Im Osten' ('In the East') addressed issues of contemporary society, provocatively playing on the east–west divide, the opening verse beginning: 'The real experts know/that men in the east kiss better./That girls in the east are prettier/is known to every child today.'[184] With its clear message that 'everything is better than in the west', it topped the east German charts and provoked an unsuccessful western response entitled 'Im Westen' ('In the West'), inevitably becoming the focus of much media attention.[185] Interestingly, it provoked a strong reaction amongst interviewees, who were either in favour of the song, ('really good', 'fun', 'brilliant', 'funny'), or in stark opposition to it ('stupid', 'rubbish', 'awful', 'crap'), with opinion divided into two equal camps across both age groups. Despite the song's exaggerated nature, it clearly offered some point of identification and a means of expressing an element of self-worth, albeit in jest; a couple of interviewees even expressed an element of Schadenfreude that the west German response had been unsuccessful. Others, however, condemned Niemann for deepening the existing divide in society and feared that his song would simply create unnecessary resentment in the west, consequently intensifying the clichés of both halves. Whichever view they adopted, the passion with which young people entered into the debate demonstrated the importance of this theme in their everyday lives. One interviewee described the song as an 'expression of protest, rather an expression of helplessness',[186] perhaps also an apt description of some young people's own reactions to the song. 'Im Osten' thus symbolises the way in which popular music culture in the east has not turned to the events of the past to attract a young following, but rather grasps the sentiments of the present. It also represents the conscious desire to move forward, for although it drew on continuing tensions its very existence pointed towards a new phase in east–west relations: ten years earlier such a hit would have been unthinkable.

Unlike consumer products and popular music, which were guaranteed a more fruitful post-*Wende* future, the *Jugendweihe* potentially faced the same fate as the GDR. By 2000, however, over 60% of all 14 year olds in the east took part, and in some areas, such as Magdeburg, almost 70%.[187] Although the ceremony is now officially independent of party politics and state influence, schools often remain the centres of activity and the ceremony is structurally altered only through the absence of the uniform oath and the GDR national anthem (which has not been replaced with that of the Federal Republic). In contrast to its structure, however, the content of the ritual has radically changed, and in place of compulsory classes on socialist themes voluntary sessions now reflect the interests of young people, from sports events and discos to themed discussions on love, relationships and careers. In the face of criticism that the ceremony has lost all didactic content and become little more than empty nostalgia for a fictitious rosy past, strong popular support for the ceremony has shown that it occupies an important place in post-*Wende* east Germany.[188] To what extent, however, does this reflect a longing for the GDR past, rather than a deeper sense of belonging in the east?

As with the purchase of eastern products, it seems that the perpetuation of the *Jugendweihe* has more to do with cultural norms than with nostalgia for the GDR. Whilst parents may cajole their offspring into taking part because of fond memories of their own *Jugendweihe*, this largely reflects nostalgia for their own childhood rather than for the GDR state. The extent to which this cultural model has become entrenched in the east is, ironically, no better demonstrated than by the attitude of the churches. Faced with low confirmation rates, a number of religious communities in the east have begun to offer an alternative to both the *Jugendweihe* and

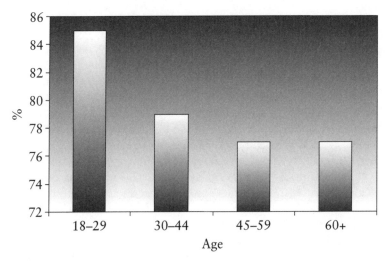

Figure 10 Percentage of east Germans in favour of keeping the *Jugendweihe*, Aug 1995

Source: Allensbacher Jahrbuch der Demoskopie 1993–1997, vol.10:
Demoskopische Entdeckungen, ed. by Elisabeth Noelle-Neumann and Renate
Köcher (Munich: Saur, 1992), p. 587.

confirmation: a coming-of-age ceremony designed to attract young people undecided about their beliefs.[189] Frowned upon by many in the west, this unusual move is only acceptable in the east because of the cultural norm that has emerged over the past decades. Interviewees' comments frequently demonstrated its accepted status: 'It was self-evident that we would participate . . . it's simply part of a young person's life, I think . . . either confirmation, communion or *Jugendweihe*.'[190] Some even believed that it was compulsory: 'Yeah, I'm not religious, I'm atheist, and so I had to, like, take part.'[191] Most who participated, however, spoke of it with fondness and, as an Allensbach survey from 1995 found, it was the youngest generation which was most in favour of its continuance (see figure 10). As in the GDR, the promise of money, gifts and family reunions inevitably forms a prime incentive for teenage participants, yet the ceremony has also regained its function as a public festival, becoming a ritual in which eastern Germans can take pride as their own and value as a source of stability in a society marked by turbulent change.

Jugendweihe ceremonies and preparatory activities have thus frequently been marked by a strong eastern character, particularly in the immediate post-*Wende* years. One songwriter's performance at a ceremony in east Berlin in 1992, for example, included a lesson in West German acronyms, teaching those present the meaning of GmbH (Ltd): 'Gehört meinem Bruder Helmut' (belongs to my brother Helmut).[192] More than a decade later, *Jugendweihe* discussions have continued to focus on the immediate problems of life in the east, such as unemployment and urban renewal, and speeches are often characterised by references to the 'people's revolution' of 1989, stressing the role played by the masses in bringing down the Wall.[193] Furthermore, the local press takes an avid interest in ceremonies, and mayors, politicians and local personalities present teenagers with their certificates, thus welcoming young people into the community of eastern Germany at large. The ritual has thus often created the feeling of a close-knit community in the face of westerners who are perceived as arrogant and lacking understanding, and provided a sense of identity and security to teenagers who may be experiencing the knock-on effect of parents' unemployment or involuntary retraining. Ironically, the collective thus appears to have adopted a similar role to the 'niche' in the GDR, offering an escape from the pressures of everyday life and providing a positive, alternative identity. Whilst this is marked by an eastern character, it is one which is defined according to the tensions of the present-day community rather than the nostalgic pull of the past.

Eastern consumer products, pop music and the *Jugendweihe* have all found renewed popularity as they have adapted to meet the needs of the population. Although some critics, such as Thomas Rausch, claim that the result has been a simple reduction of complexities for many east Germans, in which the west is blamed for all eastern problems,[194] this has rarely been the case for the young generation. Whilst contrast with the west has provided definition in the east, the above examples show that young people's identity is not based solely on the negation of the west but also on the acceptance of cultural norms in the east. These provide the region with a sense of stability and self-worth, forging a new sense of 'easternness' which can exist alongside an all-German identity and a sense of patriotism. Although this eastern identity has often proved stronger than any sense of all-German identity, it is rarely directed against the federal state but rather creates for eastern Germans a specific place within it.

Loyalties in the political arena

Social, economic and cultural divisions in united Germany are naturally reflected in political behaviour and, as in the GDR, the political engagement of young people is considered central to the state's future. Political education has thus remained a compulsory part of the school curriculum, yet in contrast to the ideologically sated *Staatsbürgerkunde* today's *Sozialkunde* aims to encourage the political responsibility of the individual and promote democracy.[195] Revised teaching methods thus reflect a more democratic learning process, in the hope that young people will feel greater social responsibility and inclusion. Outside school, attempts to involve young people actively in local and regional politics have been notable: the age of voting in Sachsen-Anhalt was lowered to 16 for local elections (one of five *Länder* – three western, two eastern – to do so), pupils' elections were organised to coincide with *Bundestag* elections,[196] and in 1997, an annual 'youth parliament' was introduced, inviting 'parties' from different schools to discuss youth issues and concerns with ministers.[197] Election campaigns also attempted to promote the participation of young voters, from the nationwide initiative of 2001 which promoted the slogan 'I'm making politics',[198] to a more eye-catching regional poster campaign in 2002, which pictured a row of toilet rolls, under which the slogan read: 'You have to give a shit.'[199] In an area which continues to suffer from economic hardship and social deprivation, the need to encourage young people to participate actively in the political development of their environment bears all the more weight, for those who face uncertain futures are more likely to show dissatisfaction with the political system of united Germany.[200]

In view of an increase in both political apathy and extremism, it seems that such initiatives met with limited success. Whilst the *Wende* continued to inspire an interest in politics amongst young east Germans during the early 1990s, with interest levels surpassing those in the west,[201] this trend was reversed in the later half of the decade, with only 35% of young people in the east and 45% in the west declaring an interest in politics in 1999 (compared to 50% and 46%, respectively, in 1996).[202] Disillusionment in the east was evident as early as the *Bundestag* elections of 1994, when turnout rates in all five eastern *Länder* lagged behind those in the west,[203] and in the regional elections of the same year the lowest participation rate was to be found amongst the under-30s, at 35% in

Sachsen-Anhalt.[204] These statistics correlate with reports from *Jugendweihe* organisers and teachers that enthusiasm for political activities was minimal, and that school elections even witnessed a low turnout.[205] As one headteacher in Sachsen-Anhalt stated: 'if the pupils themselves were to define the term *Sozialkunde*, they would . . . say "anything but politics!" '[206] This sense of political apathy stems primarily from young people's distrust of the party system, for surveys have not only revealed that eastern youth show lower levels of confidence in political institutions than western youth, but also considerably less trust in established political institutions and parties than groups such as citizens' movements and Greenpeace.[207] This mistrust relates primarily to young people's immediate environment, for many interviewees, especially teenagers, expressed concern that little was being done to provide adequate youth facilities in their area. As one young unemployed reader of the *Magdeburger Volksstimme* explained: 'Politics is taking the wrong path. They'd be better putting money into jobs and attracting investors . . . soon, when all the young people have left, there will have to be a sign at the state boundary: "You are entering the old people's home of Sachsen-Anhalt".'[208] Few thus appear willing to support a political system which offers them little, and as one group of teenagers, who were disappointed not to gain support from the town council for their youth club, stated: 'It's always claimed that the youth are disenchanted with politics. But we have the feeling that politicians are disenchanted with the youth.'[209] Similar sentiments were expressed by interviewees, and only a matter of weeks before the local elections of 2002 many lamented the fact that no parties represented their views. A large number in fact showed indifference towards the different policies of parties, believing that a change of government would change little in reality: 'for us at the grass roots . . . nothing ever changes. Whether they're called Schröder, Kohl, Waigel, whoever's up there in the government, nothing ever basically changes for us . . .'[210] As a result, a feeling of impotence prevailed, and many decided not to vote: 'my vote wouldn't count anyway, as one single one.'[211]

Mistrust of politicians also appears to be grounded in scepticism towards the political system as a whole, with few young easterners expressing satisfaction with democracy as it is practised in Germany.[212] This appears to find different roots amongst the two generations. Firstly, teenagers' frequently sketchy understanding of democracy gave rise to misconceptions concerning the political system. Benjamin, for example, claimed not to vote, as he found frequent changes of leadership disruptive: 'it should somehow be the same person for a longer period, that would be more correct.'[213] Patrick voiced similar discontent and concern over too much plurality: 'Even just all the different opinions . . . between left and right, all the parties . . . they should make one party for everyone, I'd find that much better.'[214] Whilst it should be noted that these were the views of teenagers with lower than average levels of education, the study 'Youth and Democracy in Sachsen-Anhalt' also reveals a widespread misunderstanding of democracy, finding that 69.2% of pupils agreed with the statement 'the opposition should not criticise the government, but support it'.[215] This failure to grasp the basic principles of democracy results largely from limited interest amongst younger age groups,[216] and the perception that the political sphere is reserved for adults. Schools clearly still have far to go in involving and engaging pupils, for without being able to trust or understand the basic functioning of their state these young people are unable to display fundamental civic loyalties.

In contrast to many teenagers, older interviewees held a firmer grasp of the concept of democracy, yet they remained critical of the contemporary system, often as a result of their experiences of the GDR. Johannes, for example, lamented the fact that all elements of the former system had been jettisoned in exchange for widespread freedoms, some of which do not compensate for the loss of some basic principles.[217] Eva, on the other hand, found the lack of change in the political world to be disheartening: 'You have to find contentment just for yourself, because it's no use, you won't get anywhere if you want to change the big things . . . we didn't manage it in the GDR . . . you have to provide for yourself, and then be happy with this.'[218] Despite the opposing perspectives of these two views, both displayed a scepticism towards the present political system which was based not on a lack of knowledge, but rather on experience of the GDR.

Despite the different causes of scepticism amongst teenagers and young adults, the apathy of both groups was an expression of distance to the political machinery of Germany, and thus the realisation of politics in their own sphere of influence, rather than the concept of democracy itself. Despite the radical changes since 1990, and the plurality of today's system, this situation bears resemblance

Table 3 Voting patterns of 18–24 year olds in the 1998 *Bundestag* elections (%)

	Western Germany		Eastern Germany	
	Total	Young voters	Total	Young voters
SPD	42.3	37.3	35.2	27.8
CDU/CSU	37.0	31.4	27.4	21.3
FDP	6.9	6.7	3.3	5.4
PDS	1.2	2.4	21.5	**21.7**
B90/Grüne	7.3	11.5	4.0	5.7
DVU, NPD, REP	2.9	6.0	5.0	**12.7**
Other	2.4	4.7	3.6	5.4

Source: Infratest dimap 1998, cited by Hans-Peter Kuhn, 'Jungwähler und die Bundestagswahl 1998', in Hans-Peter Kuhn, Karin Weiss and Hans Oswald, *Jugendliche Wähler in den neuen Bundesländern: Eine Langsschinttstudie zum Verhalten von Erstwählern bei der Bundestagswahl 1998* (Opladen: Leske & Budrich, p. 82.

to that witnessed in the GDR, where the ideal of socialism retained respect, yet political practices did not (see chapter 2). In both cases, young people's individual experiences of their own past and present hold most influence over their acceptance of the system in which they live, rather than formal education in either system.

Frustration with the larger established political parties has not only led to apathy, but also created very fickle political loyalties amongst young people, who are more frequently drawn to smaller fringe parties.[219] In the 1998 national elections, for example, the political extremes gained a large percentage of young eastern voters' loyalty (see table 3), and in 2002 in Sachsen-Anhalt the two largest parties (the CDU and SPD) received least support from young voters.[220] It is primarily support for the extreme right which causes widespread concern, and the DVU's 1998 election success of 12.9% in the Sachsen-Anhalt regional elections drew considerable attention towards the phenomenon of right-wing extremism amongst young people, for 32% of young (aged 18–24) males' votes went to this party.[221] Supporters of this party were more likely to have lower levels of education, to discuss political affairs with their peers rather than their parents and to feel greater economic deprivation than average.[222] Furthermore, 75% of DVU voters claimed to have little or no confidence in the way democracy functioned in Germany,[223] and large fluctuations in support for the party have suggested the influence of passing trends, rather than a strong core of activists. It would thus seem that a large number of DVU votes constituted protest votes in reaction to social and economic circumstances, rather than reflecting deep-rooted beliefs in right-wing politics. Clearly this was a specific type of protest vote, for supporters also revealed more nationalistic, xenophobic and authoritarian characteristics than average,[224] and consequently ethnic loyalty rather than civic pride. As seen earlier in this chapter, however, such characteristics have also resulted largely from the turbulent changes in the east, rather than directly from socialist education, and the fact that support for this party was strongest amongst young voters with little memory of the GDR, who relied on the peer group rather than the parental home for advice, suggests that this protest vote had little to do with GDR socialisation.

In contrast to the DVU, which saw a sharp rise and fall in popularity during and after 1998, the PDS maintained relatively constant levels of support in regional elections, attaining approximately 20% in the Sachsen-Anhalt elections of 1994, 1998 and 2002. PDS supporters were also revealed as the most loyal of all party supporters, and the party regularly attracted an above-average proportion of young voters during this period.[225] Similar to right-wing supporters, however, PDS sympathisers also expressed discontent with the current political, economic and social development of Germany, with 50% describing themselves as 'losers' from unification, and as many as 79% claiming to have little or no confidence in the way in which democracy was realised.[226] Yet interestingly, young supporters could not be identified according to their social status or levels of education,[227] and they regularly talked about political issues with their parents; whilst they advocated socialism, they distanced themselves from all forms of authoritarian behaviour.[228] The fact that a variety of social strata was represented indicated that social deprivation was not the primary motivation for PDS support; whilst many felt they were losers from unification, this would appear to be a reference to their identification with the state rather than their direct living circumstances. The election campaigns of the PDS demonstrated this very point, for they played on the loss of identity and feelings of discrimination amongst the eastern German population. Its 1994 election posters, for example, simply read 'We', referring to 'We *Ossis*',[229] and in more recent years the party has used the adverse reception of other party campaigns (using slogans such as 'red socks' and 'red hands') to advertise itself as a credible alternative in the east.[230] In this way, it claims to represent the interests of a group which feels stigmatised and misunderstood by the west. PDS votes could thus be understood as a protest against the west and western democracy and, as one *Spiegel* reporter polemically noted, this has achieved some success, for 20% PDS has frequently caused more consternation in the west than 20% unemployment.[231] Constant levels of support, even amongst a young generation which has few memories of socialism, thus reflects the need of a considerable sector of east German society to create for itself a stable and viable alternative identity. As in the cultural sphere, there is no reason why this identity may not exist alongside a sense of patriotism for the German state, yet the perception of many PDS voters that the German state is dominated by western forces has frequently prevented the comfortable co-existence of these loyalties.

Whilst it must not be forgotten that some young people were actively involved in promoting democratic politics in the post-*Wende* years, this active core remained a small minority.[232] Instead, the majority appeared disillusioned with traditional party politics and, as in the GDR, the masses retreated into a state of apathy. Young people who felt the need to protest rather than remain silent chose to support parties on the political fringes, where ideology was often not the deciding factor for their loyalty. One young right-wing supporter demonstrated this phenomenon: 'Socialism isn't right-wing, but all the same I could have lived with it, perhaps lived better. There you always had safety and security, at school, everywhere. For this reason I would vote PDS, despite its left-wing content, but only when all of the wrongs committed by the SED are gone.'[233] As in the GDR, the far left and extreme right share similar features, most notably the desire to overturn the nature of contemporary political structures. Along with the apathetic masses, their experiences of life in unified Germany have created a distrust and suspicion of the political system, proving more influential than official efforts to engage young people with their state. As a result, political participation, one of the fundamental principles of patriotic loyalty, has lacked widespread support in the east.

Conclusion

Whilst young east Germans have rapidly adapted to western lifestyles in Germany, many maintain a critical stance towards the

Table 4 The national identification of 14–18 year olds in
Sachsen-Anhalt, 2000 (%)

	I feel myself to be a. . .	
	Federal citizen	German
Not at all true	10.3	4.1
Not really true	25.9	7.3
Fairly true	42.0	28.9
Completely true	21.7	59.7

Source: Nicolle Pfaff: 'Auswertung aus dem Projekt "Jugend und Demokratie in Sachsen-Anhalt" ' Martin-Luther-Universität Halle-Wittenberg, unpublished report provided in private correspondence, 13 Jun 2002, p. 9.

society of united Germany through their political behaviour and support of 'eastern' values. As *Jugend 2000* states, young Germans are far from displaying a euphoric 'hurrah patriotism', and those in the east demonstrate greater distance from the German state than their western compatriots.[234] These results doubtless reflect the real and perceived discrimination and deprivation experienced in the east, for those with poorer education and low social status hold the most critical attitudes.[235] Discontent is, however, frequently directed towards the political and social system, rather than the concept of Germany as a historical and cultural nation. In this respect, the results of the study 'Youth and Democracy' shown in table 4 are revealing. Although 'federal citizens' and 'Germans' inhabit the same geographical area, the former identity, which is essentially weighted in political meaning and indicative of civic loyalty, proves less popular amongst young people in Sachsen-Anhalt. Interestingly, parallels to the later GDR years can be identified here, when the choice of 'German' over 'GDR citizen' also proved popular amongst young people (see chapter 2).[236] Although identification with one's status as 'German' is not detrimental to the values of patriotism today (as it was to the ideal of socialist patriotism), this alone cannot provide the basis of patriotic loyalty to the federal state.

For those who were old enough to consciously experience the *Wende*, a distanced attitude towards the FRG often developed during the initial phases of transition. Erich remembered how he refused to sing the national anthem of the FRG shortly after unification, finding the changes all too sudden: 'For me it was somehow unbelievable, just as unbelievable as, uh, former NVA soldiers, who just, like, put on a different coat.'[237] The memories of this older age group are undoubtedly important in moulding their perceptions of post-*Wende* Germany, and when asked to name key words to describe the FRG, about a quarter of all named items referred to concepts connected to freedom (freedom to travel, freedom of speech, free elections and plurality), clearly in contrast to the nature of the GDR regime. The second largest category of key words, however, was connected to greed, superficial behaviour and egoism, once again in contrast to the frequently mentioned concept of solidarity in the GDR. Whilst personal experience of the limitations of the GDR thus enforced this age group's recognition of the benefits of the present system, these were often compromised by positive memories of the GDR. In contrast, teenagers' descriptions of contemporary Germany were rarely based on comparisons with the GDR. This age group in fact found it difficult to name any key words to describe the FRG, for unified Germany simply represented the 'norm', and without a clear point of comparison, they found it hard to characterise their country. Many thus took today's political system for granted, and as a result concepts of freedom featured less prominently. On the other hand, unemployment and unequal rates of pay were more frequently mentioned by this age group, demonstrating that their perception of the contemporary state was based primarily on their experiences in contemporary society rather than historical comparison.

Distanced attitudes towards politically defined territories have also been witnessed on a regional level. In Sachsen-Anhalt, for example, there have been numerous attempts to foreground regional identity, yet a proposal in 2000 that eastern Germany should be divided into two *Länder*, thus dividing Sachsen-Anhalt in half, was supported by as many as 43.6% of respondents to a survey in the *Magdeburger Volksstimme*.[238] Many in northern parts of the *Land* claimed to feel more loyalty to neighbouring regions, some regarding the Altmark as belonging to Brandenburg, and the Harz to Niedersachsen. Similar attitudes were reflected in interviewees' comments, for only a quarter claimed to identify with Sachsen-Anhalt, and as many as half found no identity in the region at all. This stems not only from Sachsen-Anhalt's lack of historical unity but also from its evident economic and social difficulties, with many young people leaving to seek work elsewhere, thus perpetuating its

Table 5 Identification of 18–27 year olds in Sachsen-Anhalt, 1998 (%)

Attachment to. . .	Strongly attached		Quite attached		Barely attached		Not at all attached	
	18–21	22–27	18–21	22–27	18–21	22–27	18–21	22–27
Community/ town/ municipal district	24	31	40	37	28	26	7	5
Sachsen-Anhalt	11	13	35	33	44	44	8	9
East Germany	24	28	40	40	26	27	7	4
Federal Republic	11	11	36	36	39	40	13	10

Source: Einstellungen und Handlungsorientierungen von Jugendlichen und jungen Erwachsenen in Sachsen-Anhalt (Magdeburg: Ministerium für Arbeit, Frauen, Gesundheit and Soziales der Landes Sachsen Anhalt, 1998, p. 28.

negative image. In contrast, however, interviewees identified strongly with their immediate surroundings, for familiarity with their locality, as well as the presence of family and friends, offered them a sense of positive identity. Consequently, thirty-four out of forty-three interviewees claimed that they would not leave the area, or would do so only if forced to find work elsewhere.[239] This sense of local loyalty came to the fore in 2001, when the Magdeburg handball team won the European cup, and 20,000 people celebrated in the market square.[240] More significantly, however, one player's criticisms of Magdeburg on a popular TV chat show provoked many residents, including young people, vehemently to defend their town, not wanting to see its name discredited.[241] As in the northern parts of Sachsen-Anhalt, a localised identity in Magdeburg proved much closer to the hearts of young people than the larger administrative region.

The identification of young people with areas considered less political in nature was confirmed by a survey carried out in 1998, which revealed that the entities offering the strongest identities to young people were their immediate local surroundings and eastern Germany as a whole (see table 5). Interviewees' comments frequently revealed an overlap between these two areas, for in contrast to the two 'administrative' entities of Sachsen-Anhalt and the FRG, which represent the civic state, eastern Germany and the locality both offered a strong emotional identity. Whilst this was often predicated on personal relationships, cultural and sporting achievements also proved important, as demonstrated by Frank's comment concerning the handball team's victory in Magdeburg: 'Of course you can identify with this a bit, you are also happy when a club from east Germany achieves success in Europe and also Germany as a whole, yeah. Last year they became handball champions, that was definitely important for the acceptance of east Germans, for the self-confidence of east Germans.'[242] A victory for Magdeburg was thus considered a victory for eastern Germany as a whole, demonstrating the overlap between a specific local identity and a broader eastern identity, the former representing the interests of the latter as a region and extending far beyond the world of sport. Interestingly, this phenomenon was lacking in GDR sport, where loyalties were aligned rather with West German teams, in clear opposition to the official sporting interests of the socialist state. Only since sport has become depoliticised and freed from its association with the SED have young people thus felt able to turn to it as a form of identification.

Whilst the interests of both 'apolitical' geographical areas appear to overlap, the smaller locality proves more accessible to young people, and is free from the political agenda that is often perceived to characterise an eastern German identity. For this reason, 75% of older interviewees and 65% of the younger group rejected the term *Ossi* to describe themselves, regarding it to be too polemic. A large number in both age groups, however, still felt drawn to eastern Germany as a whole: 'Ossi? No, I'm a human being! . . . Okay, yeah, I come from the east, and I stand by that, but I would never say from the start that I'm an "Ossi".'[243] Whilst a stereotypical eastern identity was commonly rejected, affinity with the east often presented itself through the expression of local identities which were considered less politically laden, and thus more acceptable to the young generation. A similar stance could be seen on a supranational level, for many teenagers appeared reticent towards Europe as a political union, and failed to see it as a marker of identity. Interestingly, however, a number instead identified with their status as world citizens: 'I feel like an "earthling". . . because we all live on the earth . . . there aren't really any true borders anywhere'; 'I think I mainly identify myself as a human being . . . not as a German, not as an Irishman, not as European, but as a human being.'[244] Although this identity is not geographically limited, it bears similarity with the expression of local and east German identities, for none is based on set political boundaries, but is rather founded on a common set of accepted morals, in this case those of humanity.

The interplay of historical, social, political and geographical loyalties demonstrates the complex nature of identity formation in post-*Wende* Germany. Whilst some identities appear to conflict in interest, it is clear that none can exist independently, for each complements or contrasts the other. As Markus stated:

> I'm definitely European, but I'm just as equally German. 'Sachsen-Anhalter', this term is perhaps a little difficult, but I am someone here from central Germany, and deep down I'm perhaps also a 'Naumburger' . . . I am also a Catholic Christian, and find another group there. But just European, that wouldn't be enough for me. Just German would also be too little.[245]

Some identities and loyalties are clearly stronger than others, each shifting in importance according to an individual's personal experiences in the past and present. Whilst young adults' knowledge of GDR society provided both positive and negative comparisons to today's system, teenagers frequently drew on western Germany as a point of comparison, creating a more bi-polar vision of the 'united' German state. The survival of an eastern identity thus appears to have little to do with memory of the GDR, but rather with the economic, social and political climate of the east and, as the example of Sachsen-Anhalt demonstrates, experiences on a local level largely dictate the expression of civic loyalties. To a certain extent, distance amongst today's eastern youth towards the FRG can thus be equated with their elders' former lack of attachment to the GDR regime. Patriotism, a concept which still colours political rhetoric and educational policies, rarely appears present in the attitudes and behaviour of young people, for it is frequently undermined by developments within the personal sphere. As in the GDR, the attitudes of young people demonstrate that patriotism and civic unity cannot be imposed from above, but are instead formed through personal experiences on the local level.

Notes

1 *Verfassung des Landes Sachsen-Anhalt vom 16 Juli 1992* (Magdeburg: Landeszentrale für politische Bildung Sachsen-Anhalt, 2000), art. 27.1, p. 17.

2 E.g. *Allensbacher Jahrbuch der Demoskopie 1993–1997*, vol. 10: Demoskopische Entdeckungen, ed. by Elisabeth Noelle-Neumann and Renate Köcher (Munich: Saur, 1997), p. 497; *Jugend 2000*, pp. 283–303; Elmar Brähler and Horst Eberhard Richter, 'Deutsche – zehn Jahre nach der Wende'; 'Stolz aufs eigene Leben', *Der Spiegel*, 27 (1995), 40–64.

3 Der Bundeswahlleiter, 'Bundestagswahl 1998 – Ergebnisse nach Ländern', www.bundeswahlleiter.e/wahlen/ergeb98/d/lanu.htm, accessed on 30 Aug 2005.

4 Everhard Holtmann and Bernhard Boll, *Sachsen-Anhalt: Eine politische Landeskunde* (Magdeburg: Landeszentrale für politische Bildung des Landes Sachsen-Anhalt, 1997), p. 52.

5 Der Bundeswahlleiter, 'Bundestagswahlen', www.bundeswahlleiter.de/wahlen/btw98/btwahl_btw98.htm, accessed on 30 Aug 2005.

6 Rosalind M.O. Pritchard, 'Education Transformed? The East German School System since the *Wende*', *GP*, 7/3 (1998), 126–46 (p. 136).

7 Kultusministerium des Landes Sachsen-Anhalt, Pressemitteilung Nr 128/02, Magdeburg, Oct 2002, www1.sachsen-anhalt.de/presseapp/data/mk/2002/128_2002.htm, accessed on 21 Aug 2003.

8 *Neunter Jugendbericht: Bericht über die Situation der Kinder und Jugendlichen und die Entwicklung der Jugendhilfe in den neuen Bundesländern*, Deutscher Bundestag, 13 Wahlperiode, 9 Dec 1994, Drs. 13/70, p. 122.

9 *Ibid.*, p. 481.

10 *Ibid.*, p. 442.

11 Such as the *Kinder- und Jugendring Magdeburg e.V.* (KIJUMA), to which nineteen youth organisations belonged in 2000.

12 *Neunter Jugendbericht*, p. 444.

13 *Schulgesetz des Landes Sachsen-Anhalt in der Fassung vom 27. August 1996* (Magdeburg: Kultusministerium des Landes Sachsen-Anhalt, Mar 2003), art. 1.2, pp. 10–11.

14 Daniel Jonah Goldhagen, *Hitler's Willing Executioners: Ordinary Germans and The Holocaust* (London: Little, Brown, 1996). For further detail on all debates, see Bill Niven, *Facing the Nazi Past: United Germany and the Legacy of the Third Reich* (London: Routledge, 2001).

15 'Gemeinsam akzeptiertes DDR-Bild', *MV*, 22 Mar 1999, p. 1.

16 E.g. *Zeiten und Menschen B4* (Paderborn: Schöningh, 1978), p. 198; see also Rosalind M.O. Pritchard, *Reconstructing Education: East German Schools and Universities after Unification* (New York, Oxford: Berghahn, 1999), p. 69.

17 Val D. Rust, 'Transformation of History Instruction in East German Schools', *Compare*, 23/3 (1993), 205–17, p. 213; 'Dick sind sie und teuer, aber gut', *JW*, 25 May 1990, p. 5.

18 E.g. Joachim Hoffmann and Wolfgang Hug, *Geschichtliche Weltkunde, Klasse 10* (Frankfurt am Main: Diesterweg, 1991), pp. 117–38.

19 Peter Maser, 'Die Gesellschaft der DDR im Spiegelbild aktueller Schulbücher', in *Geschichte der DDR und deutsche Einheit*, Studien zu Politik und Wissenschaft, ed. by Günter Buchstab (Schwalbach: Wochenschau Verlag, 1999), pp. 122–59 (153).

20 *Geschichtsbuch 4: Die Menschen und ihre Geschichte in Darstellungen und Dokumenten*, ed. by Bernd Müller *et al.* (Berlin: Cornelsen, 1996), p. 238.

21 E.g. *Politik, Wirtschaft, Gesellschaft*, edn A, ed. by Dieter Grosser and Stephan Bierling (Braunschweig: Westermann, 1997), p. 185; *Bildungspolitische Information Nr 4.: Die inhaltliche Reform der Schule: Rahmenrichtlinien* (Magdeburg: Kultusministerium des Landes Sachsen-Anhalt, Jan 1992), p. 11.

22 'Gauck-Behörde: Über DDR-Unrecht wird in der Schule kaum gesprochen', *MV*, 3 Jul 2001, p. 1.

23 'Sächsische Schüler lernen ein anderes Deutschland kennen als Sachsen-Anhalter', *MV*, 27 Sep 1996.

24 'Vereinbarung soll Lehrer unterstützen', *MV*, 25 Aug 2001; *Rahmenrichtlinien Gymnasium/Fachgymnasium* (Magdeburg: Kultusministerium des Landes Sachsen-Anhalt, 1999), pp. 62, 68; *Rahmenrichtlinien Sekundarschule: Schuljahrgänge 7–10* (Magdeburg: Kultusministerium des Landes Sachsen-Anhalt, 1999), pp. 56, 60.

25 E.g. Patricia Block, Christian John and Regina Malskies, *Einmal im Leben! Ein Elternratgeber zur JugendFEIER/Jugendweihe* (Berlin: Humanistischer Verband Deutschlands, Landesverband Berlin, 2001), pp. 21–6; Humanistischer Verband Deutschlands (ed.), *Zwischen Nicht mehr und Noch nicht* (Berlin: Reschke und Partner, 2000), pp. 110–13.

26 E.g. Marianne Birthler, in 'Vereinbarung soll Lehrer unterstützen', *MV*, 25 Aug 2001; 'Gauck-Behörde: über DDR-Unrecht wird in der Schule kaum gesprochen', *MV*, 3 Jul 2001; Jörg-Dieter Gauger, 'Der Einigungsprozeß in Geschichts- und Politikbüchern', in *Geschichte der DDR und deutsche Einheit*, pp. 199–239 (236–7).

27 See Udo Margedant and Bernhard Marquardt, 'Partei und Herrschaft', in *Geschichte der DDR und deutsche Einheit*, pp. 67–121 (116–17).

28 *Rahmenrichtlinien Gymnasium/Fachgymnasium*, pp. 69, 115; *Geschichtsbuch 4 . . .*, p. 249.

29 Gauger, 'Der Einigungsprozeß in Geschichts- und Politikbüchern', p. 237.

30 Matthias Arning, 'Wenn sich junge Enkel alte Nazis als Außerirdische vorstellen', *Frankfurter Rundschau (FR)*, 26 Jan 2002.

31 *Allensbacher Jahrbuch der Demoskopie 1993–1997*, p. 516.
32 *Ibid.*, p. 518.
33 'Naumann: "Ohne Erinnerung sind wir verloren"', *MV*, 10 Mar 2000.
34 See also *Jugend 2000*, p. 315.
35 Frank, 30, 6/4/02 and Erich, 27, 25/9/01. In contrast, according to a *Spiegel* survey of 2001, 60% of Germans (of all ages), felt neither guilt nor responsibility for such crimes. See Gerhard Spörl, 'Die Kraft des Grauens', *Der Spiegel*, 19 (2001), 58–61 (p. 61).
36 Erich, 27, 25/9/01.
37 Kassandra, 18, 2/4/02; Daniela, 31, 4/4/02.
38 Mathias, 20, 3/4/02.
39 Antje, 29, 6/4/02.
40 Simone, 27, 13/4/02. Similar attitudes in: 'Naumann: "Ohne Erinnerung sind wir verloren"'; Irina Repke, 'Ganz rüde Anmache', *Der Spiegel*, 12 (2003), 46.
41 Katharina, 31, 15/4/02.
42 Robert, 28, 25/9/01; Jens, 27, 25/9/01.
43 Simone, 27, 13/4/02.
44 See Harald Welzer, Sabine Moller and Karoline Tschuggnall, *Opa war kein Nazi: Nationalsozialismus und Holocaust im Familiengedächtnis* (Frankfurt am Main: Fischer, 2002); 'Bei uns waren sie immer dagegen', *FR*, 6 Jan 2001, p. 7.
45 'Rollerblades und Pittiplatsch', *Der Spiegel*, 36 (1995), 138.
46 E.g. Detlef Oesterreich, 'Verzerrte Bilder (I)', *DJ*, 6 (1994), 272–81 (p. 274).
47 Bodo von Borries, *Das Geschichtsbewußtsein Jugendlicher* (Weinheim, Munich: Juventa, 1995), pp. 80–2. Emphasis in original.
48 *Allensbacher Jahrbuch der Demoskopie 1993–1997*, p. 583.
49 Barbara, 30, 9/4/02.
50 Katya, 18, 22/9/01.
51 'Stolz aufs eigene Leben', *Der Spiegel*, 27 (1995), 40–52 (p. 49).
52 Detlef Oesterreich, 'Verzerrte Bilder (II)', *DJ*, 7–8 (1994), 342–50 (p. 349).
53 Borries, *Das Geschichtsbewußtsein Jugendlicher*, pp. 351–2.
54 Henryk M. Broder, 'Wir lieben die Heimat', *Der Spiegel*, 27 (1995), 54–64 (p. 64).
55 See also 'Stolz aufs eigene Leben', *Der Spiegel*, 27 (1995), 40–52 (pp. 42–6).
56 Karin, 27, 24/9/01.
57 Paul, 27, 25/9/01.
58 Anna, 31, 10/4/02.
59 Johannes, 31, 23/9/01; Birgit, 30, 5/4/02; Anna, 31, 10/4/02.

60 *Allensbacher Jahrbuch der Demoskopie 1993–1997*, p. 504.
61 Antje, 29, 6/4/02.
62 Kassandra, 18, 2/4/02.
63 E.g. Benjamin, 19, 9/4/02.
64 Thorsten, 17, 8/4/02.
65 Annette, 18, 19/9/01.
66 E.g. Dirk, 17, 28/3/02.
67 Karl, 19, 9/4/02.
68 Karl, 19, 9/4/02; Patrick, 20, 9/4/02.
69 Mathias, 21, 3/4/02; Benjamin, 19, 9/4/02.
70 See Bernd Okun, 'Distanz, Enttäuschung, Haß', *Der Spiegel*, 32 (1992), 30–7 (p. 36); Stefan Berg, Florian Gless, Horand Knaup *et al.*, 'Das rote Gespenst', *Der Spiegel*, 10 (1999), 22–33 (p. 27).
71 Daniel, 18, 9/4/02; similarly Simon, 20, 9/4/02; Benjamin, 19, 9/4/02.
72 Dirk, 17, 28/3/02.
73 *Bildungspolitische Information Nr 4 . . .*, p. 11.
74 E.g. 'Spannende Geschichtsreise führte zu Bruno Thiem', *MV*, 21 May 1996; 'Schüler legten am Francke-Denkmal Blumen nieder', *MV*, 25 May 2001.
75 *Armee der Einheit 1990–2000* (Bonn: Bundesministerium der Verteidigung, Sep 2000), pp. 10–11.
76 *Jugend, Bundeswehr und deutsche Einheit Beitrag zum 9. Jugendbericht der Bundesregierung*, ed. by Heinz-Ulrich Kohr *et al.* (Munich: SOWI, 1993), p. 9.
77 *Bundeswehr heute* (Bonn: Bundesministerium der Verteidigung, Jul 1999), pp. 59–60.
78 *Ibid.*, p. 16.
79 Ulrike C. Wasmuht, Ina Plath and Eva Volke, *Sicherheitspolitik und Bundeswehr im Schulunterricht* (Strausberg: SOWI, Aug 1997), pp. 110–36.
80 Heinz-Ulrich Kohr, *Wertewandel, Sicherheitsverständnis und Sicherungsfunktionen der Bundeswehr* (Munich: SOWI, Jan 1992), p. 8.
81 Eva Volke, *Jugendliche Trendsetter und ihre Einstellungen zum Wehr- und Zivildienst* (Strausberg: SOWI, 1996), p. 12.
82 Birgit, 30, 5/4/02.
83 *Soldatengesetz*, art. 9.2, 1 Jan 2002, www.wehrpflichtrecht.de/normen/sg.html, accessed on 9 Sep 2003.
84 Kohr *et al.*, *Jugend, Bundeswehr und deutsche Einheit*, p. 28.
85 See Volke, *Jugendliche Trendsetter und ihre Einstellungen*, pp. 25–7; Heinz-Jürgen Ebenrett *et al.*, *Lagebild 'Jugend heute'* (Strausberg: SOWI, Feb 2001), pp. 177–9.
86 Karl, 19, 9/4/02.

87 Young man cited in Sabine Collmer and Georg-Maria Meyer, *Früher 'zur Fahne' – heute 'zum Bund' – soziale Deutungsmuster von wehrpflichtigen Soldaten aus den neuen Bundesländern* (Munich: SOWI, Jun 1992), p. 5.

88 Simon, 20, 9/4/02.

89 Ebenrett *et al.*, *Lagebild 'Jugend Heute'*, p. 177; Kohr *et al.*, *Jugend, Bundeswehr und Deutsche Einheit*, pp. 36–7; 'Plenarprotokoll 2/67', Landtag von Sachsen-Anhalt, zweite Wahlperiode, 4 Sep 1997, p. 5055.

90 Kohr *et al.*, *Jugend, Bundeswehr und deutsche Einheit*, p. 26. See also *Allensbacher Jahrbuch der Demoskopie 1993–1997*, pp. 1125–6.

91 Michael, 21, 25/9/01; Eva, 31, 12/4/02.

92 Thorsten, 17, 8/4/02.

93 *Allensbacher Jahrbuch der Demoskopie 1993-1997*, p. 1123.

94 Heiko Biehl, *Wendepunkt Kosovo? Sicherheitspolitische Einstellungen in den alten und neuen Ländern* (Strausberg: SOWI, 2001), p. 34.

95 Heinz-Hermann Krüger *et al.*, 'Projekt "Jugend und Demokratie in Sachsen-Anhalt": Zwischenbericht' (Martin-Luther-Universität Halle-Wittenberg, 2001), p. 121.

96 Benjamin, 19, 9/4/02.

97 E.g. Katya, 18, 22/9/01.

98 Heiko Biehl, *Wendepunkt Kosovo?*, p. 33. This trend was first noted in 1991, when 63.5% of young easterners (41.8% in the west) rejected possible German participation in a UN mission and 71.9% (41.8% in the west) in a NATO intervention. See Heinz-Ulrich Kohr, *Wertewandel, Sicherheitsverständnis und Sicherungsfunktionen . . .*, pp. 16, 19.

99 Sabine Collmer and Georg-Maria Meyer, *Früher 'zur Fahne' – heute 'zum Bund'*, p. 22.

100 Karl, 19, 9/4/02.

101 Also confirmed in Kohr, *Wertewandel, Sicherheitsverständnis und Sicherungsfunktionen*, p. 19.

102 Kohr *et al.*, *Jugend, Bundeswehr und deutsche Einheit*, p. 26.

103 Simone, 27, 13/4/02.

104 As stated by the 'Beirat für Fragen der Inneren Führung', 1993, cited in Kohr *et al.*, *Jugend, Bundeswehr und deutsche Einheit*, p. 76.

105 'Drucksache 2/1553', 1 Nov 1995 and 'Stenographischer Bericht über die 31. Sitzung des Landtages von Sachsen-Anhalt', 10 Nov 1995, pp. 71–82.

106 'Stenographischer Bericht über die 31. Sitzung des Landtages von Sachsen-Anhalt', 10 Nov 1995, p. 78.

107 'Stenographischer Bericht über die 25. Sitzung des Landtages von Sachsen-Anhalt', 31 Aug 1995, pp. 102–5.

108 Landtag von Sachsen-Anhalt, zweite Wahlperiode, 'Plenarprotokoll 2/67', 4 Sep 1997, pp. 5064, 5059.

109 Volke, *Jugendliche Trendsetter und ihre Einstellungen*, p. 3.

110 Collmer and Meyer, *Früher 'zur Fahne' – heute 'zum Bund'*, pp. 9–11.

111 Kohr *et al.*, *Jugend, Bundeswehr und deutsche Einheit*, p. 128.

112 Julia, 21, 9/4/02; Nadia, 18, 27/9/01.

113 Kohr *et al.*, *Jugend, Bundeswehr und deutsche Einheit*, pp. 49–65; Ebenrett *et al.*, *Lagebild 'Jugend heute'*, p. 171.

114 Kohr *et al.*, *Jugend, Bundeswehr und deutsche Einheit*, pp. 72–3.

115 Landtag von Sachsen-Anhalt, zweite Wahlperiode: 'Drs. 2/3206', 18 Feb 1997, pp. 17–18; 'Drs. 2/4717', 9 Mar 1998, p. 10; dritte Wahlperiode: 'Drs. 3/1085', 22 Feb 1999, p. 6.

116 Landtag von Sachsen-Anhalt, zweite Wahlperiode, 'Drs. 2/3886', 25 Aug 1997.

117 Landtag von Sachsen-Anhalt, zweite Wahlperiode, 'Plenarprotokoll, 2/67', 4 Sep 1997, pp. 5054–64.

118 *Rahmenrichtlinien Sekundarschule, Schuljahrgänge 8–10: Sozialkunde* (Magdeburg: Kultusministerium des Landes Sachsen-Anhalt, Apr 1999), pp. 45–7.

119 *Schule mit Zukunft: Bildungspolitische Empfehlungen und Expertisen der Enquete-Kommission des Landtages von Sachsen-Anhalt*, ed. by Karl-Heinz Braun *et al.* (Opladen: Leske & Budrich, 1998), p. 41.

120 'Wir leben mit Menschen anderer Kulturen zusammen', in *Rahmenrichtlinien Sekundarschule, Schuljahrgänge 8–10: Sozialkunde*, pp. 42–4.

121 'Miteinander Jahresbericht 2000', Magdeburg, Miteinander e.V.; www.miteinander-ev.de, accessed on 16 Mar 2001; *Projektschultage: Ein Angebot der außerschulischen Jugendbildung*, 'Projekt für Toleranz und Demokratie', pamphlet, no date [2001?].

122 'Jugendaustausch wächst', *MV*, 27 Mar 2003, p. 1.

123 Ronald Freytag and Dietmar Sturzbecher, *Die zweite Entdeckung Amerikas: Einstellungen ostdeutscher Jugendlicher zu den USA* (Potsdam: Verlag für Berlin-Brandenburg, 1998), p. 42; Irina Repke, 'Ganz rüde Anmache', *Der Spiegel*, 12 (2003), 46.

124 Freytag and Sturzbecher, *Die zweite Entdeckung Amerikas*, pp. 6, 21, 39, 80.

125 Matthias, 20, 3/4/02; Stefan, 29, 12/4/02.

126 Paul, 27, 25/9/02.

127 Daniel, 18, 9/4/02.

128 Richard Münchmeier, 'Europa – Fassade oder Chance?', in *Jugend 2000*, pp. 327–42 (329).

129 See Melanie Piepenschneider, *Die europäische Generation: Europabilder der Jugendlichen in der Bundesrepublik Deutschland* (Bonn: Europa Union Verlag, 1992), pp. 185–6.
130 Dirk, 17, 28/3/02.
131 Daniel, 18, 9/4/02.
132 Harry Müller and Wilfried Schubarth, 'Rechtsextremismus und aktuelle Befindlichkeiten von Jugendlichen in den neuen Bundesländern', *APuZG*, B38 (1992), 16–28 (p. 18).
133 *Verfassungsschutzbericht des Landes Sachsen-Anhalt 1999* (Magdeburg: Ministerium des Innern des Landes Sachsen-Anhalt, 1999), p. 17.
134 E.g. Karl-Peter Fritzsche, 'Ich habe nichts gegen Ausländer, aber . . . Eine deutsch-deutsche Schülerbefragung', *GEP*, 8/1 (1997), 15–17; Detlef Oesterreich, *Authoritäre Persönlichkeit und Gesellschaftsordnung: Der Stellenwert psychischer Faktoren für politische Einstellungen. Eine empirische Untersuchung von Jugendlichen in Ost und West* (Weinheim, Munich: Juventa, 1993), p. 188; *Jugend 2000*, p. 240.
135 Thomas Claus and Detlev Herter, 'Jugend und Gewalt', *APuZG*, B38 (1994), 10–20 (p. 19); Thomas Claus *et al.*, *Jugend in Europa im Spannungsfeld von Demokratie und Extremismus*, Forschungsbericht (Magdeburg, Innsbruck, Amsterdam: GISA Gender-Institut Sachsen-Anhalt, 2001), p. 158.
136 Eva Thalhammer, *Attitudes towards Minority Groups in West and East Germany* (Vienna: European Monitoring Centre on Racism and Xenophobia, April 2001), p. 4, www.eumc.eu.int/publications/euro-barometer/east-west-ger_en.pdf, accessed on 27 Nov 2001; Walter Friedrich, 'Ist der Rechtsextremismus im Osten ein Produkt der autoritären DDR?', *APuZG*, B46 (2001), 16–23 (p. 20).
137 Peter, 20, 27/9/01; Julia, 21, 9/4/02.
138 *Jugend 2000*, p. 224.
139 Stefan, 29, 12/4/02.
140 E.g. Dietmar Sturzbecker and Detlef Landua, 'Rechtsextremismus und Ausländerfeindlichkeit unter ostdeutschen Jugendlichen', *APuZG*, B46 (2001), 6–15 (p. 10); Detlef Oesterreich, *Authoritäre Persönlichkeit und Gesellschaftsordnung*, p. 173.
141 Karl-Peter Fritzsche, 'Ich habe nichts gegen Ausländer, aber . . .', p. 17; *Jugend 2000*, p. 258.
142 E.g. Peter Förster, Walter Friedrich, Harry Müller and Wilfried Schubarth, *Jugend Ost: Zwischen Hoffnung und Gewalt* (Opladen: Leske & Budrich), p. 133; Michael Minkenberg, 'German Unification and the Continuity of Discontinuities: Cultural Change and the Far Right in East and West', *GP*, 3/2 (1994), 169–92 (p. 173); Corinna

Kleinert, Wilfried Krüger and Helmut Willems, 'Einstellungen junger Deutscher gegenüber ausländischen Mitbürgern und ihre Bedeutung hinsichtlich politischer Orientierung', *APuZG*, B31 (1998), 14–27 (p. 22).

143 Johannes, 31, 23/9/01.

144 Julia, 21, 9/4/02.

145 Marlies, cited in Arim Soares do Bem, *Das Spiel der Identitäten in der Konstitution von 'Wir'-Gruppen* (Frankfurt am Main: Lang, 1998), p. 181.

146 Wilhelm Heitmeyer, *Die Bielefelder Rechtsextremismus-Studie* (Weinheim, Munich: Juventa, 1993).

147 See, for example, Detlef Oesterreich, 'Jugend in der Krise', *APuZG*, B19 (1993), 21–31; *Jugend 2000*, pp. 283–303.

148 Ulrike, 30, 5/4/02.

149 Johannes, 31, 23/9/01.

150 *Xenophobia and Racism in Europe*, European Monitoring Centre on Racism and Xenophobia, http://www.eumc.int/publications/eurobarometer.htm, accessed on 27 Nov 2001.

151 Wolfram Brunner and Dieter Walz, 'Selbstidentifikation der Ostdeutschen 1990–1997', in *Werte und nationale Identität im vereinten Deutschland*, ed. by Heiner Meulemann, pp. 229–50 (p. 230).

152 Thomas Gensicke, *Die neuen Bundesbürger: Eine Transformation ohne Integration* (Opladen, Wiesbaden: Westdeutscher Verlag, 1998), p. 43.

153 Peter Förster, 'Jugend von heute in der Gesellschaft von morgen', in *Jugend Morgen*, ed. by Staatskanzlei des Landes Sachsen-Anhalt (Halle, Saale: Mitteldeutscher Verlag, 2001), pp. 15–43 (17).

154 Anna, 31, 10/4/02.

155 Benjamin, 19, 9/4/02; similarly Simon, 20, 9/4/02; Matthias, 20, 3/4/02.

156 Stefan Berg, 'Die neue deutsche Sippenhaft', *Der Spiegel*, 39 (1996), 51–3 (p. 53).

157 E.g. in titles such as 'Ossi, benimm dich!'; 'Ratgeber: Wie wird man Wessi', see http://www.eulenspiegel-verlag.de, accessed on 5 May 2003.

158 Thomas Rausch, 'Zwischen Freiheitssuche und DDR-Nostalgie', *APuZG*, B45 (1999), 32–8.

159 Thorsten, 17, 8/4/02.

160 Landtag von Sachsen-Anhalt, 4. Wahlperiode, Drucksache 4/183, 6 Sep 2002.

161 Both in *MV*, 12 Feb 2001 and 22 Mar 2002.

162 Statistisches Bundesamt Deutschland 2002, http://www.destatis.de/cgi-bin/printview.pl, accessed on 7 Jan 2002. See also: 'Lehrlingsgehälter sind knapp bemessen', *MV*, 13 Feb 1999.

163 'Differenzierung statt Kollektivismus', *MV*, 10 Apr 2000.
164 Michael, 21, 25/9/01.
165 Anna, 31, 10/4/02.
166 Robert, 28, 25/9/01.
167 Katya, 18, 22/9/01.
168 'Ostdeutschland steht auf der Kippe', *MV*, 4 Jan 2001.
169 Simone, 27, 13/4/02.
170 Paul, 27, 25/9/01.
171 Ralf, 21, 27/9/01.
172 Thorsten, 17, 8/4/02.
173 Wolfram Brunner and Dieter Walz, 'Selbstidentifikation der Ostdeutschen 1990–1997', in *Werte und nationale Identität im vereinten Deutschland: Erklärungsansätze der Umfrageforschung*, ed. by Heiner Meulemann (Opladen: Leske & Budrich, 1998), pp. 229–50 (242).
174 See Beth Linklater, 'Narratives of the GDR: What Parents Tell their Children', in *Relocating Germanness: Discursive Disunity in Unified Germany*, ed. by Patrick Stevenson and John Theobald, (Basingstoke: Macmillan, 2000), pp. 150–66 (161).
175 Andreas Staab, 'Testing the West: Consumerism and National Identity in Eastern Germany', *GP*, 6/2 (1997), 139–49 (p. 145). See also Cortina Gaumann, 'Ost-Identität: Mehr als Trotznostalgie?', in *Die DDR in Deutschland: Ein Rückblick auf 50 Jahre*, ed by Heiner Timmermann (Berlin: Duncker & Humblot, 2001), pp. 763–79 (764).
176 'Ostprodukte drei Tage der Renner', *Neues Deutschland (ND)*, 11 May 1999, p. 10.
177 Rainer Gries, 'Der Geschmack der Heimat', *DA*, 27/10 (1994), 1041–58 (pp. 1052–3).
178 See Helen Kelly-Holmes, 'United Consumers? Advertising Discourse and Constructions of German Identity', in *Relocating Germanness*, pp. 91–108 (98).
179 Rainer Gries, 'Der Geschmack der Heimat', pp. 1050–1.
180 Thomas Ahbe, 'Ostalgie als Laienpraxis', *Berliner Debatte INITIAL*, 10/3 (1993), pp. 87–97 (87).
181 Andreas Staab, for example, makes the polemic claim: 'This virtual GDR reality imposes a severe obstacle to inner unification. Germany's democratic stability is challenged when people selectively and affectionately remember the totalitarian past and disproportionately criticise the present.' In 'Testing the West', p. 148.
182 'Die Puhdys kommen – auch nach Magdeburg', *MV*, 9 Mar 1999; 'Zwei Möhren aus Holz für Puhdys', *Mitteldeutsche Zeitung*, 2 Apr 2002, p. 11.

183 E.g. 'Gestammel oder Klartext – Aufregung um "Prinzen"-Lied', *MV*, 25 Aug 2001.

184 Kai Niemann, *Im Osten* (Sony Music Entertainment (Germany), 2001).

185 Klaus, *Im Westen* (Papagayo M (Carlton), 2001).

186 Markus, 30, 5/4/02.

187 Figures from the records of the *Landesverband Sachsen-Anhalt der Interessenvereinigung Jugendweihe e.V.*

188 'Bei Meiers Thesen blutet mir das Herz', *MV*, 4 Feb 2000.

189 'Jugendfeier für Nicht-Christen', *MV*, 10 May 2001.

190 Thorsten, 16, 8/4/02.

191 Karl, 19, 9/4/02.

192 Barbara Bollwahn, 'Vom Staatsakt zum Kulturprogramm', *taz-Berlin*, 30 Mar 1992, p. 5.

193 For example in a speech given by Frau Budde, AMO Kultur- und Kongreßhaus, Magdeburg, 5 May 2001.

194 Thomas Rausch, 'Zwischen Freiheitssuche und DDR-Nostalgie', p. 38.

195 *Rahmenrichtlinien Sekundarschule Schuljahrgänge 8–10: Sozialkunde*, p. 6.

196 See Frank Tillmann and Wolfgang Langer, *Demokratische Vor-Laute* (Opladen: Leske & Budrich, 2000).

197 *Jugendparlament 1998* (Magdeburg: Landtag von Sachsen-Anhalt, 1998); 'Frischer Wind im Plenarsaal', *Mitteldeutsche Zeitung*, 14 Sep 1998, p. 3.

198 'Bundesinitiative Beteiligungsbewegung', *Elfter Kinder- und Jugendbericht*, Deutscher Bundestag – 14. Wahlperiode, 4 Feb 2002, Drs. 14/8181, p. 19.

199 As seen on posters, and in youth magazines, e.g. *DATEs*, Magdeburg, Apr 2002, pp. 46–7.

200 Förster, 'Jugend von heute in der Gesellschaft von morgen', p. 40; *Jugend 2000*, p. 16.

201 See *Jugend '92*, p. 25; Ursula Hoffmann-Lange, Martina Gille and Helmut Schneider, 'Das Verhältnis von Jugend und Politik in Deutschland', *APuZG*, B19 (1993), 3–12 (p. 7); Soares do Bem, *Das Spiel der Identitäten*, p. 299.

202 *Jugend 2000*, p. 264.

203 Ursula Feist, 'Nichtwähler 1994', *APuZG*, B51–52 (1994), 35–46 (p. 42).

204 *Ibid.*, pp. 36, 42; see also *Landtagswahl in Sachsen-Anhalt 2002* [pamphlet].

205 Tillmann and Langer, *Demokratische Vor-Laute*, pp. 10, 41.

206 Krüger *et al.*, 'Projekt "Jugend und Demokratie"', p. 104.

207 Wolfgang Gaiser, Martina Gille, Winfried Krüger and Johann de Rijke, 'Politikverdrossenheit in Ost und West? Einstellungen von Jugendlichen und jungen Erwachsenen', *APuZG*, B19–20 (2000), 12–23 (pp. 17–18); Nicolle Pfaff, 'Auswertung aus dem Projekt "Jugend und Demokratie" ' (unpublished), pp. 4–7.

208 Letter from Axel Schulenburg, 'Ohne Arbeit geht die Jugend', *MV*, 6 Apr 2002.

209 'Junge "Zone"-Besucher fühlen sich von Stadt im Stich gelassen', *MV*, 3 May 2001. See also *Jugend '97*, ed. by Jugendwerk der deutschen Shell (Opladen: Leske & Budrich, 1997), p. 17.

210 Michael, 21, 25/9/01.

211 Karl, 19, 9/4/02.

212 Krüger *et al.*, 'Projekt "Jugend und Demokratie" ', pp. 125–6. See also *Jugend 2002*, ed. by Deutsche Shell (Frankfurt am Main: Fischer, 2003), p. 22, which finds 52% of eastern youth and 27% of western youth to be critical of the way in which democracy is carried out in Germany.

213 Benjamin, 19, 9/4/02.

214 Patrick, 20, 9/4/02.

215 Krüger *et al.*, 'Projekt "Jugend und Demokratie"', p. 123.

216 E.g. *Jugend 2000*, p. 263; Hoffmann-Lange *et al.*, 'Das Verhältnis von Jugend und Politik in Deutschland', p. 8.

217 Johannes, 31, 23/9/01.

218 Eva, 31, 12/4/02.

219 See Hans-Peter Kuhn, 'Jungwähler und die Bundestagswahl 1998', *Jugendliche Wähler in den neuen Bundesländern: Eine Längsschnittstudie zum Verhalten von Erstwählern bei der Bundestagswahl 1998*, ed. by Hans-Peter Kuhn, Karin Weiss and Hans Oswald (Opladen: Leske & Budrich, 2001), pp. 75–86 (82); 'Junge Menschen bleiben Parteien nicht lange treu', *MV*, 3 Aug 2002.

220 *Landtagswahl in Sachsen-Anhalt 2002* [pamphlet].

221 Sibylle Reinhardt and Frank Tillmann, 'Politische Orientierungen Jugendlicher: Ergebnisse und Interpretationen der Sachsen-Anhalt-Studie', *APuZG*, B45 (2001), 3–13 (p. 3).

222 See Hans Oswald and Karin Weiss, 'Die Brandenburger Erstwählerstudie im Überblick', in *Jugendliche Wähler in den neuen Bundesländern*, pp. 245–58 (252–3).

223 Everhard Holtmann, *Protestpartei am rechten Rand* (Magdeburg: Landeszentrale für politische Bildung Sachsen-Anhalt, 1999), p. 26.

224 *Ibid.*, p. 20.

225 'Junge Menschen bleiben Parteien nicht lange treu', *MV*, 3 Aug 2001; *Was Deutschland bewegt: Der forsa-Meinungsreport 2002* (Frankfurt am Main: Eichborn, 2002).

226 Holtmann, *Protestpartei am rechten Rand*, pp. 25–6; Hoffmann-Lange *et al.*, 'Das Verhältnis von Jugend und Politik in Deutschland', p. 12.

227 *Einstellungen und Handlungsorientierungen von Jugendlichen und jungen Erwachsenen in Sachsen-Anhalt* (Magdeburg: Ministerium für Arbeit, Frauen, Gesundheit und Soziales des Landes Sachsen-Anhalt, 1998), p. 43.

228 Oswald and Weiss, 'Die Brandenburger Erstwählerstudie im Überblick', pp. 250–1.

229 Stefan Berg, 'Die neue deutsche Sippenhaft', *Der Spiegel*, 39 (1996), 51–3 (p. 52).

230 Meredith A. Heiser-Durón, 'PDS Success in the East German States, 1989–1999: "Colorful calling card from the Forgotten Communist Past?" ', in *After the GDR: New Perspectives on the Old GDR and the Young Länder*, German Monitor 54, ed. by Laurence McFalls and Lothar Probst (Amsterdam, Atlanta, GA: Rodopi, 2001), pp. 247–69 (251–2).

231 Stefan Berg, 'Die neue deutsche Sippenhaft', p. 52.

232 As demonstrated in discussions with regional representatives of the *Junge Union* and *Jusos* in Sachsen-Anhalt. (Holger Wegener, 19/9/01; Yves Metzing, 13/9/01).

233 Jens, 23, cited in Eberhard Seidel-Pielen, *Stinos, Glatzen und Trinker: Jugend auf der Suche nach neuen Normen und Umgangsformen* (Magdeburg: Fraktion Bündnis 90/Die Grünen im Landtag von Sachsen-Anhalt, 1995), p. 16.

234 *Jugend 2000*, pp. 310–12, 325.

235 *Ibid.*, pp. 313–17.

236 SAPMO-BArch, DY24/11803, 'Einschätzung der politischen Lage . . .', 9 Oct 1989, p. 18.

237 Erich, 27, 25/9/01.

238 ' "Die Landesregierung nimmt die Altmark sowieso nicht wahr" ' and 'Fast jeder Zweite meint, dass Sachsen-Anhalt geteilt werden soll', *MV*, 17 Mar 2000.

239 See also 'Wenn wir hier einen Job finden, bleiben wir natürlich', *MV*, 25 Feb 2002.

240 'Jubel-Meer am Alten Markt: 20 000 Fans feiern Handballer des SC Magdeburg', *MV*, 21 May 2001.

241 See *MV* between 25 May and 2 June 2001, e.g. 'Kretschmars skandalöser Auftritt in der Harald-Schmidt-Show: "Arrogant" ', 25 May 2001.

242 Frank, 30, 6/4/02.

243 Michaela, 29, 20/9/01.

244 Thorsten, 17, 8/4/02; Michael, 21, 25/9/01.

245 Markus, 30, 5/4/02.

Conclusion: death of the GDR – rebirth of an eastern identity?

I am proud to be German. (Laurenz Meyer, CDU General Secretary, March 2001)[1]

Laurenz Meyer has the mentality of a skinhead and not only the appearance of one . . .That is typical of the insipidness, the numskull attitude, that marks out every racist thug in this republic. (Jürgen Trittin, Federal Environment Minister, March 2001)[2]

During the months following Laurenz Meyer's declaration of pride in March 2001 and Jürgen Trittin's virulent riposte, the concept of pride became a subject of heightened public debate in Germany. Whilst the extreme nature of Trittin's attack was widely condemned, a number of high-profile public figures such as President Johannes Rau and the singers Peter Maffay and Udo Lindenburg also rejected this outright expression of pride, largely as a result of its associations with the Nazi past.[3] Others, however, including Chancellor Schröder, defended Meyer's statement, and the CDU defiantly produced posters for regional elections bearing the slogan 'Proud of Germany'.[4] Yet in contrast to Willy Brandt's successful 1972 election campaign, headed by the slogan 'Germans – We can be proud of our country', the 2001 poster campaign was loaded with controversy. Despite recent claims that unified Germany has regained a sense of 'normality', the expression of collective German pride is clearly still considered anything but 'normal'.

The attitudes of young east Germans exemplify the unease that surrounds the expression of patriotic pride in contemporary Germany yet, in contrast to their elders, they often have little personal memory of divided Germany, and none of National Socialism. For the majority, unified Germany thus represents the accepted norm, typically described by one teenager as 'normal reality'.[5] Few, however, choose to make the same claim as Meyer, many instead simply stating: 'I just am German'; 'I'm happy to be born here'; 'I can't help that I'm German.'[6] As the examination of their patriotic behaviour both during the GDR period and in unified Germany has revealed, it is less the 'normality' of living in unified Germany (or indeed the 'abnormality' of division) that has shaped young people's patriotic sentiment in recent years, but rather the perceived normalities and abnormalities of life in the private sphere, as determined by the public framework. Individuals' personal experiences of employment, education or military service, for example, have proved more influential in their assessment of each state than any official rhetoric or propaganda.

This phenomenon is central to the three major questions posed in this book. Firstly, how was patriotism encouraged in the GDR state and post-unification Germany, and to what extent can it successfully be imposed on a population from above? Secondly, what does the relationship between young people and these two states reveal about the nature of each system, and how did young people's patriotic behaviour (or lack of it) impact on the East German state's apparent stability and demise? Thirdly, what are the longer-term effects of GDR socialisation and socialist patriotic education: have they influenced young people's civic loyalties in post-*Wende* Germany, or are they subordinate to the conditions and circumstances of life in the present day?

The primacy of personal experience within patriotic sentiment is central to each of the above questions, yet it is most pertinent to the first, for it helps to explain the way in which patriotism is formed. This is demonstrated by four parallels that can be drawn between young people's behaviour in the GDR and united Germany, despite the radically different nature of these two political systems. The first concerns the way in which young people responded to the immediate conditions of their everyday lives, for confidence in both states was severely diminished by problems concerning goods and services, creating reticence towards the expression of patriotism. In the GDR, the shortage and nature of basic material goods, suitable housing, fashion accessories and cultural entertainment provoked increasing criticism of the authorities, whereas in unified Germany employment shortages have provided a major cause of fear and discontent. Although both cases are different, the result is similar: a lack of confidence in the state and a consequent unwillingness to contribute actively to its development, whether this is demonstrated through low levels of military commitment, reluctant political activity, or ambivalence towards supposedly legitimising international alliances.

Insecurities caused by material or labour shortages have been most visible with respect to attitudes towards foreigners both before and after the *Wende*. In the GDR, competition for material goods and housing caused tensions between young people and foreign residents in the same way that fear of losing one's status through unemployment after unification created resentment towards foreigners who were perceived to be living off the state. As both cases demonstrate, it is clearly difficult to be content with the presence of foreign cultures if one's own situation appears insecure and vulnerable, and as a result they are frequently perceived as a threatening and destabilising force. In this way, personal insecurities can become ethnic in nature, endangering the civic basis of patriotism and creating identities and loyalties marked by exclusivity. Right-wing extremism has existed as a minority phenomenon throughout both periods, largely in protest against the contemporary state of affairs rather than as a result of deep-rooted ideological beliefs. This is demonstrated by the fact that supporters of both political extremes have frequently shared similar concerns and interests, especially in the GDR, where movement between minority groups, such as punks and skinheads, was common. In contrast to Martin Walser's claim that right-wing extremism is caused by 'the neglect of the national',[7] it would seem, rather, that quite the opposite cause is true: the neglect of the private.

Despite notable instances of extremism, political apathy marks the second major parallel between both systems. With the exception of the *Wende* period, which saw a brief phase of mass politics alongside a new-found sense of purpose and responsibility, both systems have been marked by a lack of commitment to political activity, and thus to the civic basis of patriotism. This was considered to be futile by most, especially in the GDR, where the large-scale official political demonstrations achieved little real change, and attempts to bring reform to the system were simply ignored or quashed. Whilst the situation has since changed, many still feel impotent within the post-*Wende* political sphere, believing themselves to be unable to change the status quo as individuals, and consequently withdrawing from the political process. In both cases, young people have experienced alienation from the political world and a consequent lack of responsibility within society.

Widespread apathy is a phenomenon which can be witnessed internationally amongst young generations, yet attitudes within both German states have demonstrated that this does not result simply from typical youthful demeanour but also from an active distrust of party politics. In the GDR this was founded in the stagnant and undemocratic nature of the political system, where the act of voting had no real effect, FDJ meetings simply relayed the SED's latest policies to young people and ageing leaders failed to listen to the needs of young people. Following unification, politicians still failed to elicit the trust of young citizens, who felt that their needs were not being served and that no parties truly represented their interests. In both periods it was not the fundamental principle of the respective political system that was considered at fault but rather the realisation of the system in question. Socialism as it was experienced by young people thus failed to match up to the socialist ideal in the same way that the realities of a free-market democracy have not lived up to young people's post-*Wende* expectations. As a result, politics has remained a sphere devoid of emotional involvement for young people, and areas primarily defined by their political and civic boundaries (such as the GDR, the FRG or Sachsen-Anhalt) have consequently evoked few feelings of loyalty.

Thirdly, the way in which materials are presented to young people greatly influences the effective transmission of their content, a phenomenon which was evident in both states. This was most apparent under socialism, where the dry teaching methods, repetition and old-fashioned language of the SED's patriotic education simply sapped enthusiasm and produced boredom amongst pupils. Whilst this approach has largely been revised in united Germany, and attempts to produce support for the state prove more subtle in nature, evidence still reveals that the dry or politicised presentation of certain materials (e.g. concerning the European Union and the formal unification process) have caused a lack of interest. Furthermore, efforts to emphasise specific subject areas have frequently resulted in the opposite of the desired effect. In the area of historical consciousness, for example, attempts to foreground official GDR history simply turned young people away from this area; instead they were drawn towards historical periods which were considered taboo, such as Stalin's crimes or the true causes of the 1953 uprising. Similarly, attempts since 1990 in Sachsen-Anhalt to fore-ground older, less controversial regional history as a basis for regional pride appear to have had little effect in the face of interest in twentieth-century controversies. Moreover, the western bias in history teaching shortly after the *Wende* created amongst many a defensive interest in the east. Outside the education system, the same pattern of behaviour can be identified, demonstrating that the cultural dominance of any phenomenon does not necessarily secure its popularity. In the GDR, the overbearing emphasis on proletarian internationalism, and particularly Soviet culture, caused many young citizens to reject these values and look elsewhere for inspiration; in contrast, the dominance of American values in unified Germany has caused resistance towards some elements of its mass culture.[8] Clearly the more young people feel that their lifestyles and loyalties are being dictated to them, the more they are likely to resist.

The fourth and final parallel concerns the dominant nature of West(ern) Germany. The presence of this 'other half' of Germany (both before and after the *Wende*) illustrates the extent to which collective identities are created in the face of difference, and patriotic sentiment is influenced by an element of competitiveness or rivalry. In the GDR, West German culture was clearly idolised by young people, as it represented the inaccessible, and provided a source of valuable material items which were lacking under SED socialism. Despite this idolisation, an element of competitiveness was also evident, and the desire not to appear as the poor German relative created a defensive protection of East German distinctiveness. This feeling came to the fore during the *Wende*, when West German attempts to become involved in what was perceived as an East German affair caused increasing resistance. Since the fall of the Wall, the new proximity of these two cultures has caused east Germans to reassess dramatically their own situation in the face of 'the other', both materially and psychologically. Whilst they have adopted (willingly or otherwise) numerous elements of western life, east Germans' self-definition has increasingly been shaped in contrast to the West, particularly where they have felt negative discrimination. Although a sense of 'easternness' need not conflict with patriotic sentiment, it is this feeling of negative discrimination which potentially undermines loyalty to the united state. As Meulemann states: 'The east Germans are becoming more similar to the west Germans, yet their identity as east Germans is becoming stronger.

The "wall of values" is crumbling, albeit slowly; but the "wall of self-categorisation" is growing.'⁹ The death of the GDR clearly did not imply the death of young people's loyalty to an eastern set of values, but in many ways its rebirth.

As the above parallels show, young people's reticence about the expression of patriotism in both systems has resulted primarily from their unsatisfactory experiences of everyday life in the personal sphere. Indeed, personal insecurities and dissatisfactions can frequently lead to unpatriotic behaviour, as witnessed in negative attitudes towards foreigners, or the opposing trends of extremism and apathy. Attempts to shape patriotic sentiment from above, most prominently in the GDR through its comprehensive patriotic programme, but also in united Germany through school classes such as *Sozialkunde*, political initiatives and historical exhibitions, have thus frequently failed. Young people see their immediate concerns to lie elsewhere, and their collective self-image is defined as much in relation to others as in a common set of values. Instances concerning the creation of positive collective identities amongst young people both before and after the *Wende* demonstrate the importance of these elements. The church-based peace movements of the 1980s, for example, attracted large numbers of young people, as they addressed many of their immediate concerns and frustrations, instilled in participants a sense of empowerment and responsibility that had previously been lacking and provided a sphere of influence away from the omnipresence of the SED. In more recent years, a number of cultural phenomena, such as the *Jugendweihe*, popular music and consumer products, have found appeal as they have been adapted to suit the needs of the east German community, providing a positive focus of attention away from the dominant west and centring on the immediate challenges facing young people in the east. On the one hand, these examples suggest that patriotism is not a burning issue amongst young people in post-unification Germany and is subordinate to a number of personal concerns. On the other hand, however, they demonstrate that formal attempts to create a sense of patriotism can find resonance amongst this generation only if they address the physical and emotional states of young people in the personal sphere before, or at least alongside, issues concerning the civic state.

Whilst the similarities between young people's relationship to patriotism in both states reveal important elements relating to the formation of patriotic sentiment, they say little about the character of the two states themselves, particularly the nature of the GDR regime – the second question addressed in this book. Here the different effects of resistance to patriotic behaviour on the functioning of each system prove enlightening, particularly with reference to the demonstration of opposition to the state, and the withdrawal into apathy.

As illustrated in chapter 2, the demonstration of opposition to the GDR state was varied in nature and widespread amongst the young generation. Instances ranged from small-scale individual acts, such as the defacement of school certificates, the refusal to participate in the *Jugendweihe*, or the burning of the FDJ shirt, through to localised protests as witnessed at the Carl-von-Ossietzky school in 1988, or participation in nationwide actions frequently organised under the umbrella of the churches, such as those which carried the motto 'Swords into ploughshares'. These incidents clearly revealed that the SED's goal of uniformity within the education system and the sphere of young people was never reached during the 1980s. Instead, young people's growing desire to break out of the SED's patriotic mould endangered the regime, weakening its hold on the young generation and ultimately helping to cause its demise. Ironically, many who demonstrated against the regime revealed surprising patriotic potential, for they were engaged in the public debate and often believed in the basic principles of socialism; their aim was to improve the GDR rather than to overthrow the state. The SED, however, made little attempt to listen to the real concerns of these people, and in its drive for uniformity and ultimate control it punished them, whilst tolerating those who had retreated into the private sphere. In doing so, it lost numerous potential supporters.

In contrast, the plural democratic system of united Germany has accepted and allowed demonstrations of protest against the workings of the state. As a result, many instances of protest in the GDR, such as a pupil defacing his or her certificate, do not warrant attention today, for they have lost all political meaning. Instead, the act of engaging in critical political debate is actively encouraged, even when this results in highlighting problematic or contentious elements of state policy, for true democracy demands the representation of all citizens' interests. Protests which have, however, aroused concern are those which are potentially directed against the democratic order, such as right-wing extremist demonstrations. Whilst these are strictly policed, they have often been allowed to take place, thus revealing the confident nature of the state, in contrast to the constant paranoia of the SED.

The importance of political protest in each regime is countered by the presence of apathy. Whilst this phenomenon was dominant during both periods, it adopted a radically different function within each. In the GDR, the large number of apathetic conformists ultimately maintained the system for, as long as they participated to the necessary minimum, yet refrained from overt forms of protest, the state was able to function smoothly. Although the aim of GDR socialisation and patriotic education was to create a young generation which would be fully active in the pursuit of socialism, in reality only a minority of young people was needed to commit to this course; the withdrawal of the masses into the private sphere ironically enabled the SED to present a semblance of stability to the outer world, as well as to its own citizens. As young people began to emerge from this state of apathy, however, the GDR found itself resting on unstable foundations, and as soon as genuine political activity became a mass phenomenon the future of the state was severely limited.

Young people's apathetic stance towards the affairs of the state in united Germany, however, has far from supported the democratic order, for apathy endangers the nature of true democracy by creating an environment in which political decisions fall into the hands of a minority, rather than being representative of the masses. Whilst mass apathy is unlikely to endanger the existence of the FRG in the same way that the politicisation of young people helped bring about the demise of the GDR, it does, however, limit the functioning of the state. As the contrasting natures of the GDR and united Germany demonstrate, the importance of patriotic behaviour to the maintenance of a state clearly depends on the nature of its political foundations: whilst the maintenance of a true democracy requires a high level of patriotic commitment, the absence of this commitment may actually help sustain a single-party state.[10]

These findings help deepen our understanding of the GDR regime, for the fact that inadequate commitment to official socialist patriotic values in the GDR helped maintain the regime shows that stability was based on more than simple repression and central control. As demonstrated by the apathetic conformity of many young people who co-operated with the system to suit their own needs, yet whose disaffection with the regime was largely tolerated, the boundaries between state and society were far from clear-cut. The evident interaction between both spheres not only proved essential in shaping the loyalties of young people – and, indeed, the nature of state control – but it also seriously undermined the validity of firstly the totalitarian paradigm and secondly the model of the 'niche society' for the GDR, both of which failed to recognise such interaction. The classification of the GDR as 'totalitarian' allows no space for the complex and often changeable nature of the relationship between state and society, for rather than describing the actual structures of power this model relies on the aims of the state to intimate the nature of the regime. As Mary Fulbrook argues: 'The primary focus on ideology and repression misses the crucial importance of *Anpassung*, grumbling conformity and the isolation of dissent, as key aspects tending towards political stability despite lack of commitment, as well as failing to explore the conditions for the organisation of alternative movements which can mount effective challenges to the regime under particular conditions.'[11] Although the portrayal of the GDR as a 'niche society' clearly allows for a more differentiated view, and captures the importance of private circles within the regime, this concept also fails to recognise the significance of interaction between the private and public spheres. As Thomas Lindenberger claims, the concept of the 'niche' is rather misleading, if not somewhat idyllic, for the private sphere was never entirely free from the influence of GDR politics.[12]

   In contrast to the concepts of totalitarianism and the 'niche society', the idea of *Eigen-Sinn* is largely supported by the findings of this study. As Corey Ross states, this concept 'points towards ways of bridging the divide between the competing images of ubiquitous dissent and widespread conformity by emphasizing how the pursuit of one's interests – indeed, the very definition of one's interests in the first place – is integrally related to social and political circumstances'.[13] This idea can be found in numerous areas of young people's lives throughout the 1980s, and aptly reflects their frequently complex relationship with the state. This is perhaps best symbolised by the GDR *Jugendweihe*, a ceremony which was mobilised by the SED to encourage and demonstrate high levels of state loyalty in the GDR. Despite its official nature, it became a popular and emotionally laden ritual for young people and their families, who adapted it to their own needs. Whilst some took part simply to ensure their future career paths, many also saw it as a family celebration and an important turning point in their lives. In response, the SED also adapted its approach in order to maintain the popularity of the ritual; whilst the preparatory *Jugendweihe* classes continued to propagate socialist ideology, shops were allowed to market clothes and presents specifically for this occasion, and the importance of family values and the coming of adulthood were often emphasised in official discourse. This interaction between state and society clearly demonstrates the limitations of totalitarian theory and concepts of the 'niche society' to characterise the GDR. Instead, the pursuit of *Eigen-Sinn* captures the essence of this relationship and, as Lindenberger highlights, the true nature of the GDR can only be understood once we recognise 'the individual [*eigen-sinnig*] experiences of east Germans with "their" dictatorship'.[14]

The concept of *Eigen-Sinn* also relates closely to the way in which GDR socialisation has affected young people in the longer term – the third point of investigation in this study. The nature and extent of young people's personal interaction with the GDR state has thus clearly impacted on their post-unification identities, as demonstrated by the differences in attitude between the two groups of interviewees: teenagers and young adults. Teenagers had few memories of the GDR, yet their minimal experiences of life under socialism often gained a disproportional over-importance in their assessment of united Germany. In this way, personal experience of the GDR (however minimal) created amongst many the impression that they knew what life there was like, and consequently they felt part of an exclusive group which was able to legitimately pass judgement on the GDR. Furthermore, rosy childhood memories have frequently painted an image of a world in which young people lived easy, straightforward lives, free from the immediate worries of unemployment and financial insecurity and, as a result, those growing up post-1989 have often felt hard done by and disadvantaged. This image is often strengthened by their parents' own difficult experiences since unification, and subsequently their positive appraisal of life in the GDR. Others, however, who experienced negative discrimination during the GDR, paint a rather different picture for their offspring. It is consequently no surprise that teenagers' views of the socialist past were biased in nature, through their limited experiences and reliance on 'second-hand' sources. The tendency to adopt a black and white viewpoint was also evident in many teenagers' attitudes towards their immediate environment, which were frequently shaped by the opposition of east and west within united Germany, each half often simply negating the other, rather than being valued (or criticised) for its own individual nature. Indeed, as a result of growing up during a time marked by western dominance and perceived eastern inferiority, teenagers' categorisation of both east and west was highly stereotyped, and their loyalties were based primarily on the perception of east–west difference in the present, rather than past divisions.

In contrast, young adults' attitudes towards the past and present were more moderate. As a result of their longer socialisation in the GDR, their views of the socialist state were varied and more likely to be neutral and descriptive in nature than those of teenagers. Having encountered both the positive and the negative aspects of life under SED socialism and experienced life there as a daily normality, their memories proved less susceptible to manipulation than those of teenagers (although, as with all memories, they have been altered by the passage of time). These memories were consequently more influential in this age group's assessment of their contemporary state, and in contrast to teenagers' reliance on western difference as a point of comparison for their own situation, young adults were more likely to look to the GDR past as a reference point for the present. Rather than defining themselves in the face of the west, members of this cohort thus more frequently drew on past personal experiences to judge the present. The strong solidarity that was felt during the GDR, or the appreciation of non-material values, for example, highlighted for them the cut-throat competitiveness and economic greed of contemporary society. In contrast, however, the regulated nature of public life and the lack of personal freedoms in the GDR underlined for them the liberal nature of post-*Wende* Germany, and allowed for greater appreciation of the benefits of its political system. As a result of young adults' greater reliance on the past–present comparison, their self-definition in the face of the west was more moderate than that of teenagers, and their descriptions of east and west were consequently less biased.

In both age groups, personal experiences have played a vital role in influencing attitudes towards united Germany. The influence of GDR socialisation has thus continued to be highly relevant in the lives of young adults, and as claimed in *Good Bye Lenin!*, 'the GDR lives on', yet rarely in the sense of formal education, and propaganda. In contrast to the views of psychologists and social scientists such as Hans-Joachim Maaz and Christian Pfeiffer on the one hand, who claim that education and socialisation in the GDR created authoritarian characteristics amongst young people, and Peter Förster and Detlef Oesterreich on the other, who suggest that contemporary circumstances are primarily responsible for identity formation today, the findings of this study suggest that it is rather young people's experiences of life in the private sphere (in both the past and present) which throw light on contemporary attitudes. GDR courses in military defence, for example, had little long-lasting ideological effect, yet the unofficial solidarity that formed amongst pupils during such lessons has had a much longer-lasting influence. Similarly, the most influential post-unification experiences have been those which have directly affected the private sphere, such as unemployment and financial insecurity.

The relationship between the past and present is clearly two-way: whilst personal experiences of the present have influenced young people's assessment of the past, personal experiences of the past have equally influenced attitudes towards the present. Whereas the former was more prevalent amongst teenagers, the latter was witnessed more frequently amongst young adults. As Elisabeth Noelle-Neumann and Renate Köcher state: 'The Cold War has made a lasting impression on the historical consciousness of west and east Germans.'[15] This is true to the extent that the Cold War was responsible for the division of Germany, for it was the various experiences on each side of the Wall that have clearly shaped subsequent historical consciousness. It is more doubtful where ideology is concerned, however, for the long-term effects of GDR patriotic education have proved negligible in the attitudes of young adults over a decade later. Similarly, formal education in schools since 1990 has appeared secondary to personal experience in shaping young people's behaviour. It is thus no surprise that those who have experienced most difficulties in the private sphere are more likely to be critical of the present state, and lenient in their assessment of the GDR past.

Despite the importance assigned to the debate concerning the influence of socialisation versus contemporary circumstances, one final factor that has been a recurrent theme throughout this study proves equally prominent in shaping young people's loyalties today: the National Socialist past. Following the suppression of many elements of this part of German history during the GDR, it has gained a new importance in the east, particularly amongst young people. Indeed, this period has regained the emotional involvement of young people, providing a strong source of shame and often preventing the expression of pride in Germany and its institutions, particularly the *Bundeswehr*, for fear that history may repeat itself. As the debate initiated by Meyer and Trittin suggests, this period of history is likely to remain central to the formation of collective loyalties in Germany for the immediate future.

The relationship of young adults to the National Socialist past also supports the thesis that personal experience in the GDR claimed greater importance in the formation of patriotic sentiment than formal GDR socialisation. Firstly, the influence of this period in shaping young people's loyalties soon after the demise of the GDR suggests that the SED's anti-fascist propaganda had little, if any, long-lasting effect. Their apparent emotional detachment from the period of National Socialism during the 1980s changed more dramatically than any other element following unification, and thirteen years after the fall of the Wall, it evoked more emotional reaction than any other period of history. Secondly, young adults' personal experience of the *Wende* and mass opposition to the SED in 1989 has caused them to judge older generations' apparent complicity with the Nazi past particularly harshly. Here we see how past personal experiences can also influence attitudes towards periods of history which were not experienced first-hand, yet which reflect on present loyalties. In this way, many young adults' reticence towards displaying patriotic pride as a result of shame in the Nazi past has ultimately been heightened by their personal involvement in demonstrations during the *Wende*. Whilst the interaction between past and present experiences can clearly be influenced by events outside one's immediate personal sphere, this sphere will still colour the light in which they are viewed. Once again, 'the GDR lives on', at least in the way that it continues to influence the attitudes and perceptions of those who experienced life there.

As the evidence of this study has demonstrated, patriotism cannot be imposed upon citizens from above, however thorough and uniform attempts to do so may be. Instead, it can only grow organically from below, where personal experiences of the past and present are central to the development of civic and national loyalties. Whilst these are further defined by perceived difference in the present as well as older historical traditions, personal experiences are also influential in these areas. Clearly the local and personal needs of the masses must be satisfied before a state can rely on the popular support and active commitment of its citizens. Contrary to common assumptions, patriotism is thus not primarily about state symbolism or national greatness, but ultimately about satisfaction within the personal sphere.

Notes

1 'Meinungen über Nationalstolz gehen weit auseinander', *MV*, 28 Mar 2001.

2 Cited in *Berlin aktuell: Die Woche im Bundestag*, 20 Mar 2001, accessed on 29 Sep 2003.

3 'Maffay und Lindenberg unterstützen Rau', *MV*, 22 Mar 2001.

4 'Stolz sind sie irgendwie alle', *MV*, 21 Mar 2001; 'CDU integriert Aktion "Stolz auf Deutschland" in OB-Wahlkampf', *MV*, 28 Mar 2001.

5 Sylvia, 17, 27/9/01.

6 Christoph, 19, 9/4/02; Michaela, 29, 20/9/01; Andre, 17, 14/9/01.

7 Martin Walser, 'Deutsche Sorgen', *Der Spiegel*, Nr 26 (1993), 40–7 (p. 43).

8 It should be noted, however, that the German government recognised this atmosphere of resistance in determining policy on the Iraq crisis in 2002, and tapped into the popular mood.

9 Heiner Meulemann (ed.), *Werte und nationale Identität im vereinten Deutschland* (Opladen: Leske & Budrich, 1998), p. 17.

10 Whilst the Third Reich and other fascist states relied heavily on popular support, this was to be founded on the basis of ethnic exclusivity and nationalist thought, rather than the civic emphasis of patriotic commitment.

11 Mary Fulbrook, 'The Limits of Totalitarianism: God, State and Society in the GDR', *Transactions of the Royal Historical Society*, 6/7 (1997), 25–52 (p. 50).

12 Thomas Lindenberger, *Herrschaft und Eigen-Sinn in der Diktatur: Studien zur Gesellschaftsgeschichte der DDR* (Cologne, Weimar, Vienna: Böhlau, 1999), p. 9.

13 Corey Ross, *The East German Dictatorship: Problems and Perspectives in the Interpretation of the GDR* (London: Arnold, 2002), p. 124.

14 Lindenberger, *Herrschaft und Eigen-Sinn in der Diktatur*, p. 12.

15 *Allensbacher Jahrbuch der Demoskopie 1993-1997*, vol. 10: *Demoskopische Entdeckungen*, ed. by Elisabeth Noelle-Neumann and Renate Köcher (Munich: Saur, 1997), p. 505.

Select bibliography

Archival sources

Bundesarchiv, Berlin (BArch)

DA3/	Zentraler Runder Tisch
DC4/	Zentralinstitut für Jugendforschung
DO1/	Deutsche Volkspolizei
DO4/	Staatssekretär für Kirchenfragen
DR2/	Ministerium für Volksbildung

Stiftung Archiv der Parteien und Massenorganisationen der DDR im Bundesarchiv, Berlin (SAPMO-BArch)

DY21/	Jugendweihe
DY24/	FDJ
DY30/	SED
DY30/825–1394	Abteilung Sicherheitfragen
DY 30/IV2/2/	Politbüro
DY30/IV2/2.036/	Büro Paul Verner
DY30/IV2/2.039/	Büro Egon Krenz
DY30/JIV2/16/	Abteilung Jugend
DY30/JIV2/9.05/	Abteilung Volksbildung
DY30/IVB2/9.05/	Abteilung Volksbildung
DY30/IVB2/14/	Arbeitsgruppe Kirchenfragen
DY59/	Gesellschaft für Sport und Technik

Bundesbeauftragte für die Unterlagen des Staatssicherheitsdienstes der ehemaligen Deutschen Demokratischen Republik, Berlin (BStU)

BV-Halle, Abt. XX/	Bezirksverwaltung Halle, Abteilung XX (Staatsapparat, Kultur, Kirche, Untergrund)
BV-Halle, AKG/	Bezirksverwaltung Halle, Auswertungs- und Kontrollgruppe
BV-Mdg, Abt. XX/	Bezirksverwaltung Magdeburg, Abteilung XX (Staatsapparat, Kultur, Kirche, Untergrund)

BV-Mdg, AKG/	Bezirksverwaltung Magdeburg, Auswertungs- und Kontrollgruppe
MfS-HA IX/	Hauptabteilung IX (Untersuchungsorgan)
MfS-HA XX/	Hauptabteilung XX (Staatsapparat, Kultur, Kirche, Untergrund)
MfS-HA XX, AKG/	Hauptabteilung XX (Staatsapparat, Kultur, Kirche, Untergrund), Auswertungs- und Kontrollgruppe
MfS-JHS/	Juristische Hochschule des MfS
MfS-ZAIG/	Zentrale Auswertungs- und Informationsgruppe des MfS

Landesarchiv Magdeburg – Landeshauptarchiv – (LA Magd.-LHA-)

Rep.41/	Rat der Stadt Magdeburg
Rep.M1/	Bezirkstag und Rat des Bezirkes Magdeburg
Rep.P13/	Bezirksleitung Magdeburg der SED
Rep.P15, IV/D–4/02/	SED-Kreisleitung Gardelegen
Rep.P15, IV/D–4/07/	SED-Kreisleitung Kalbe/M
Rep.P15, IV/D–4/08/	SED-Kreisleitung Klötze
Rep.P15, IV/D–4/09/	SED-Kreisleitung Oschersleben
Rep.P15, IV/D–4/11/	SED-Kreisleitung Salzwedel
Rep.P15, IV/D–4/15/	SED-Kreisleitung Stendal
Rep.P15, IV/D–4/16/	SED-Kreisleitung Tangerhütte
Rep.P16/	SED-Stadtleitung Magdeburg
Rep.43/	FDGB-Bezirksvorstand Magdeburg

Deutsches Institut für Internationale Pädagogische Forschung/Bibliothek für Bildungsgeschichtliche Forschung/Archiv, Berlin (DIPF/BBF/Archiv)

| 10./–16./ | Akademie der Pädagogischen Wissenschaften |
| JW/ | Junge Welt (Briefsammlung) |

Matthias-Domaschk-Archiv, Berlin (M-D-A)

| 10.11/2 | Thematische Sammlung/Bausoldaten |
| 13.1.1/ | Samisdat-Hefte zur Wehrdienstverweigerung |

Private collection, Magdeburg (Fr. Dr. Kornemann-Weber)
Protokolle des Runden Tisches in Sachsen-Anhalt, 1989–90

Federal government sources

Neunter Jugendbericht: Bericht über die Situation der Kinder und Jugendlichen und die Entwicklung der Jugendhilfe in den neuen Bundesländern, Deutscher Bundestag, 13. Wahlperiode, 1994, Drs. 13/70

Zehnter Kinder- und Jugendbericht: Bericht über die Lebenssituation von Kindern und die Leistungen der Kinderhilfen in Deutschland, Deutscher Bundestag, 13. Wahlperiode, 1998, Drs. 13/11368
Elfter Kinder- und Jugendbericht, Deutscher Bundestag, 14. Wahlperiode, 4 Feb 2002, Drs 14/8181

Regional government sources

Bildungspolitische Information Nr 4: Die inhaltliche Reform der Schule: Rahmenrichtlinien (Magdeburg: Kultusministerium des Landes Sachsen-Anhalt, 1992)
Einstellungen und Handlungsorientierungen von Jugendlichen und jungen Erwachsenen in Sachsen-Anhalt (Mageburg: Ministerium für Arbeit, Frauen, Gesundheit und Soziales des Landes Sachsen-Anhalt, 1998)
Kinder- und Jugendbericht des Landes Sachsen-Anhalt, Landtag von Sachsen-Anhalt, Erste Wahlperiode, 1994, Drs 1/3775
Kinder- und Jugendpolitisches Programm des Landes Sachsen-Anhalt (Magdeburg: Ministerium für Arbeit, Frauen, Gesundheit und Soziales des Landes Sachsen-Anhalt, 2000)
Landtag von Sachsen-Anhalt, Erste Wahlperiode, Drucksache: 1/2527
Landtag von Sachsen-Anhalt, Zweite Wahlperiode, Drucksache: 2/666, 2/1538, 2/1553, 2/1948, 2/3206, 2/3886, 2/3922, 2/4717
Landtag von Sachsen-Anhalt, Dritte Wahlperiode, Drucksache: 3/43, 3/217, 3/770, 3/1085, 3/1370, 3/1547, 3/1553, 3/1991, 3/1993, 3/2804, 3/3126, 3/4214, 3/4288, 3/4717, 3/4866, 3/5354
Landtag von Sachsen-Anhalt, Vierte Wahlperiode, Drucksache: 4/137, 4/183

Interviews

Interviews for this project were carried out in September 2001 and March–April 2002 in Magdeburg with:

- twenty-three 'teenagers' (born 1980–84): sixteen male/seven female, average age 18.7
- twenty 'young adults' (born 1970–74): nine male/eleven female, average age 29.1

Interviewees were found through a variety of youth organisations in Magdeburg, as well as a number of personal contacts. The same questions were asked of all interviewees, yet these were used only as a guide to make sure that all the relevant information was solicited, rather than providing a rigid question–answer formula. The aim was to allow interviewees to talk as freely as they wished, and not to limit their answers to the specific question in hand. All interviewees have been given pseudonyms.

Other interviews
Hans-Jörg Beyerling, *Junge Humanisten*: 8 May 2001
Frau Herbig, *Interessenvereinigung Jugendweihe e.V.*: 18 Apr 2001
Manfred Köppe, *Landesheimatbund Sachsen-Anhalt e.V.*: 11 Jun 2001
Susanne Kornemann-Weber, *Diakonisches Werk in der KPS e.V.*: 26 Mar 2003
Thomas Lösche, *Amt für Kinder und Jugendarbeit der Evangelischen Kirche der KPS*: 24 Mar 2003
Yves Metzing, *JuSos*: 13 Sep 2001
Martin Rieß, *SJD-Die Falken*: 24 Sep 2001
Holger Wegener, *Junge Union*: 19 September 2001

Secondary sources

Ahrberg, Edda, '*Mit gestutzten Flügeln*': *Jugend in der DDR*, Sachbeiträge (2) (Magdeburg: Landesbeauftragte für die Unterlagen des Staatssicherheitsdienstes der ehemaligen DDR Sachsen-Anhalt, 1996)
Allinson, Mark, *Politics and Popular Opinion in East Germany 1945–68* (Manchester: Manchester University Press, 2000)
Baehr, Vera-Maria, *Wir denken erst seit Gorbatschow: Protokolle von Jugendlichen aus der DDR* (Recklinghausen: Bitter, 1990)
Barker, Peter (ed.), *The Party of Democratic Socialism in Germany: Modern Post-Communism or Nostalgic Populism?*, German Monitor 42 (Amsterdam, Atlanta, GA: Rodopi, 1998)
Barker, Peter (ed.), *The GDR and its History: Rückblick und Revision: Die DDR im Spiegel der Enquete-Kommissionen*, German Monitor 49 (Amsterdam, Atlanta, GA: Rodopi, 2000)
Becker, Arnold, *Jugendweihe: Ein unüberwindbarer Graben zwischen Ost und West?* (Frankfurt am Main: Haag & Herchen, 1999)
Behnken, Imbke, *Schülerstudie '90: Jugendliche im Prozeß der Vereinigung* (Weinheim, Munich: Juventa, 1991)
Bem, Arim Soares do, *Das Spiel der Identitäten in der Konstitution von 'Wir'-Gruppen. Ost- und Westdeutsche Jugendliche und in Berlin geborene Jugendliche ausländischer Herkunft im gesellschaftlichen Umbruch* (Frankfurt am Main: Lang, 1998)
Benz, Ute and Wolfgang (eds), *Deutschland, deine Kinder: Zur Prägung von Feindbildern in Ost und West* (Munich: dtv, 2001)
Biehl, Heiko, *Wendepunkt Kosovo? Sicherheitspolitische Einstellungen in den alten und neuen Ländern* (Strausberg: SOWI, 2001)
Billerbeck, Liane von, *Generation Ost: aufmüpfig, angepaßt, ehrgeizig? Jugendliche nach der Wende* (Berlin: Ch. Links, 1999)
Böhm, Jürgen, Joachim Brune, Heribert Flörchinger, Antje Helbing and Annegret Pinther, *Deutsch Stunden Aufsätze: Was Jugendliche von der Einheit denken* (Berlin: Argon, 1993)

Bolz, Alexander and Hartmut Griese (eds), *Deutsch-deutsche Jugend-forschung: Theoretische und empirische Studien zur Lage der Jugend aus ostdeutscher Sicht* (Weinheim, Munich: Juventa, 1995)

Borries, Bodo von, *Das Geschichtsbewußtsein Jugendlicher* (Weinheim, Munich: Juventa, 1995)

Brähler, Elmar and Horst-Eberhard Richter, 'Deutsche – zehn Jahre nach der Wende', *APuZG*, B45 (1999), 24–31

Brämer, Rainer and Ulrich Heublein, 'Studenten in der Wende? Versuch einer deutsch-deutschen Typologie vor der Vereinigung', *APuZG*, B44 (1990), 3–16

Buchstab, Günter (ed.), *Geschichte der DDR und deutsche Einheit*, Studien zu Politik und Wissenschaft (Schwalbach: Wochenschau, 1999)

Chowanski, Joachim and Rolf Dreier, *Die Jugendweihe: Eine Kulturgeschichte seit 1852* (Berlin: edition ost, 2000)

Claus, Thomas and Detlev Herter, 'Jugend und Gewalt', *APuZG*, B38 (1994), 10–20

Claus, Thomas, Ferdinand Karlhofer, Gilg Seeber and Cocky Booy, *Jugend in Europa im Spannungsfeld von Demokratie und Extremismus*, Forschungsbericht, GISA Gender-Institut Sachsen-Anhalt (Magdeburg, Innsbruck, Amsterdam, 2001)

Collmer, Sabine and Georg-Maria Meyer, *Früher 'zur Fahne' – heute 'zum Bund': Soziale Deutungsmuster von wehrpflichtigen Soldaten aus den neuen Bundesländern* (Munich: SOWI, 1992)

Cooke, Paul and Jonathan Grix (eds), *East Germany: Continuity and Change*, German Monitor 46 (Amsterdam, Atlanta, GA: Rodopi, 2000)

Decker, Kerstin and Gunnar, *Gefühlsausbrüche oder Ewig pubertiert der Ostdeutsche* (Berlin: Das Neue Berlin, 2000)

Dennis, Mike, *The Rise and Fall of the German Democratic Republic, 1945–1990* (Harlow: Longman, 2000)

Deutscher Bundestag (ed.), *Materialien der Enquete-Kommission 'Aufarbeitung von Geschichte und Folgen der SED-Diktatur in Deutschland'*, 12. Wahlperiode des Deutschen Bundestages (Baden-Baden: Nomos, 1995), 18 vols

Deutsches Jugendinstitut (ed.), *Schüler an der Schwelle zur deutschen Einheit* (Opladen: Leske & Budrich, 1992)

Feige, Michael, *Vietnamesische Studenten und Arbeiter in der DDR und ihre Beobachtungen durch das MfS*, Sachbeiträge (10) (Magdeburg: Landesbeauftragte für die Unterlagen des Staatssicherheitsdienstes der ehemaligen DDR in Sachsen-Anhalt, 1999)

Feist, Ursula, 'Nichtwähler 1994', *APuZG*, B51–52 (1994), 35–46

Foitzik, Jan, Helga Gotschlich, Daniel Küchenmeister *et al.* (eds), *Jahrbuch für zeitgeschichtliche Jugendforschung 1994/5* (Berlin: Metropol, 1995)

Förster, Peter, "'Es war nicht alles falsch, was wir früher über den Kapitalismus gelernt haben." Empirische Ergebnisse einer Längsschnittstudie zum Weg junger Ostdeutscher vom DDR-Bürger zum Bundesbürger', *DA*, 34/2 (2001), 197–218

Förster, Peter, Walter Friedrich, Harry Müller and Wilfried Schubarth, *Jugend Ost: Zwischen Hoffnung und Gewalt* (Opladen: Leske & Budrich, 1993)

Freytag, Ronald and Dietmar Sturzbecker, *Die zweite Entdeckung Amerikas: Einstellungen ostdeutscher Jugendlicher zu den USA* (Potsdam: Verlag für Berlin-Brandenburg, 1998)

Friedrich, Walter, 'Mentalitätswandlungen der Jugend in der DDR', *APuZG*, B16–17 (1990), 25–37

Friedrich, Walter, 'Ist der Rechtsextremismus im Osten ein Produkt der Autoritären DDR?', *APuZG*, B46 (2001), 16–23

Friedrich, Walter and Peter Förster, *Jugend im Osten* (Leipzig: Rosa-Luxemburg-Verein, 1996)

Friedrich, Walter and Hartmut Griese (eds), *Jugend und Jugendforschung in der DDR: Gesellschaftspolitische Situationen, Sozialisation und Mentalitätsentwicklung in den achtziger Jahren* (Opladen: Leske & Budrich, 1991)

Friedrich, Walter, Peter Förster and Kurt Starke (eds), *Das Zentralinstitut für Jugendforschung Leipzig 1966–1990: Geschichte, Methoden, Erkenntnisse* (Berlin: edition ost, 1999)

Fritzsche, K.-Peter, "'Ich habe nichts gegen Ausländer, aber . . .": Eine deutsch-deutsche Schülerbefragung', *GEP*, 8/1 (1997), 15–17

Fulbrook, Mary, *Anatomy of a Dictatorship* (Oxford, New York: Oxford University Press, 1995)

Fulbrook, Mary, *German National Identity after the Holocaust* (Cambridge: Polity Press, 1999)

Furian, Gilbert and Nikolaus Becker, *'Auch im Osten trägt man Westen': Punks in der DDR – und was aus ihnen geworden ist* (Berlin: Tilsner, 2000)

Gaiser, Wolfgang, Martina Gille, Winfried Krüger and Johann de Rijke, 'Politikverdrossenheit in Ost und West? Einstellungen von Jugendlichen und jungen Erwachsenen', *APuZG*, B19–20 (2000), 12–23

Galenza, Ronald and Heinz Hauemeister (eds), *Wir wollen immer artig sein . . . Punk, New Wave, HipHop, Independent: Szene in der DDR 1980–1990* (Berlin: Schwarzkopf und Schwarzkopf, 1999)

Gensicke, Thomas, *Die neuen Bundesbürger: Eine Transformation ohne Integration* (Opladen, Wiesbaden: Westdeutscher Verlag, 1998)

Gibas, Monika, "'Die DDR: Das sozialistische Vaterland der Werktätigen!'", *APuZG*, B39–40 (1999), 21–30

Gille, Martina, Winfried Krüger, Johann de Rijke and Helmut Willems, 'Das Verhältnis Jugendlicher und junger Erwachsener zur Politik:

Normalisierung oder Krisenentwicklung?', *APuZG*, B19 (1996), 3–17

Göschel, Albrecht, *Kontrast und Parallele: Kulturelle und politische Identitätsbildung ostdeutscher Generationen* (Stuttgart, Berlin, Cologne: Kohlhammer/Deutscher Gemeindeverlag, 1999)

Gotschlich, Helga, *'Links und links und Schritt gehalten . . .' Die FDJ: Konzepte – Abläufe – Grenzen* (Berlin: Metropol, 1994)

Gotschlich, Helga and Edeltraud Schulze (eds), *Deutsche Teilung – Deutsche Wiedervereinigung: Jugend und Jugendpolitik im Umbruch der Systeme* (Berlin: Metropol, 1996)

Greiffenhagen, Martin and Sylvia, *Ein schwieriges Vaterland* (Munich, Leipzig: List, 1993)

Gries, Rainer, 'Der Geschmack der Heimat', *DA*, 27/10 (1994), 1041–58

Griese, Christiane, 'Patriotismus in den Farben der DDR', *GEP*, 7/2 (1996), 608–14

Griese, Christiane and Helga Marburger, *Zwischen Internationalismus und Patriotismus* (Frankfurt am Main: IKO, 1995)

Griese, Hartmut (ed.), *Übergangsrituale im Jugendalter: Jugendweihe, Konfirmation, Firmung und alternativen Positionen und Perspektiven am 'Runden Tisch'* (Münster: LIT, 2000)

Grix, Jonathan and Paul Cooke (eds), *East German Distinctiveness in a Unified Germany* (Birmingham: University of Birmingham Press, 2002)

Große, Michael, *Identitätskrise ostdeutscher Jugendlicher? Politische und gesellschaftliche Einstellungen von ost- und westdeutschen Jugendlichen im Vereinigungsprozeß* (Hamburg: Universität der Bundeswehr Hamburg, 1994)

Heinemann, Karl-Heinz and Wilfried Schubarth (eds), *Der antifaschistische Staat entläßt seine Kinder* (Cologne: PapyRossa, 1992)

Heitmeyer, Wilhelm, *Rechtsextremistische Orientierungen bei Jugendlichen* (Weinheim, Munich: Juventa, 1992)

Heitmeyer, Wilhelm, *Die Bielefelder Rechtsextremismus-Studie* (Weinheim, Munich: Juventa, 1993)

Henderson, Karen, 'The Search for Ideological Conformity: Sociological Research on Youth in the GDR under Honecker', *GH*, 10/3 (1992), 318–34

Heublein, Ulrich and Rainer Brämer, 'Studenten im Abseits der Vereinigung', *DA*, 23/9 (1990), 1397–1410

Holtmann, Everhard, *Protestpartei am rechten Rand: Die DVU in der Wählerlandschaft Sachsen-Anhalts* (Magdeburg: Landeszentrale für politische Bildung Sachsen-Anhalt, 1999)

Howard, Mark Alan, 'Die Ostdeutschen als ethnische Gruppe? Zum Verständnis der neuen Teilung des geeinten Deutschland', *Berliner Debatte INITIAL*, 6/4–5 (1995), 119–31

Jarausch, Konrad H. (ed.), *After Unity: Reconfiguring German Identities* (Providence, Oxford: Berghahn, 1997)

Jarausch, Konrad H. (ed.), *Dictatorship as Experience* (New York, Oxford: Berghahn, 1999)

Jugend '92: Lebenslagen, Orientierungen und Entwicklungsperspektiven im vereinten Deutschland, 11. Shell Jugendstudie, Jugendwerk der Deutschen Shell (Opladen: Leske & Budrich, 1992)

Jugend '97: Zukunftsperspektiven, gesellschaftliches Engagement, politische Orientierung, 12. Shell Jugendstudie, Jugendwerk der Deutschen Shell (Opladen: Leske & Budrich, 1997)

Jugend 2000, 13. Shell Jugendstudie, vols 1–2, Deutsche Shell (Opladen: Leske & Budrich, 2000)

Jugend 2002: Zwischen pragmatischem Idealismus und robustem Materialismus, 14. Shell Jugendstudie, Deutsche Shell (Frankfurt am Main: Fischer, 2002)

Kaelble, Hartmut, Jürgen Kocka and Hartmut Zwahr (eds), *Sozialgeschichte der DDR* (Stuttgart: Klett-Cotta, 1994)

Kirchhöfer, Dieter, *Aufwachsen in Ostdeutschland: Langzeitstudie über Tagesläufe 10- bis 14jähriger Kinder* (Weinheim, Munich: Juventa, 1998)

Klier, Freya, *Lüg Vaterland: Erziehung in der DDR* (Munich: Kindler, 1990)

Kohr, Heinz-Ulrich, Ekkehard Lippert, Georg-Maria Meyer and Johanna Sauter, *Jugend, Bundeswehr und deutsche Einheit: Beitrag zum 9. Jugendbericht der Bundesregierung* (Munich: SOWI, 1993)

Kowalczuk, Ilko-Sascha and Stefan Wolle, *Roter Stern über Deutschland* (Berlin: Ch. Links, 2001)

Krüger, Heinz-Hermann and Nicolle Pfaff, 'Jugendkulturelle Orientierungen, Gewaltaffinitat und Auslanderfeindlichkeit: Rechtsextremismus an Schulen in Sachsen-Anhalt', *APuZG*, B45 (2001), 14–23

Krüger, Heinz-Hermann, Sibylle Reinhardt, Catrin Kötters, Ralf Schmidt, Nicolle Pfaff, Birgit Fischer and Frank Tillmann, 'Projekt "Jugend und Demokratie in Sachsen-Anhalt": Zwischenbericht' (Martin-Luther-Universität Halle-Wittenberg, 2001)

Kuhn, Hans-Peter, Karin Weiss and Hans Oswald, *Jugendliche Wähler in den neuen Bundesländern: Eine Längsschnittstudie zum Verhalten von Erstwählern bei der Bundestagswahl 1998* (Opladen: Leske & Budrich, 2001)

Lenz, Wolfgang (ed.), *Jugend 2000: Trends – Analysen – Perspektiven* (Bielefeld: Bertelsmann, 1992)

Lindenberger, Thomas (ed.), *Herrschaft und Eigen-Sinn in der Diktatur: Studien zur Gesellschaftsgeschichte der DDR* (Cologne, Weimar, Vienna: Böhlau, 1999)

Maaz, Hans-Joachim, *Der Gefühlsstau: Ein Psychogramm der DDR* (Munich: Knaur, 1992)

Maaz, Hans-Joachim, *Das gestürzte Volk* (Munich: Knaur, 1993)

Madarász, Jeannette, *Conflict and Compromise in East Germany, 1971–1989: A Precarious Stability* (Basingstoke: Palgrave, 2003)

Mählert, Ulrich and Gerd-Rüdiger Stephan, *Blaue Hemden – Rote Fahnen: Die Geschichte der Freien Deutschen Jugend* (Opladen: Edition Deutschland Archiv/Leske & Budrich, 1996)

Mätzing, Heike Christina, *Geschichte im Zeichen des historischen Materialismus* (Hannover: Hahnsche Buchhandlung, 1999)

McDougall, Alan, *Youth Politics in East Germany: The Free German Youth Movement 1946–1968* (Oxford: Oxford University Press, 2004)

McFalls, Laurence H. and Lothar Probst (eds), *After the GDR: New Perspectives on the Old GDR and the Young Länder*, German Monitor 54 (Amsterdam, Atlanta, GA: Rodopi, 2001)

McKay, Joanna, *The Official Concept of the Nation in the Former GDR* (Aldershot: Ashgate, 1998)

Meier, Andreas, *Jugendweihe-JUGENDFEIER: Ein deutsches nostalgisches Fest vor und nach 1990* (Munich: dtv, 1998)

Meulemann, Heiner (ed.), *Werte und nationale Identität im vereinten Deutschland: Erklärungsansätze der Umfrageforschung* (Opladen: Leske & Budrich, 1998)

Meuschel, Sigrid, *Legitimation und Parteiherrschaft in der DDR* (Frankfurt am Main: Suhrkamp, 1992)

Mitter, Armin and Stefan Wolle, *Untergang auf Raten: Unbekannte Kapitel der DDR-Geschichte* (Munich: Bertelsmann, 1993)

Moericke, Helga, *Wir sind verschieden: Lebensentwürfe von Schülern aus Ost und West* (Frankfurt am Main: Luchterhand, 1991)

Möller, Sabine, 'Vielfache Vergangenheit: Das Geschichtsbewußtsein vom Nationalsozialismus im Ost-West Vergleich', Universität Hannover, 2000, www.soz.uni-hannover.de/ipsy/tradier, accessed on 14 Oct 2002

Müller, Harry and Wilfried Schubarth, 'Rechtsextremismus und aktuelle Befindlichkeiten von Jugendlichen in den neuen Bundesländern', *APuZG*, B38 (1992), 16–28

Münchmeier, Richard, '"Entstrukturierung" der Jugendphase', *APuZG*, B31 (1999), 3–13

Muszynski, Bernhard (ed.), *Deutsche Vereinigung: Probleme der Integration und der Identifikation* (Opladen: Leske & Budrich, 1991)

Mütter, Bernd, 'Probleme bei der Einführung westdeutscher Geschichtsbücher in den neuen Bundesländern', *GEP*, 5/2 (1994), 73–81

Neubacher, Frank, *Jugend und Rechtsextremismus in Ostdeutschland vor und nach der Wende* (Bonn: Forum, 1994)

Neubauer, Georg, Wolfgang Melzer and Klaus Hurrelmann, *Jugend im deutsch-deutschen Vergleich: Die Lebenslage der jungen Generation im Jahr der Vereinigung* (Berlin: Luchterhand, 1992)

Neubert, Ehrhart, *Geschichte der Opposition in der DDR 1949–1989*, 2nd edn (Bonn: Bundeszentrale für politische Bildung, 2000)

Neuhaus, Friedemann, *Geschichte im Umbruch: Geschichtspolitik, Geschichtsunterricht und Geschichtsbewußtsein in der DDR und den neuen Bundesländern 1983–1993* (Frankfurt am Main: Lang, 1998)

Noelle-Neumann, Elisabeth and Renate Köcher (eds), *Allensbacher Jahrbuch der Demoskopie 1993–1997* (Munich: Saur, 1997)

Nothnagle, Alan L., *Building the East German Myth: Historical Mythology and Youth Propaganda in the German Democratic Republic, 1945–1989* (Ann Arbor: University of Michigan Press, 1999)

Oesterreich, Detlef, *Autoritäre Persönlichkeit und Gesellschaftsordnung: Der Stellenwert psychischer Faktoren für politische Einstellungen: Eine empirische Untersuchung von Jugendlichen in Ost und West* (Weinheim, Munich: Juventa, 1993)

Oswald, Hans (ed.), *Sozialisation und Entwicklung in den neuen Bundesländern*, 2. Beiheft der Zeitschrift für Soziologie der Erziehung und Sozialisation (Weinheim, Munich: Juventa, 1998)

Pollack, Detlef, 'Die ostdeutsche Identität: Erbe des DDR-Sozialismus oder Produkt der Wiedervereinigung?', *APuZG*, B41–42 (1998), 9–23

Poutrus, Patrice G., Jan C. Behrends and Dennis Kuck, 'Historische Ursachen der Fremdenfeindlichkeit in den neuen Bundesländern', *APuZG*, B39 (2000), 15–21

Pritchard, Rosalind M. O., *Reconstructing Education: East German Schools and Universities after Unification* (New York, Oxford: Berghahn, 1999)

Probst, Lothar, 'Ost-West-Differenzen und das republikanische Defizit der deutschen Einheit', *APuZG*, B41–42 (1998), 3–8

Rauhut, Michael, *Rock in der DDR 1964 bis 1989* (Bonn: Bundeszentrale für politische Bildung, 2002)

Reinhardt, Sibylle and Frank Tillmann, 'Politische Orientierungen Jugendlicher: Ergebnisse und Interpretationen der Sachsen-Anhalt-Studie "Jugend und Demokratie"', *APuZG*, B45 (2001), 3–13

Roberts, K., S. Clark, C. Fagan and J. Tholen, *Surviving Post-Communism: Young People in the Former Soviet Union* (Cheltenham, Northampton, MA: Edward Elgar, 2000)

Rodden, John, *Repainting the Little Red Schoolhouse: A History of Eastern German Education, 1945–1995* (New York, Oxford: Oxford University Press, 2002)

Ross, Corey, *The East German Dictatorship: Problems and Perspectives in the Interpretation of the GDR* (London: Arnold, 2002)

Ross, Gordon Charles, *The Swastika in Socialism: Right-Wing Extremism in the GDR* (Hamburg: Kovac, 2000)

Rüchel, Uta, '. . . *Auf deutsch sozialistisch zu denken* . . .': *Mosambikaner in der Schule der Freundschaft*, Sachbeiträge (18) (Magdeburg: Landesbeauftragte für die Unterlagen des Staatssicherheitsdienstes der ehemaligen DDR in Sachsen-Anhalt, 2001)

Rust, Val D., 'Transformation of History Instruction in East German Schools', *Compare*, 23/3 (1993), 205–17

Sachse, Christian, *Die Entwicklung der (vor)militärischen Ausbildung in der DDR und die Auswirkungen auf das Friedensbewußtsein Jugendlicher* (Kiel: Projektverbund Friedenswissenschaften Kiel, 1995)

Sapparth, Henry, 'DDR? – Nein, Danke!', *GEP*, 6/9 (1995), 538–48

Schlegel, Ute and Peter Förster (eds), *Ostdeutsche Jugendliche: Vom DDR-Bürger zum Bundesbürger* (Opladen: Leske & Budrich, 1997)

Schmidtchen, Gerhard, *Wie weit ist der Weg nach Deutschland?*, 2nd edn (Opladen: Leske & Budrich, 1997)

Schubarth, Wilfried, 'Geschichtskult contra Geschichtsbewußtsein: Nachholbedarf der DDR-Jugend', *DJ*, 10 (1990), 449–53

Schubarth, Wilfried and Richard Stöss (eds), *Rechtsextremismus in der Bundesrepublik Deutschland: Eine Bilanz* (Bonn: Bundeszentrale für politische Bildung, 2000)

Sieber, Malte and Ronald Freytag, *Kinder des Systems: DDR-Studenten vor, im und nach dem Herbst '89* (Hamburg: Morgenbuch, 1993)

Staab, Andreas, *National Identity in Eastern Germany: Inner Unification or Continued Separation?* (Westport, CT: Praeger, 1998)

Staatskanzlei des Landes Sachsen-Anhalt (ed.), *Jugend morgen* (Halle (Saale): Mitteldeutscher Verlag, 2001)

Stevenson, Patrick and John Theobald (eds), *Relocating Germanness: Discursive Disunity in Unified Germany* (Basingstoke: Macmillan, 2000)

Stock, Manfred and Philipp Mühlberg, *Die Szene von Innen: Skinheads, Grufties, Heavy Metals, Punks* (Berlin: Ch. Links, 1990)

Sturzbecker, Dietmar, *Jugend und Gewalt in Ostdeutschland* (Göttingen: Verlag für Angewandte Psychologie, 1997)

Tillmann, Frank and Wolfgang Langer, *Demokratische Vor-Laute* (Opladen: Leske & Budrich, 2000)

Veen, Hans-Joachim *et al.* (eds), *Eine Jugend in Deutschland? Orientierungen und Verhaltensweisen der Jugend in Ost und West* (Opladen: Leske & Budrich, 1994)

Wasmuht, Ulrike C., Ina Plath and Eva Volke, *Sicherheitspolitik und Bundeswehr im Schulunterricht* (Strausberg: SOWI, 1997)

Westle, Bettina, *Kollektive Identität im vereinten Deutschland: Nation und Demokratie in der Wahrnehmung der Deutschen* (Opladen: Leske & Budrich, 1999)

Wolle, Stefan, *Die heile Welt der Diktatur: Alltag und Herrschaft in der DDR 1971–1989* (Bonn: Bundeszentrale für politische Bildung, 1998)

Zilch, Dorle, *Millionen unter der blauen Fahne* (Rostock: Norddeutscher Hochschulschriften, 1994)

Zimmermann, Hartmut *et al.*, *DDR Handbuch*, 3rd edn (Cologne: Wissenschaft und Politik, 1985), 2 vols

Index